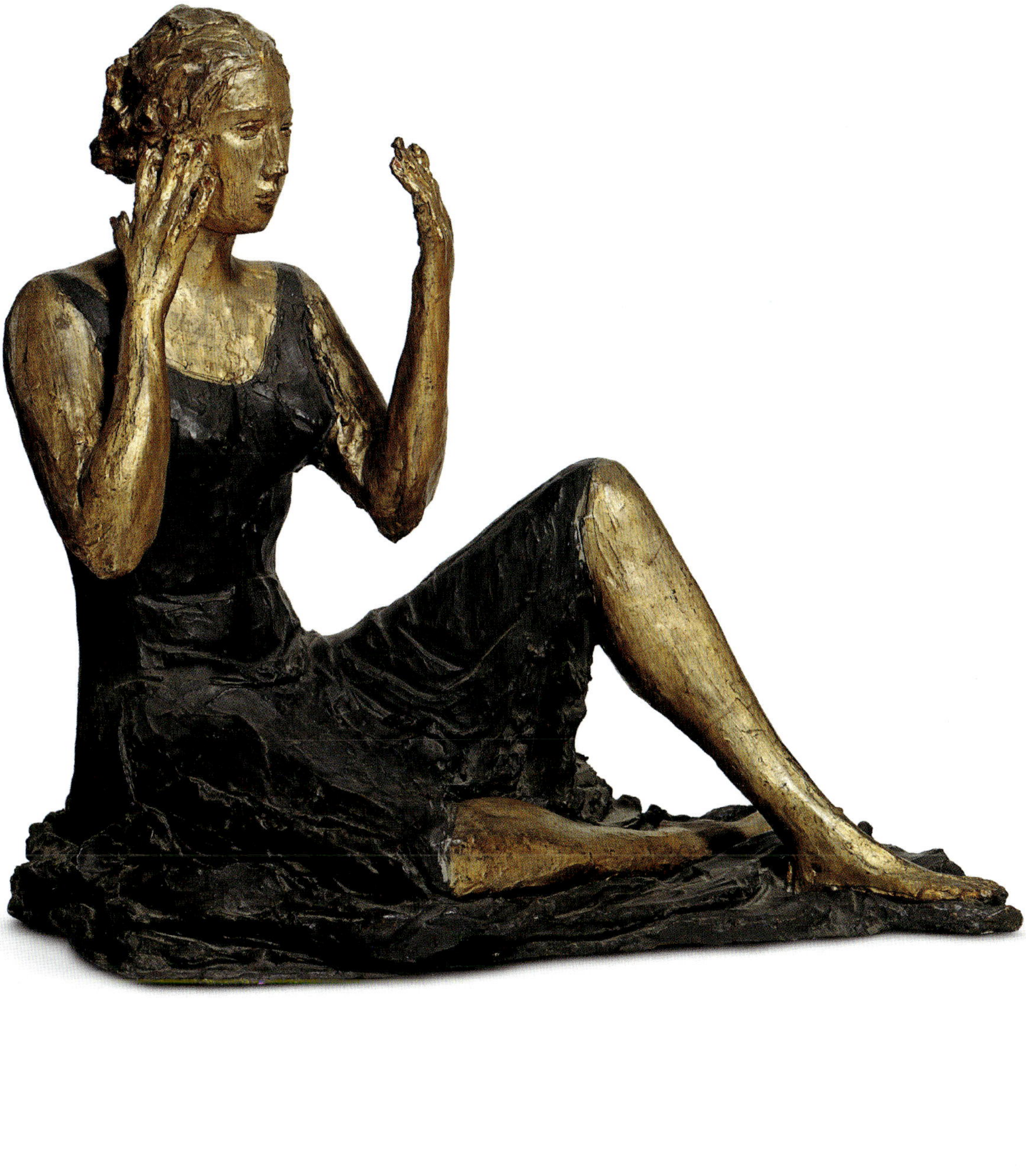

Lucio Fontana

Signorina seduta
1934
coloured bronze,
gold, black and red,
84 x 103 cm,
34 SC 1,
Courtesy Comune di Milano,

Alberto Giacometti

L'Objet invisible
1934-1935
bronze,
155 x 32 x 29 cm
inv. 310
Courtesy Fondation Marguerite
et Aimé Maeght,
Saint-Paul-de-Vence

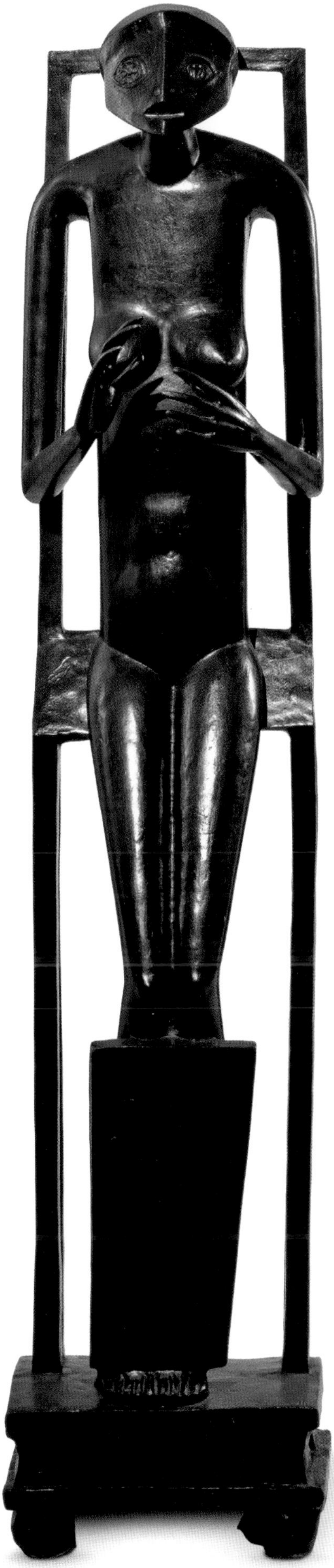

Lucio Fontana

Paulette
1938
coloured ceramic, white and black
68 x 69 x 32 cm
inv. 38 SC 2
Collezioni civiche,
dono Alberto Della Ragione,
Museo Novecento, Firenze

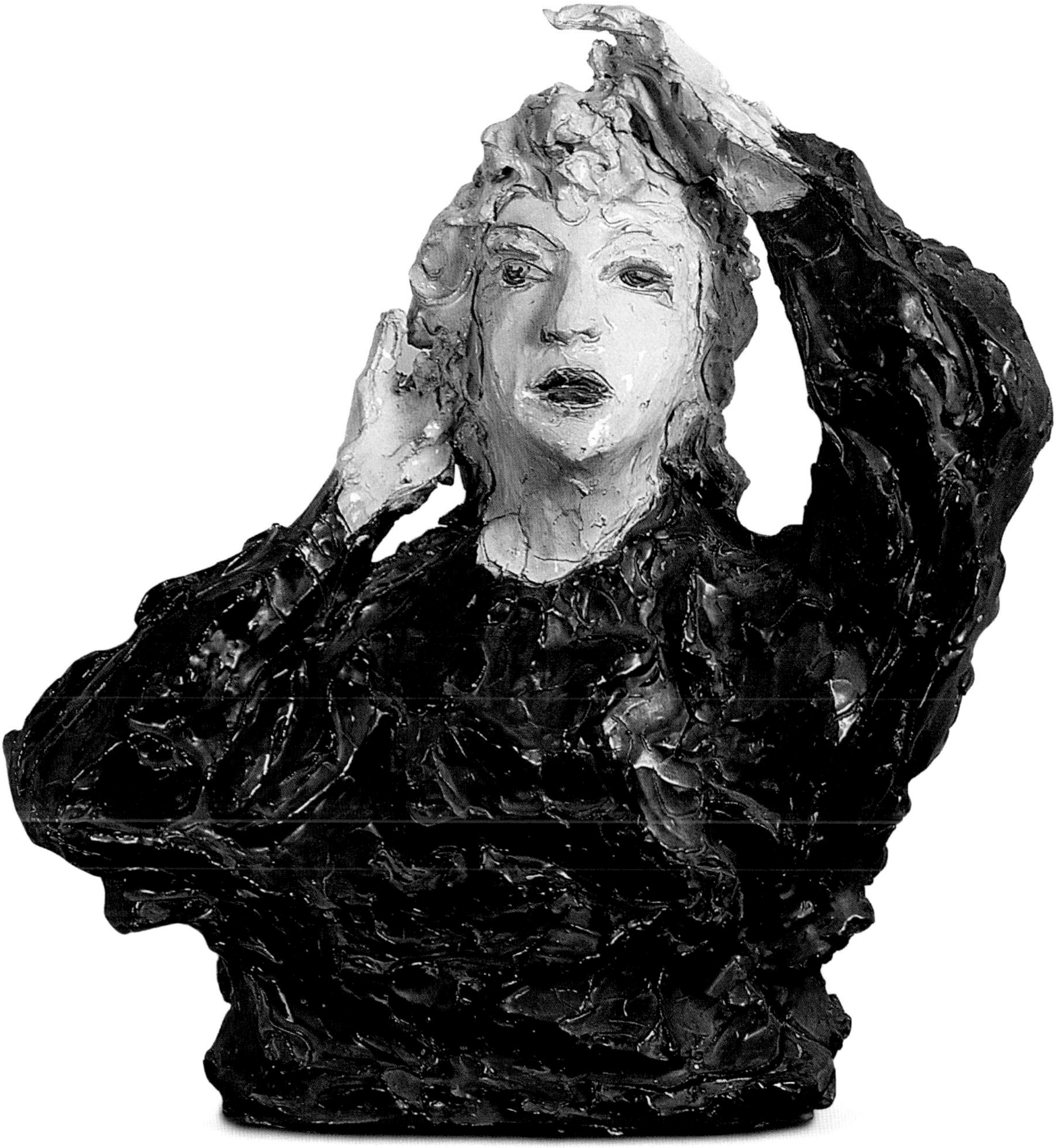

Alberto Giacometti

Groupe de trois hommes
(Trois hommes qui marchent)
1943-1949
bronze, 72 x 32 x 31,5 cm
inv. 324
Courtesy Fondation Marguerite
et Aimé Maeght,
Saint-Paul-de-Vence

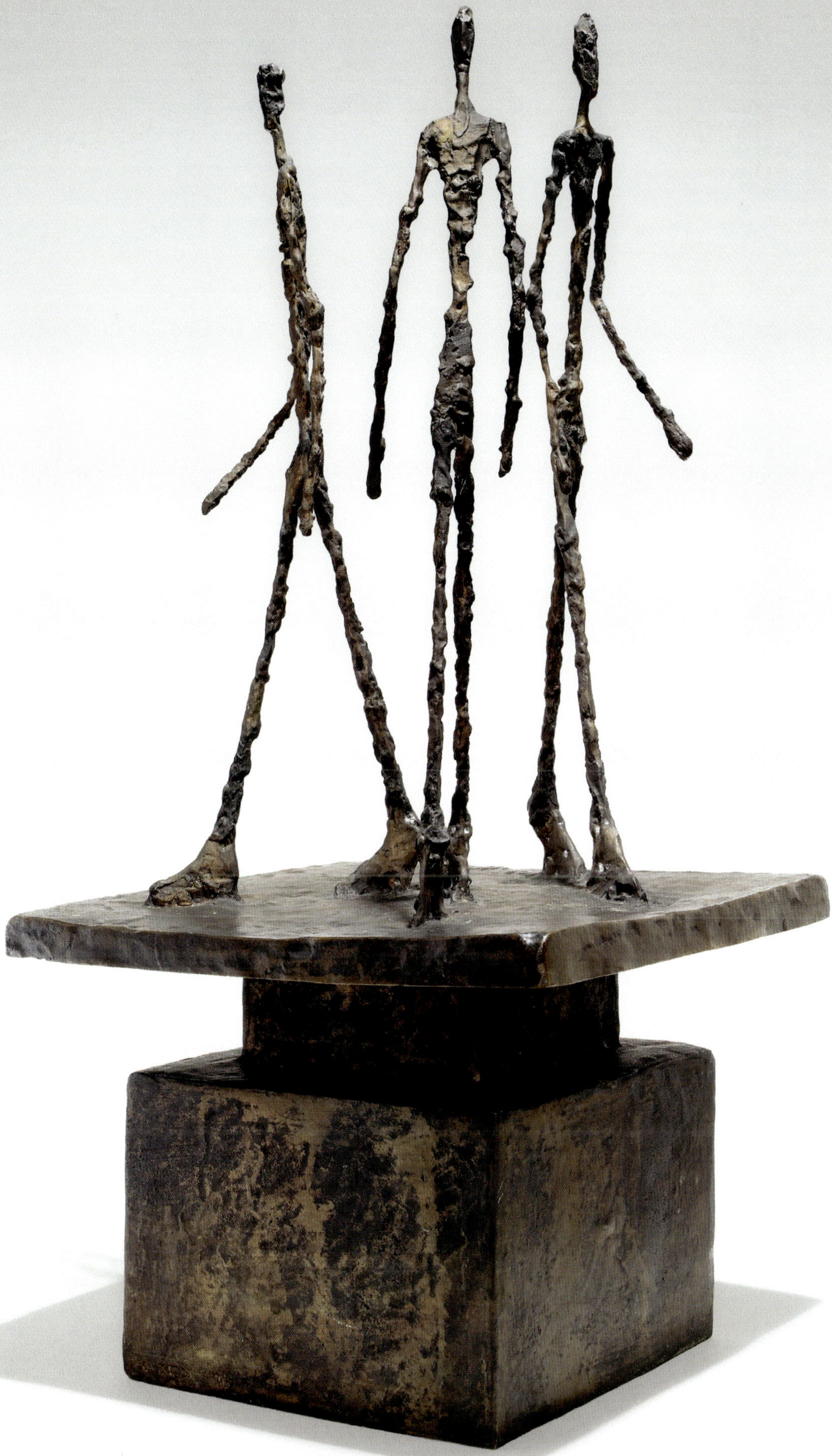

Alberto Giacometti

Femme debout II
(Grande femme debout II)
1943-1949
bronze, 270 x 35 x 53 cm
inv. 0308
Courtesy Fondation Marguerite
et Aimé Maeght,
Saint-Paul-de-Vence

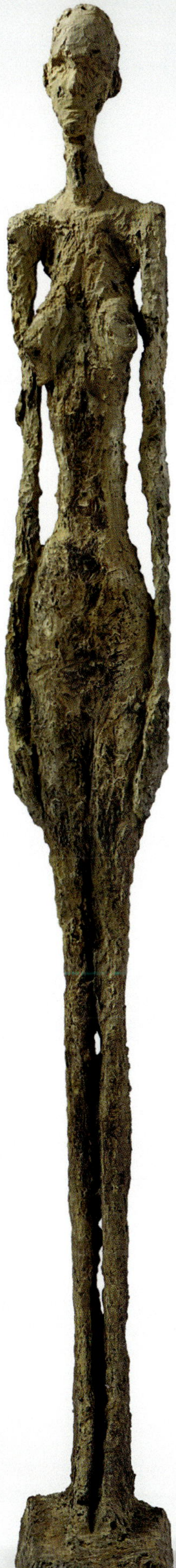

Lucio Fontana

Concetto spaziale, Forma
1958
iron, 244 x 42 x 28 cm
inv. 58 SC 1
Courtesy Fondazione
Lucio Fontana, Milano

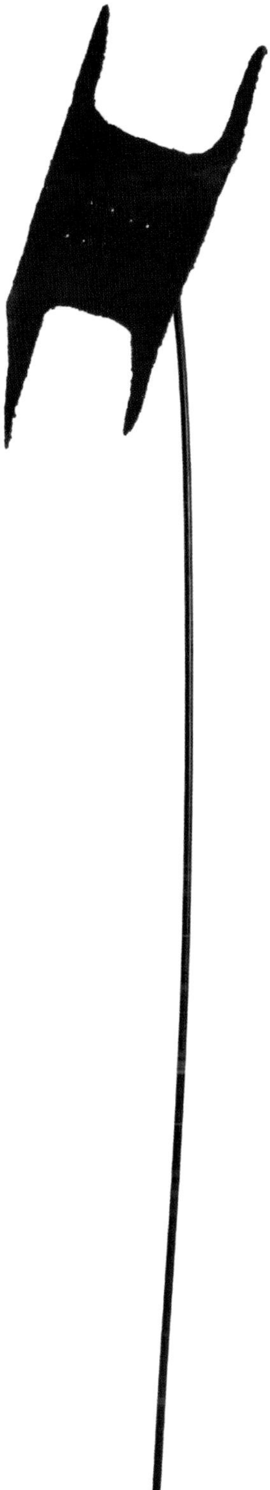

Alberto Giacometti

L'Homme qui marche I
1960
bronze, 183 x 26 x 95 cm
inv. 314
Courtesy Fondation Marguerite
et Aimé Maeght,
Saint-Paul-de-Vence

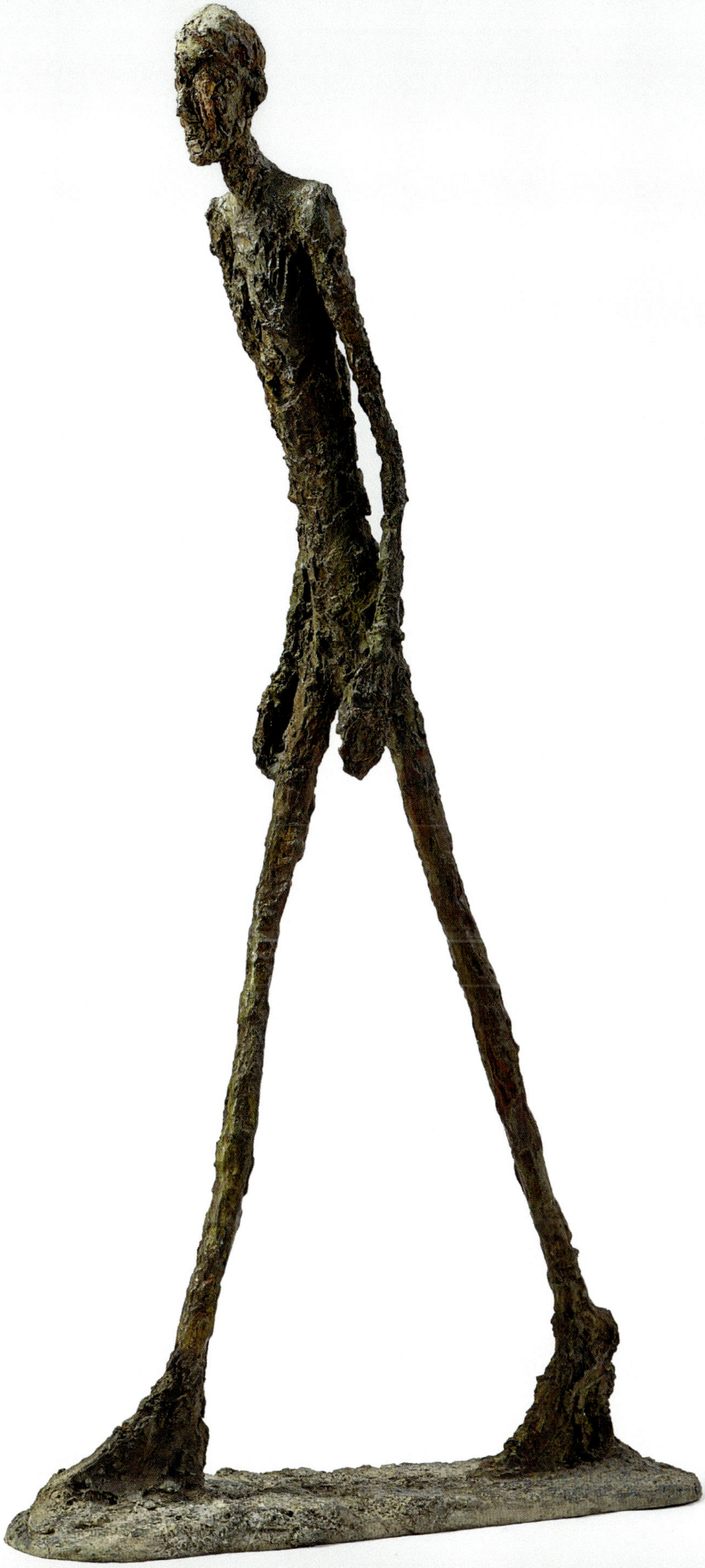

Lucio Fontana

Concetto spaziale
1959-1960
slipped terracotta, 55 x 42 cm inv.
61-62 SOS 40
Courtesy Fondazione
Lucio Fontana, Milano

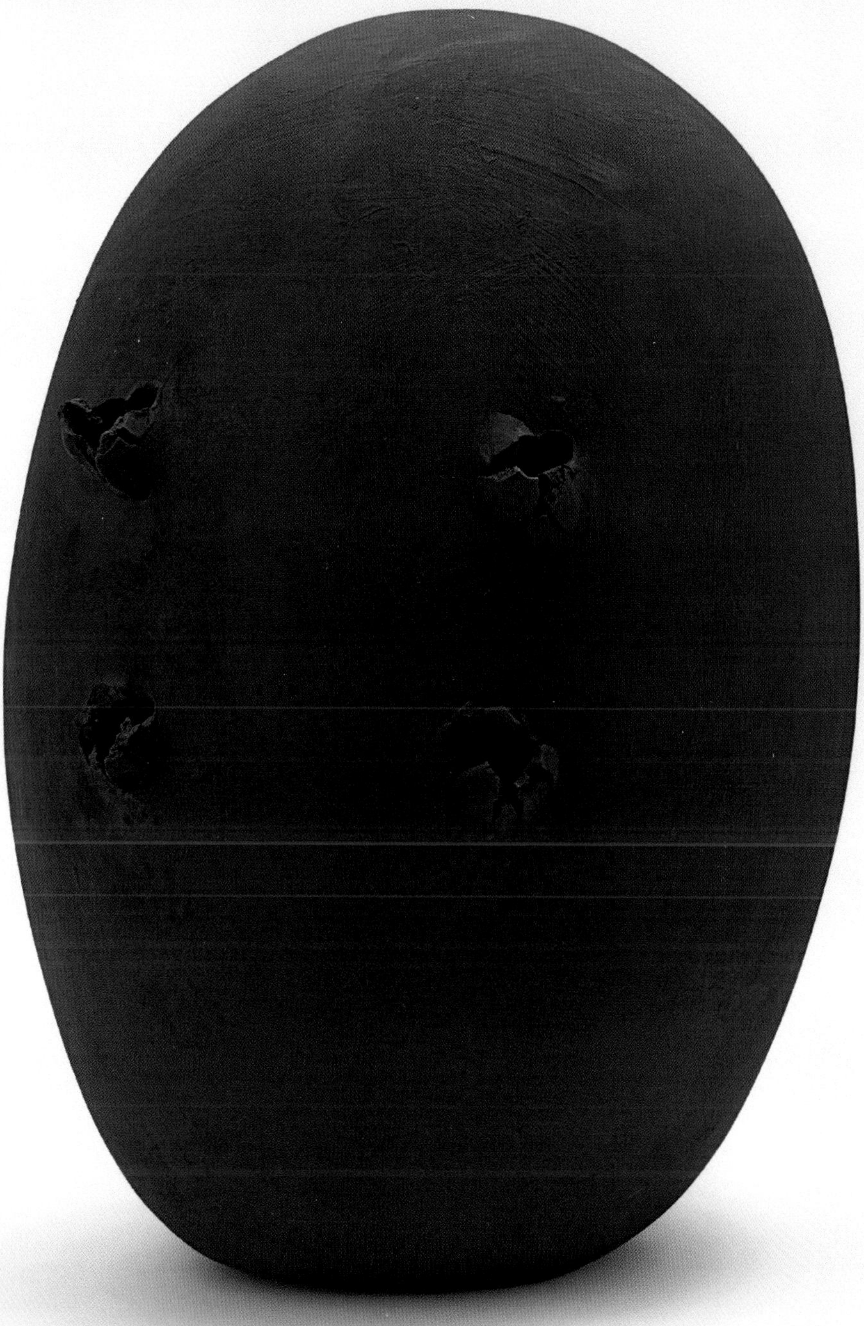

Lucio Fontana

Concetto spaziale, Natura
1959-1960
bronze, diameter 75 cm
inv. 59-60 N 32
Courtesy Fondazione
Lucio Fontana, Milano

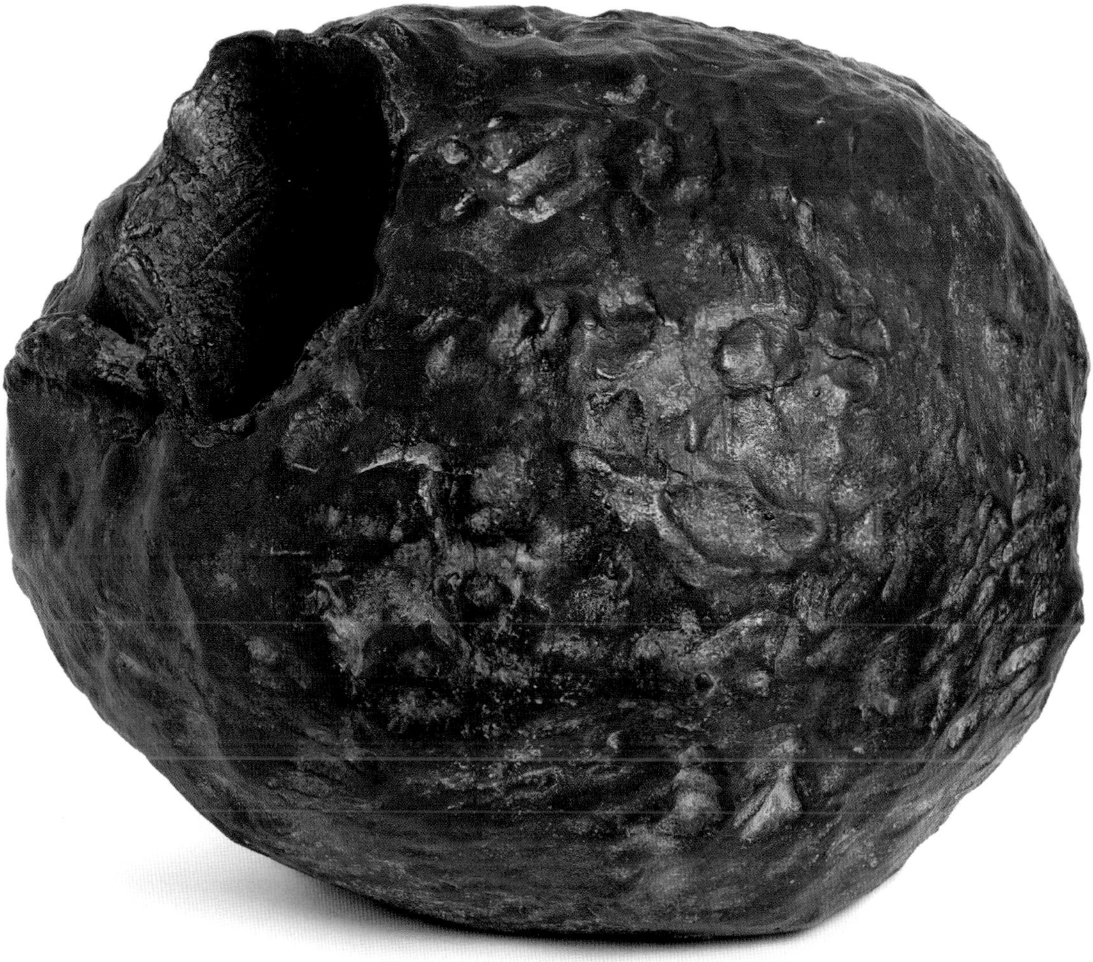

Lucio Fontana

Concetto spaziale, Natura
1959-1960
bronze, 41 x 49 x 46 cm
inv. 59-60 N 17
Courtesy Fondazione
Lucio Fontana

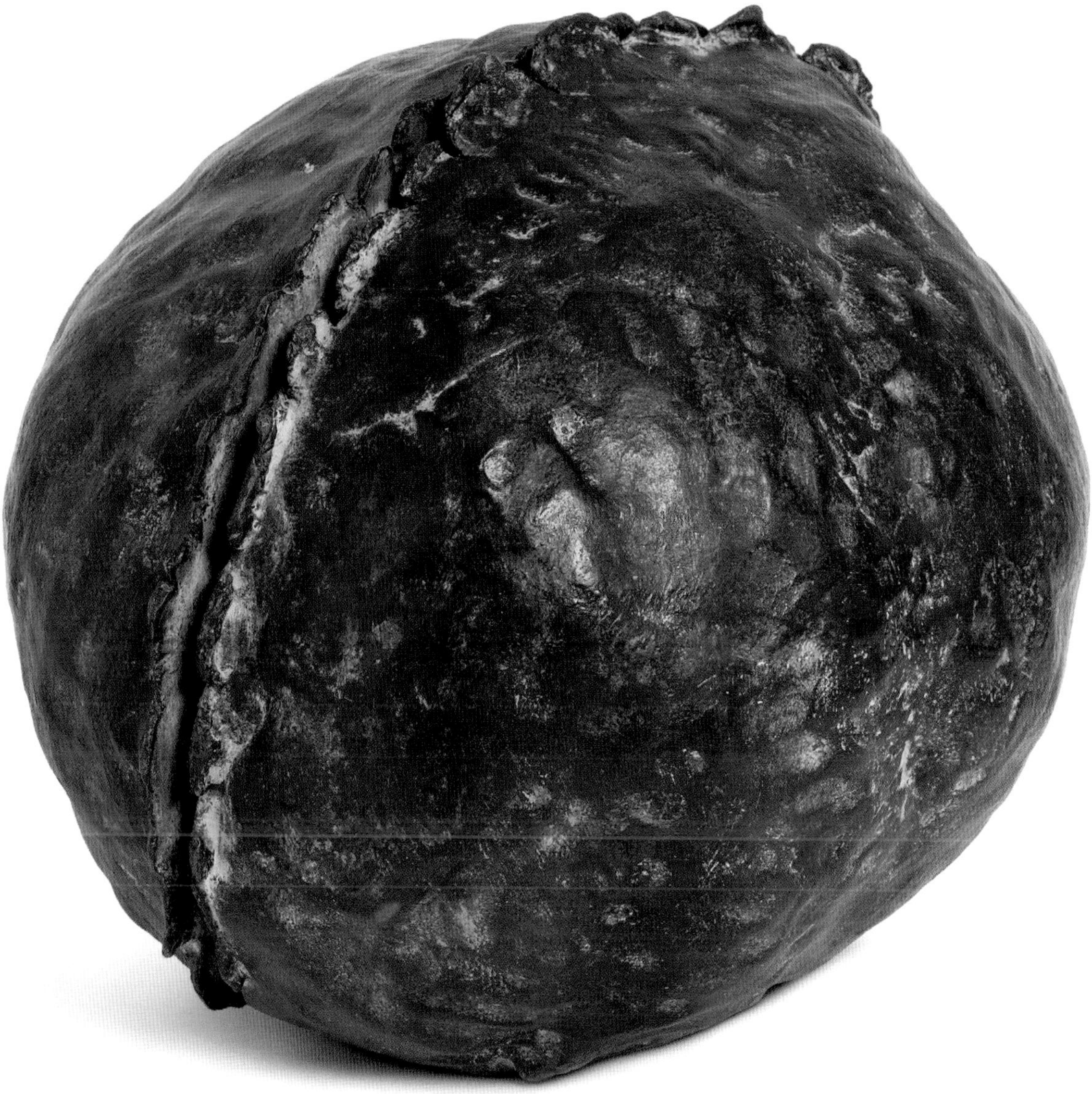

Lucio Fontana

Concetto spaziale, Natura
1959-1960
bronze, diameter 80 cm
inv. 59-60 N 7
Courtesy Private collection

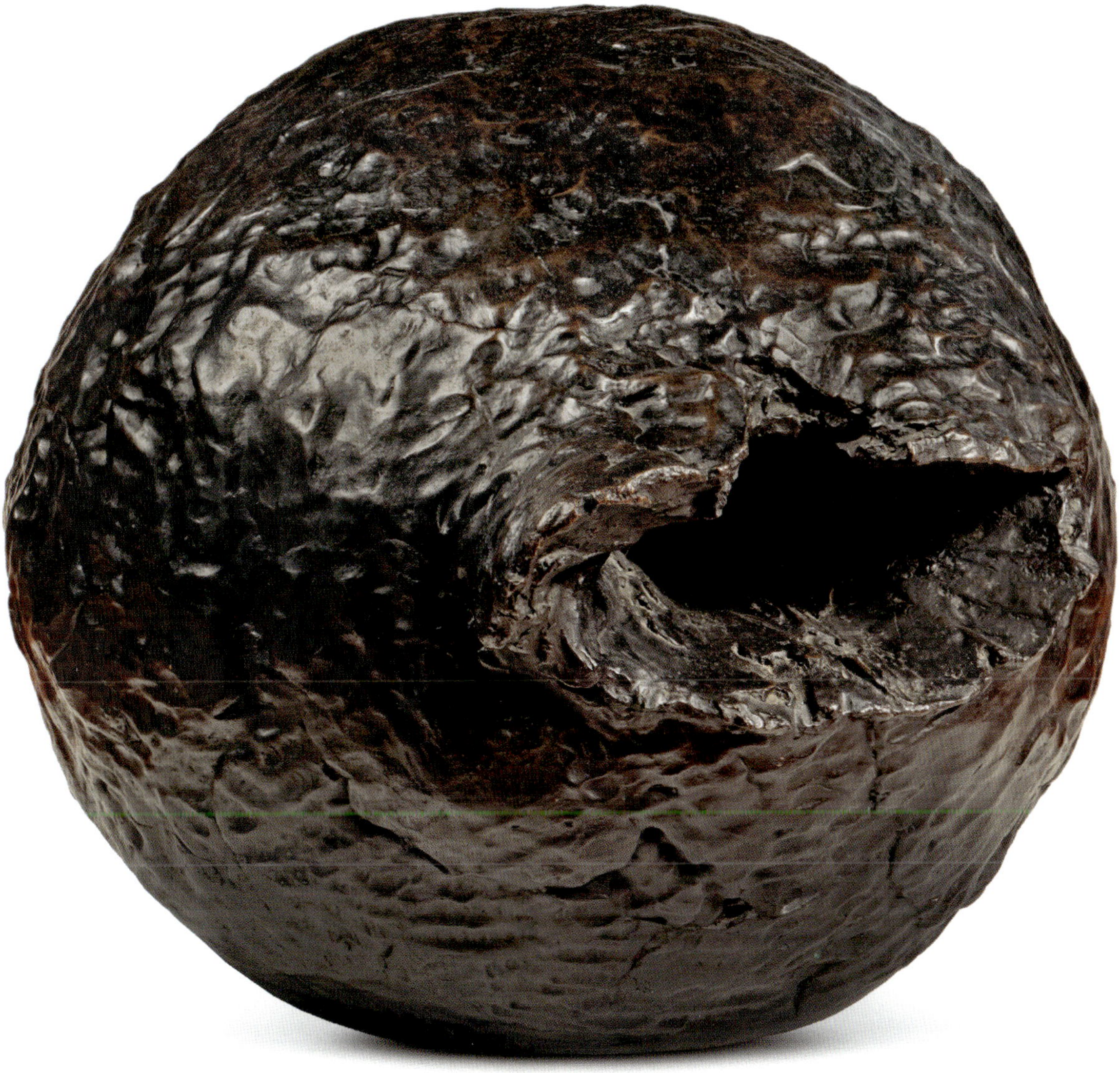

Lucio Fontana

Concetto spaziale, Natura
1959-1960
bronze, diameter 60 cm
inv. 59-60 N 3
Courtesy Fondazione
Lucio Fontana

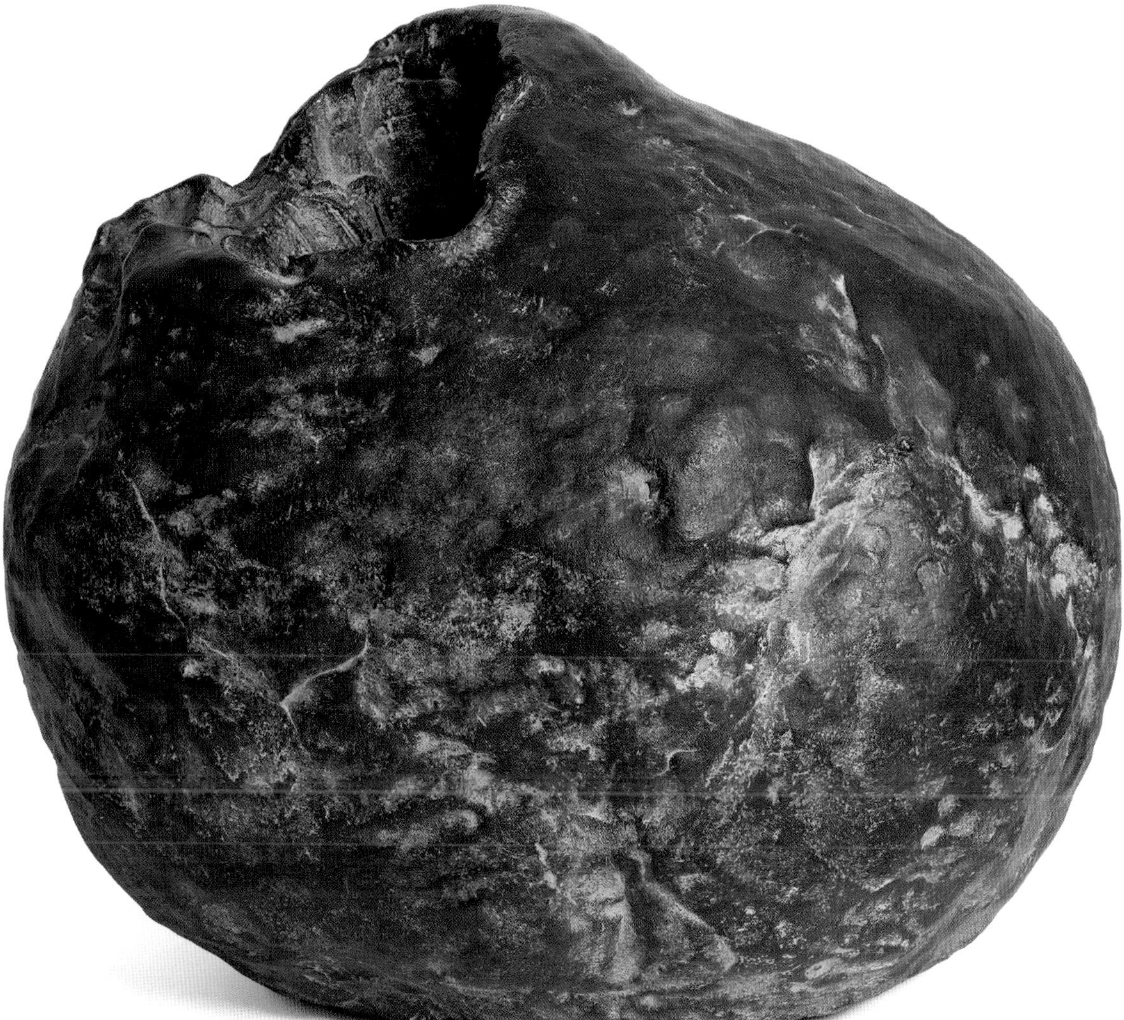

Lucio Fontana

Concetto spaziale, Natura
1959-1960,
terracotta, diameter 75 cm
inv. 59-60 N
Courtesy Private collection

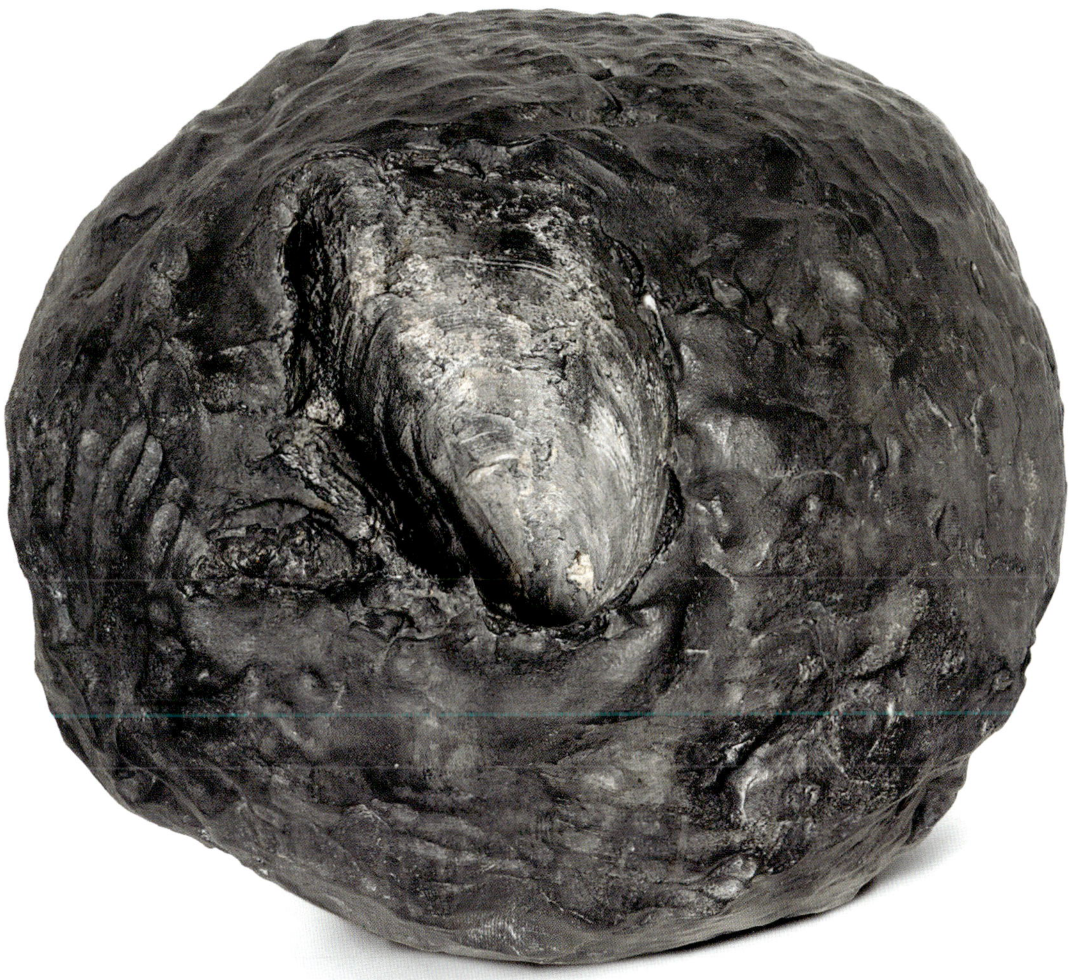

Lucio Fontana

Concetto spaziale, Natura
1959-1961
bronze, 78,8 X 88,6 X 83,2 cm
inv. 59-60 N 20
Courtesy Ben Brown Fine Art,
London, Hong Kong
and Palm Beach

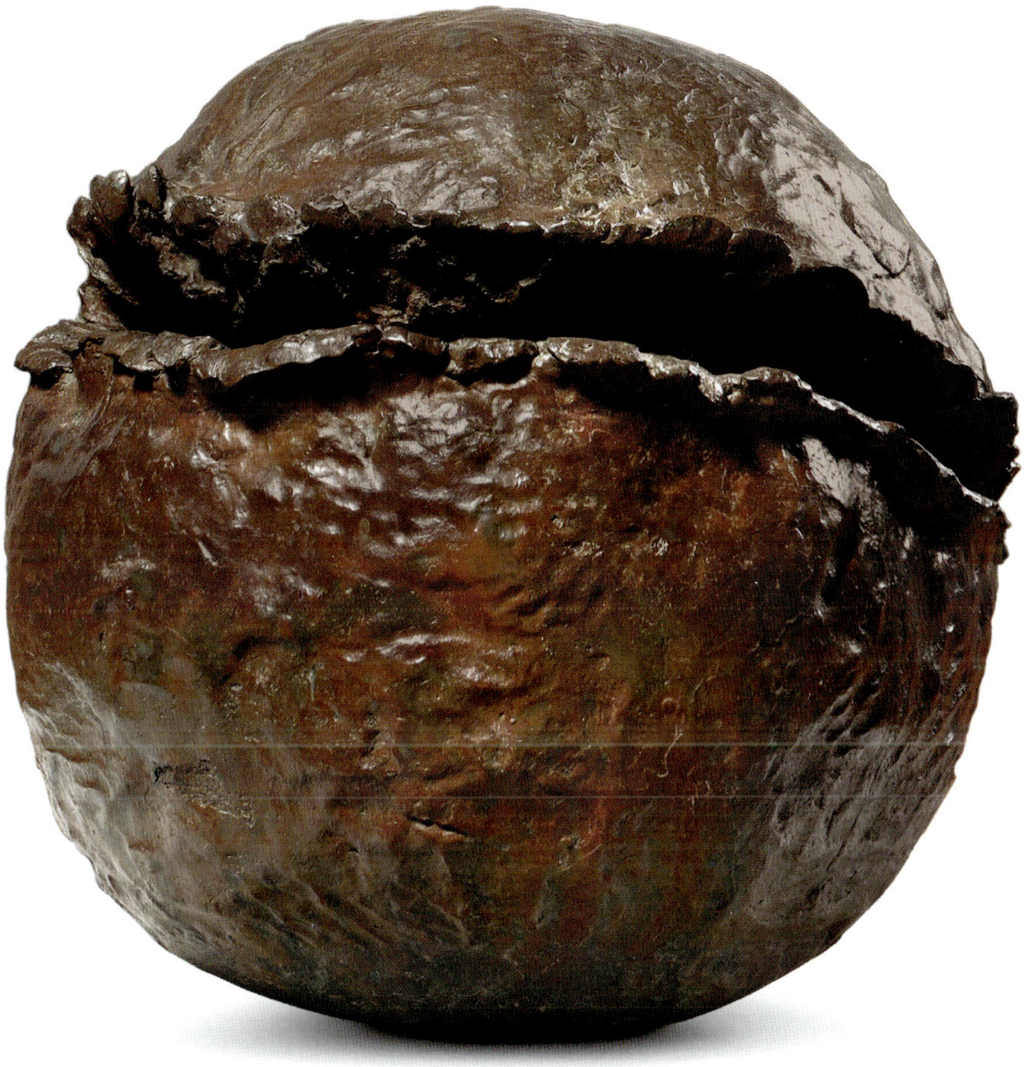

Lucio Fontana

Concetto spaziale, Natura
1982 (1959-1960)
bronze, 57 x 65 cm
inv. 59-60 N 10
Courtesy Private collection

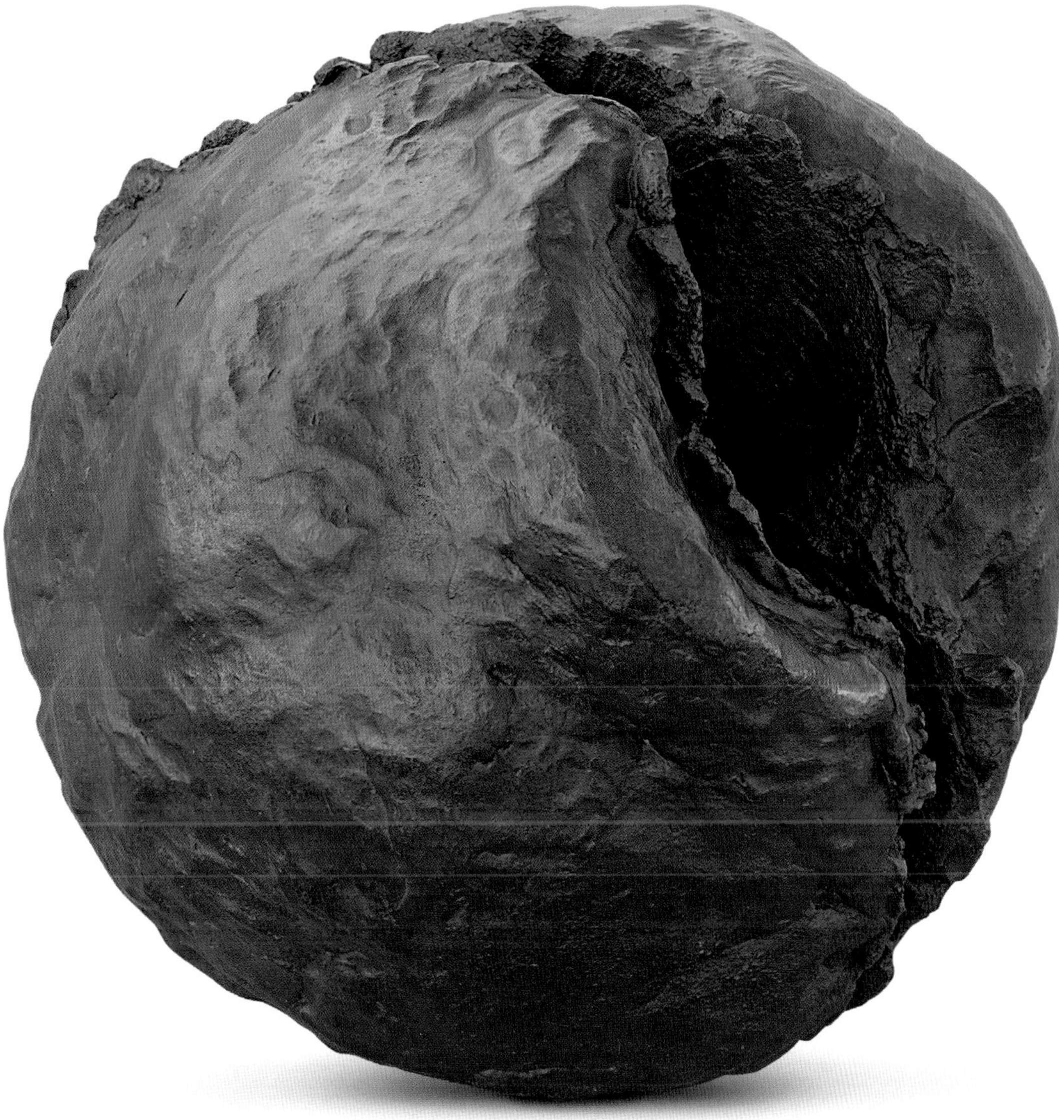

Alberto Giacometti

Buste d'homme (Lotar II),
1964-1965 (cast 1973)
bronze, 58 x 36 x 25 cm
inv. AGD 2925
Courtesy Private collection

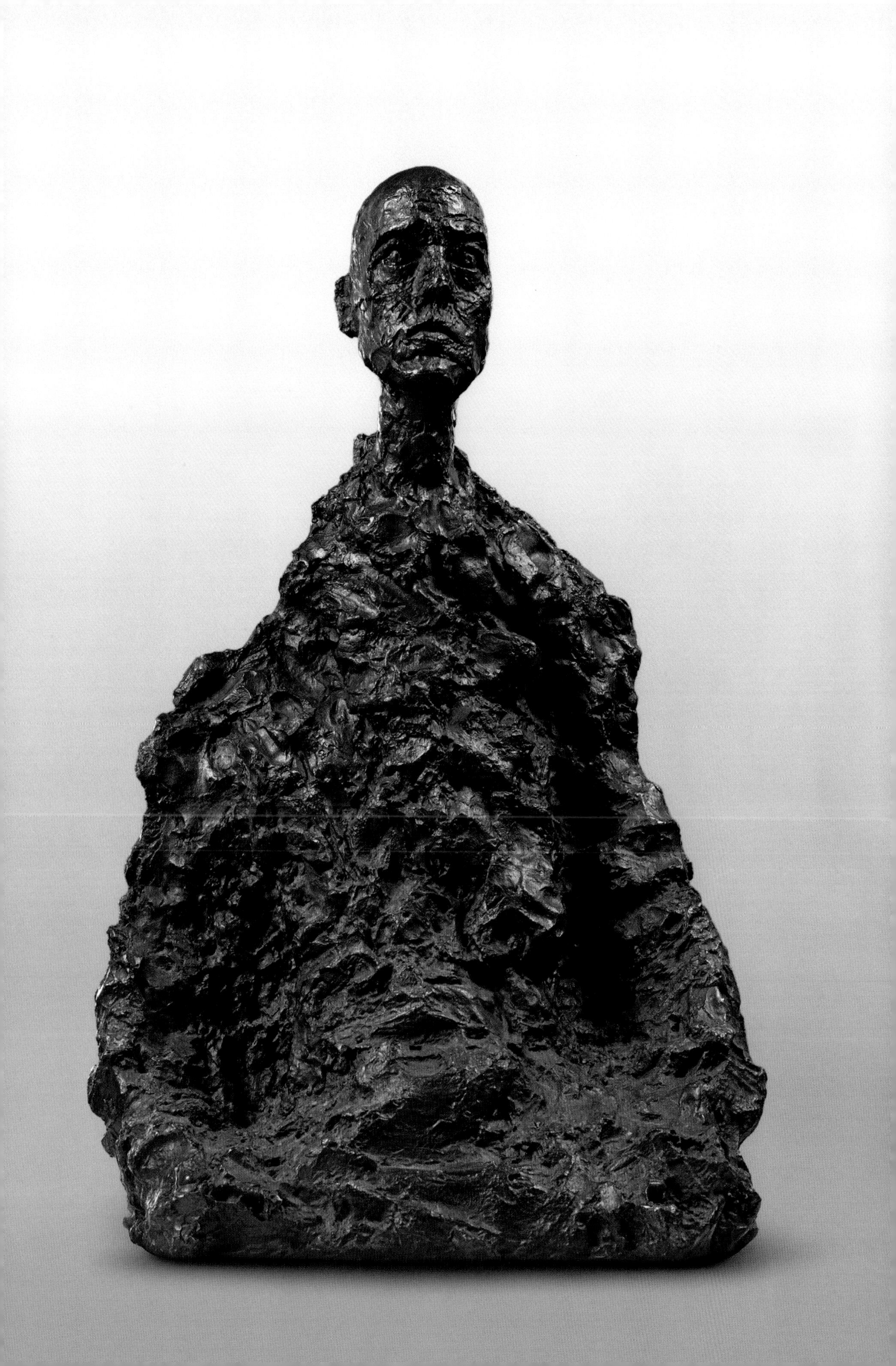

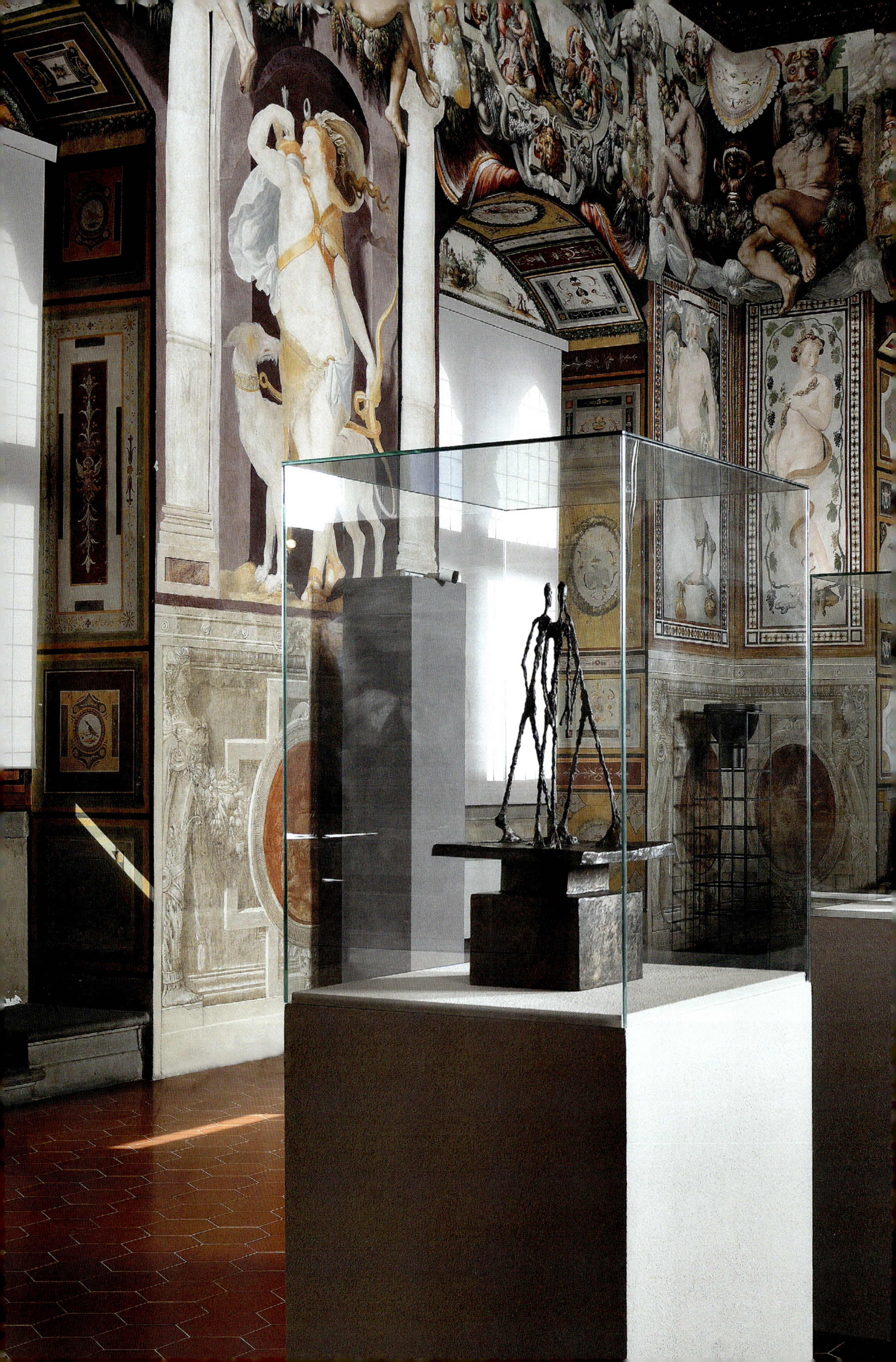

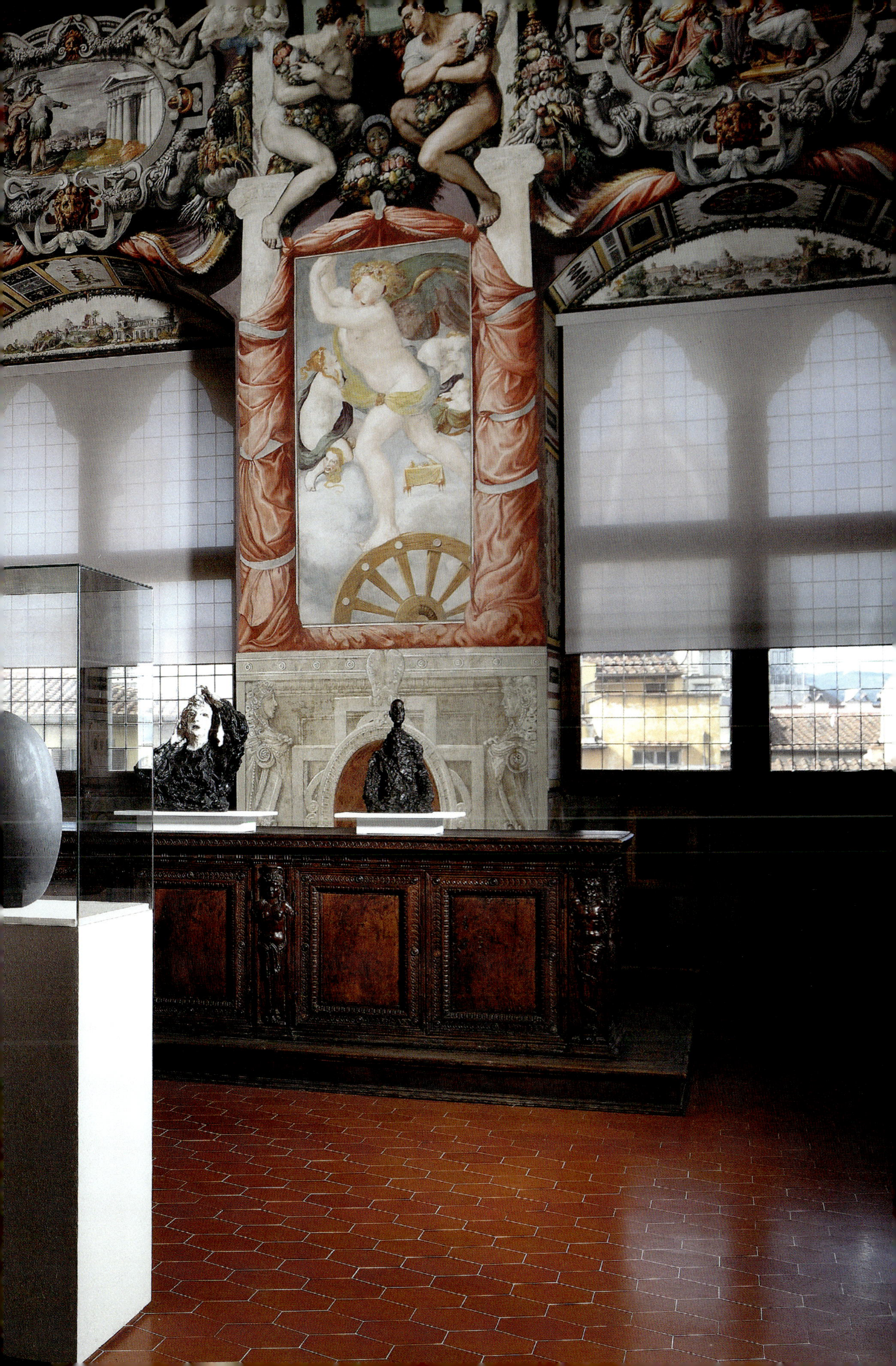

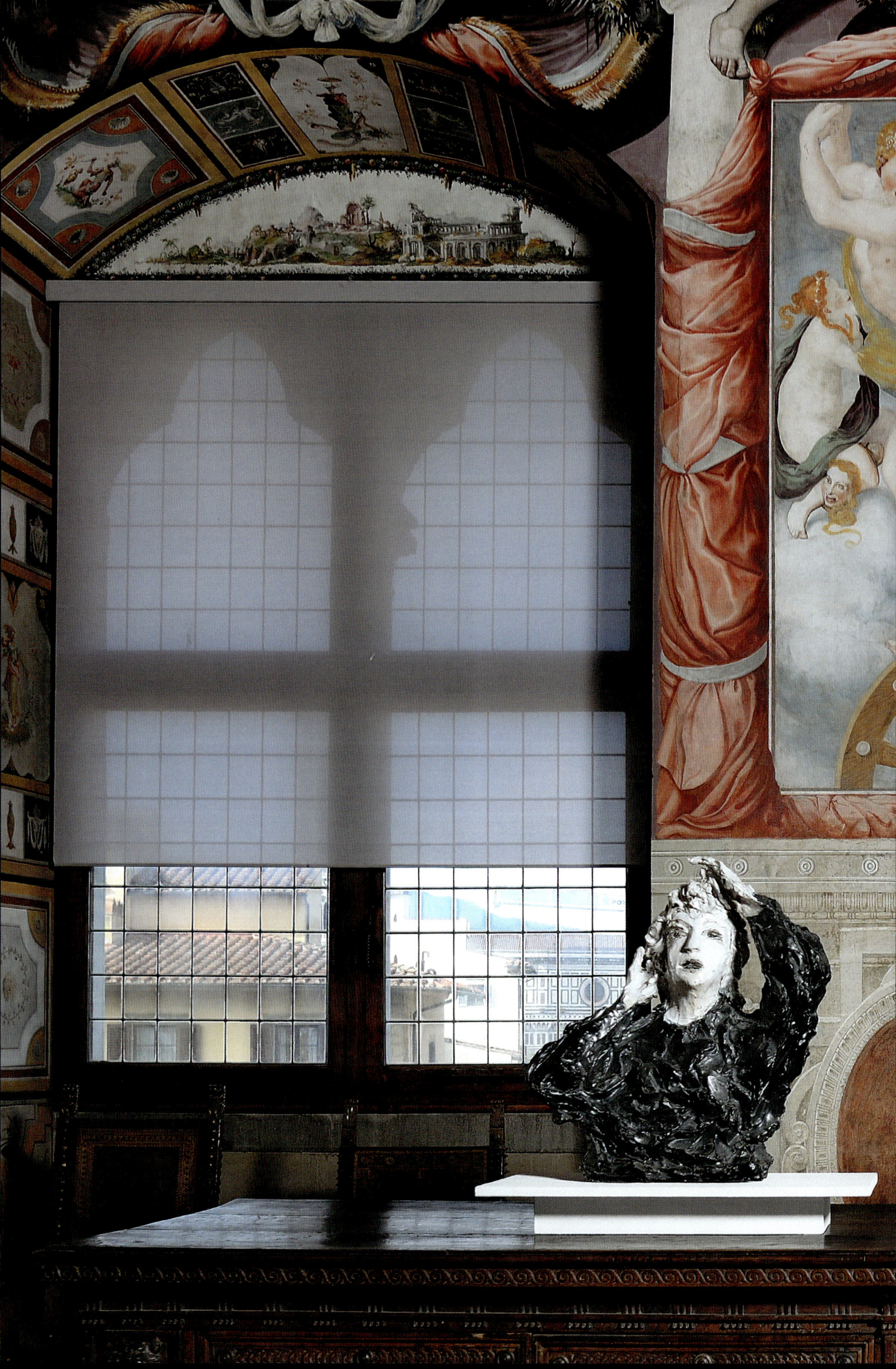

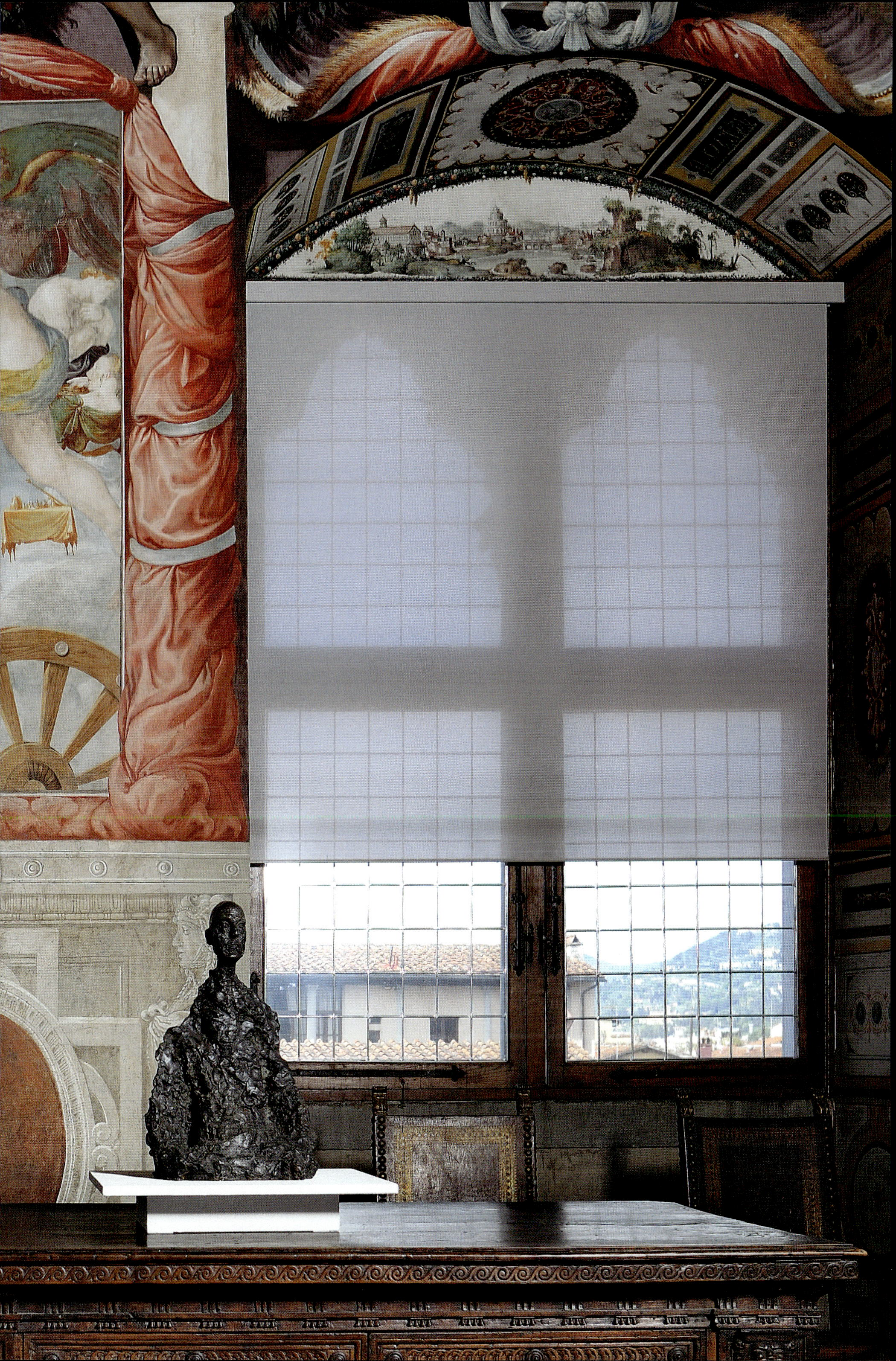

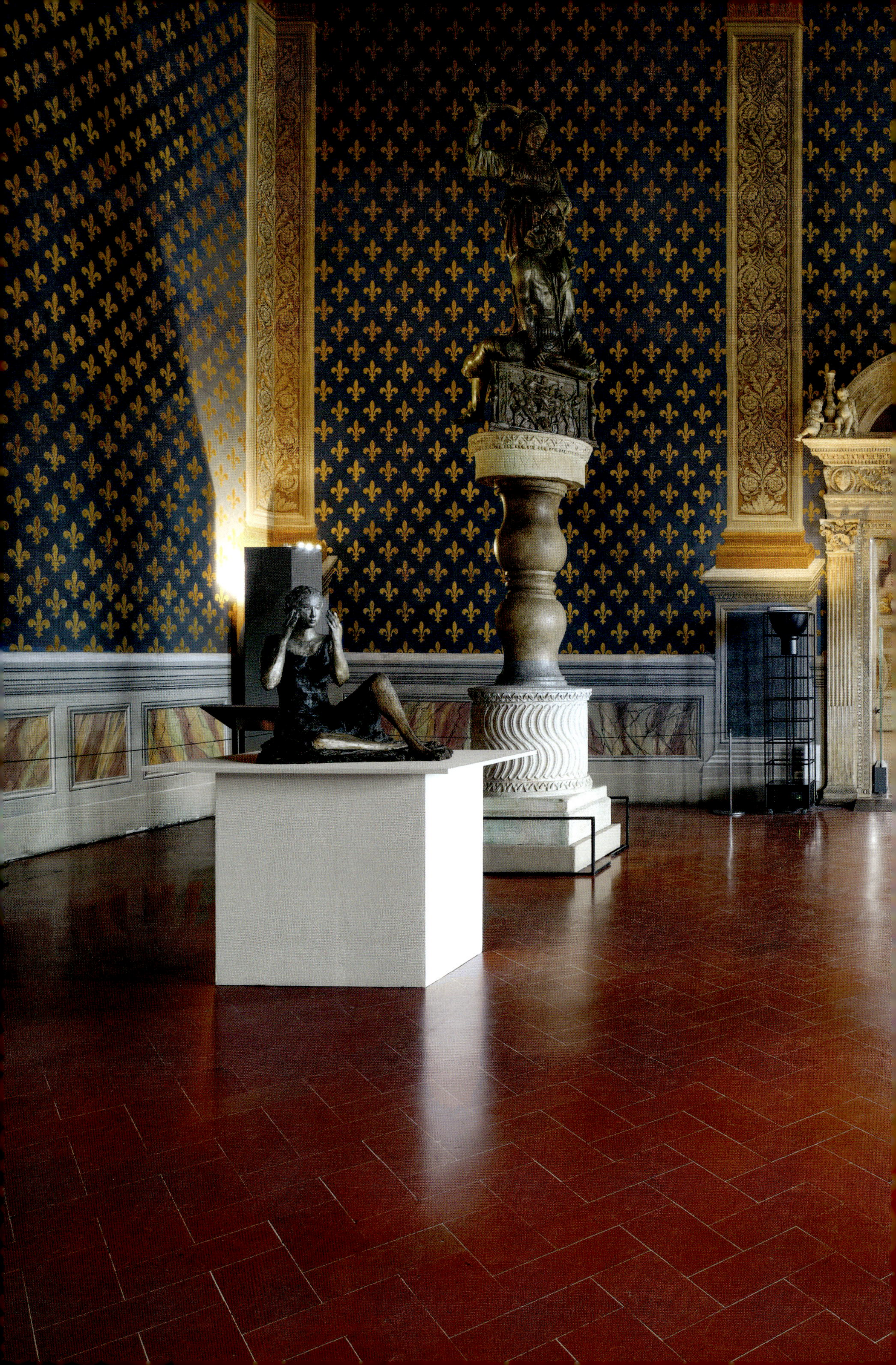

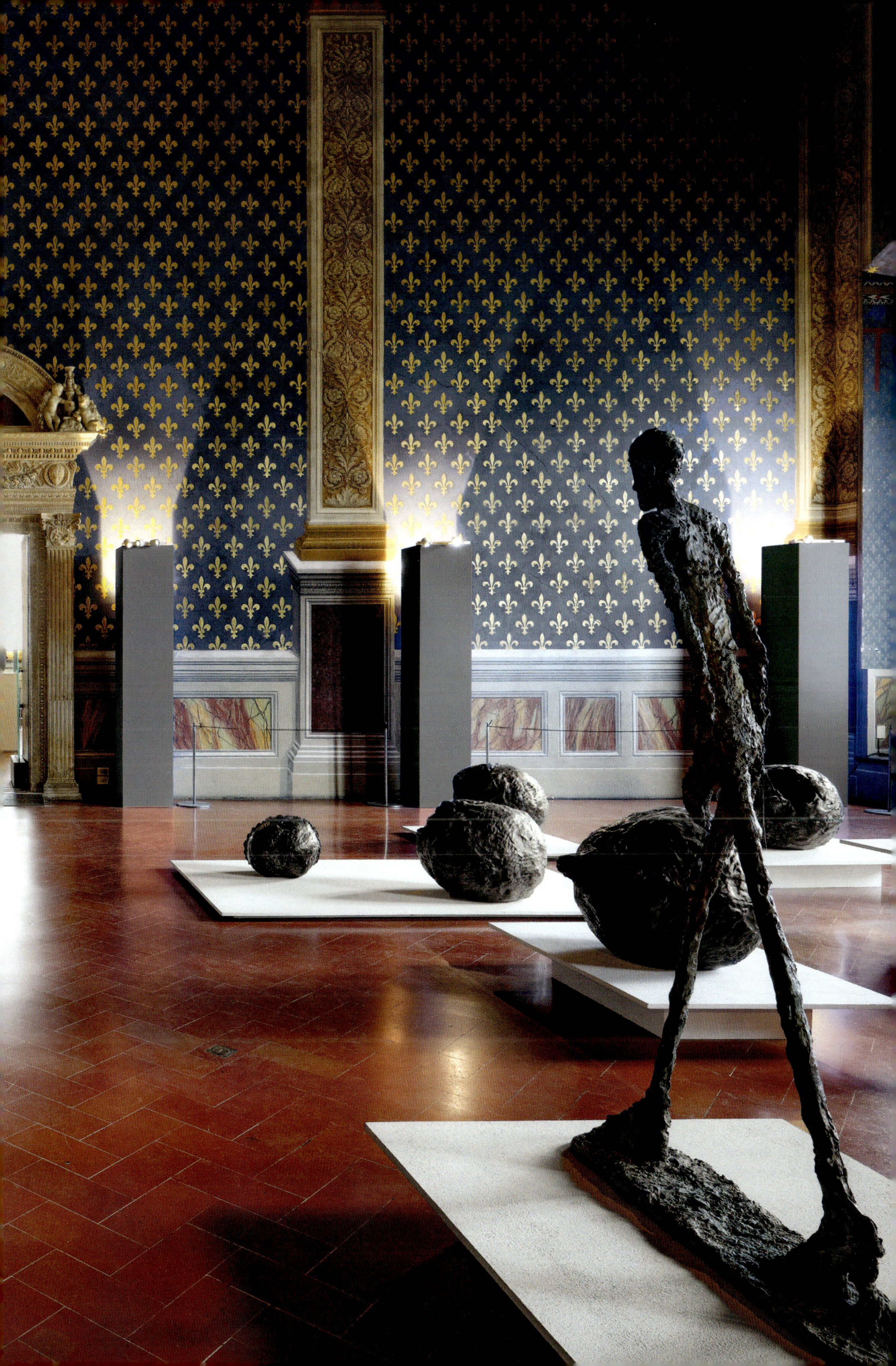

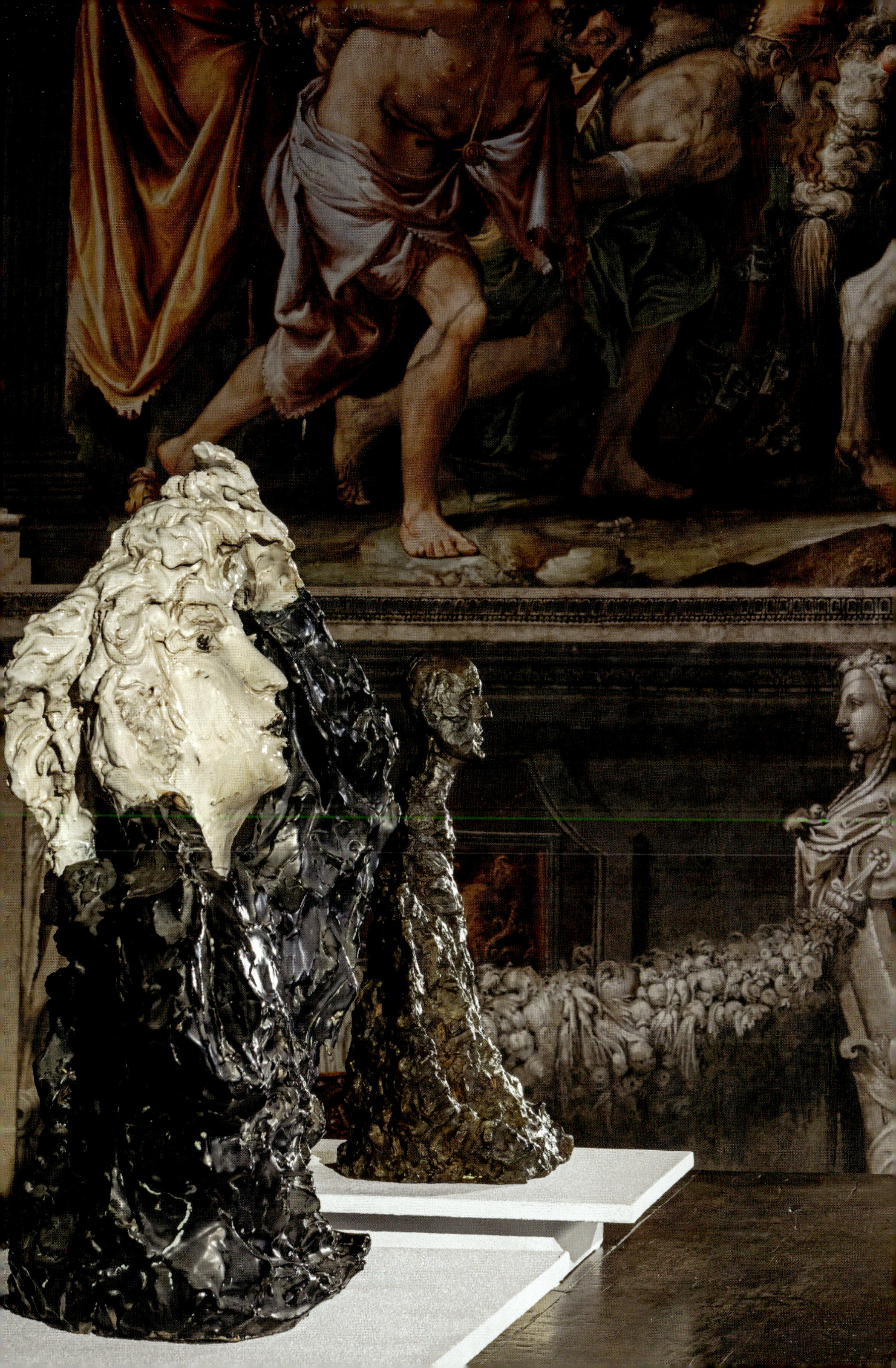

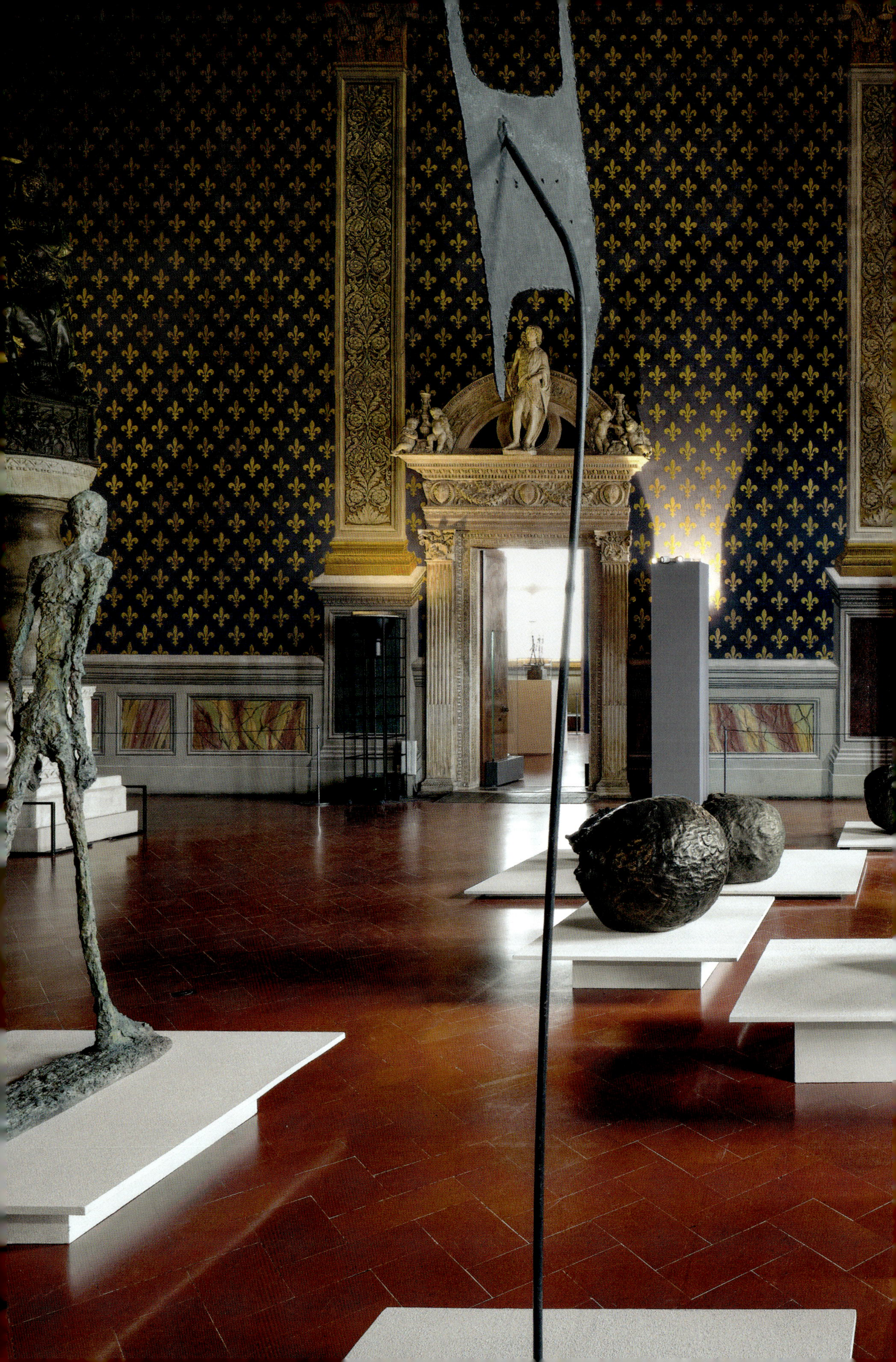

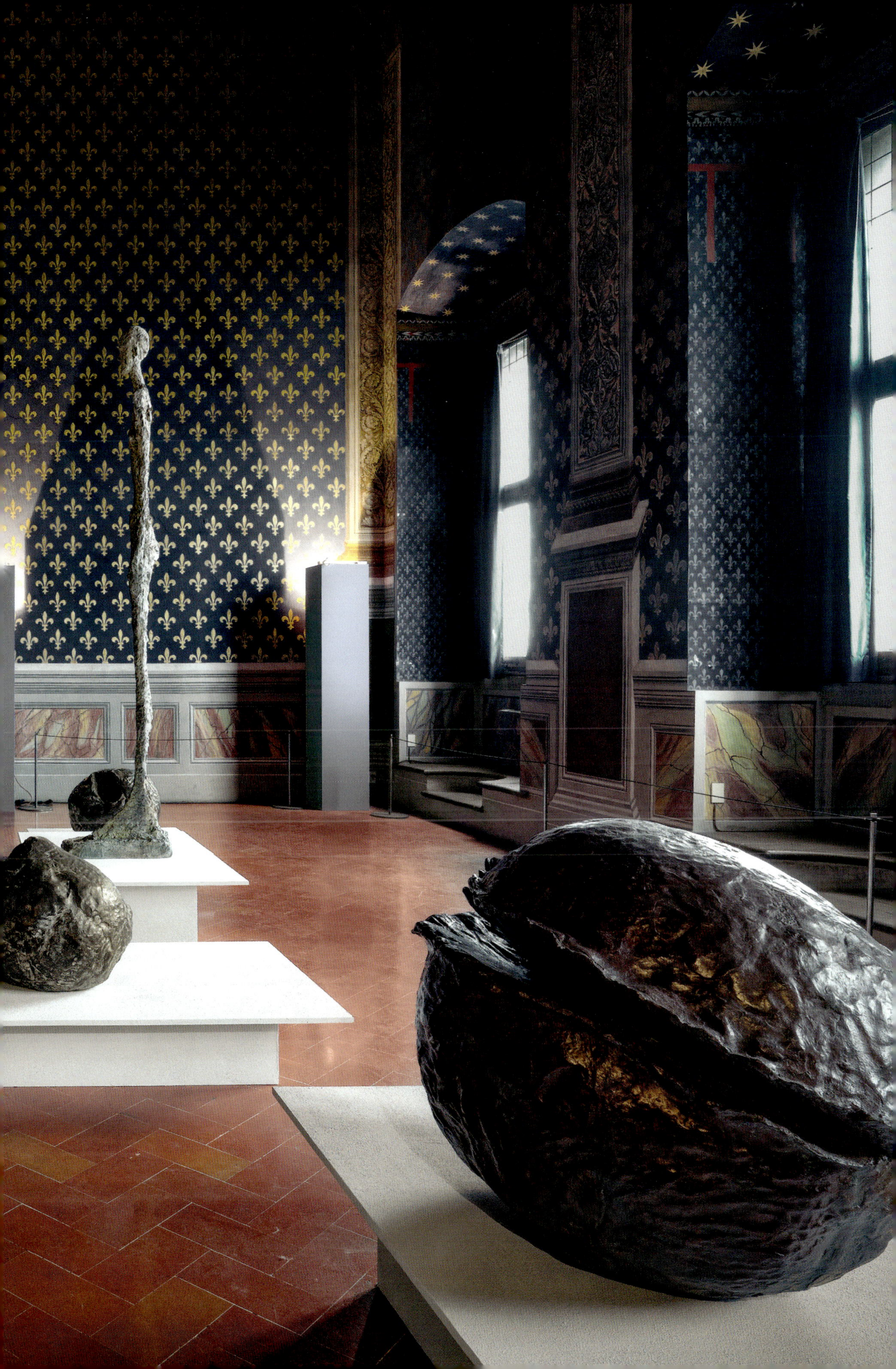

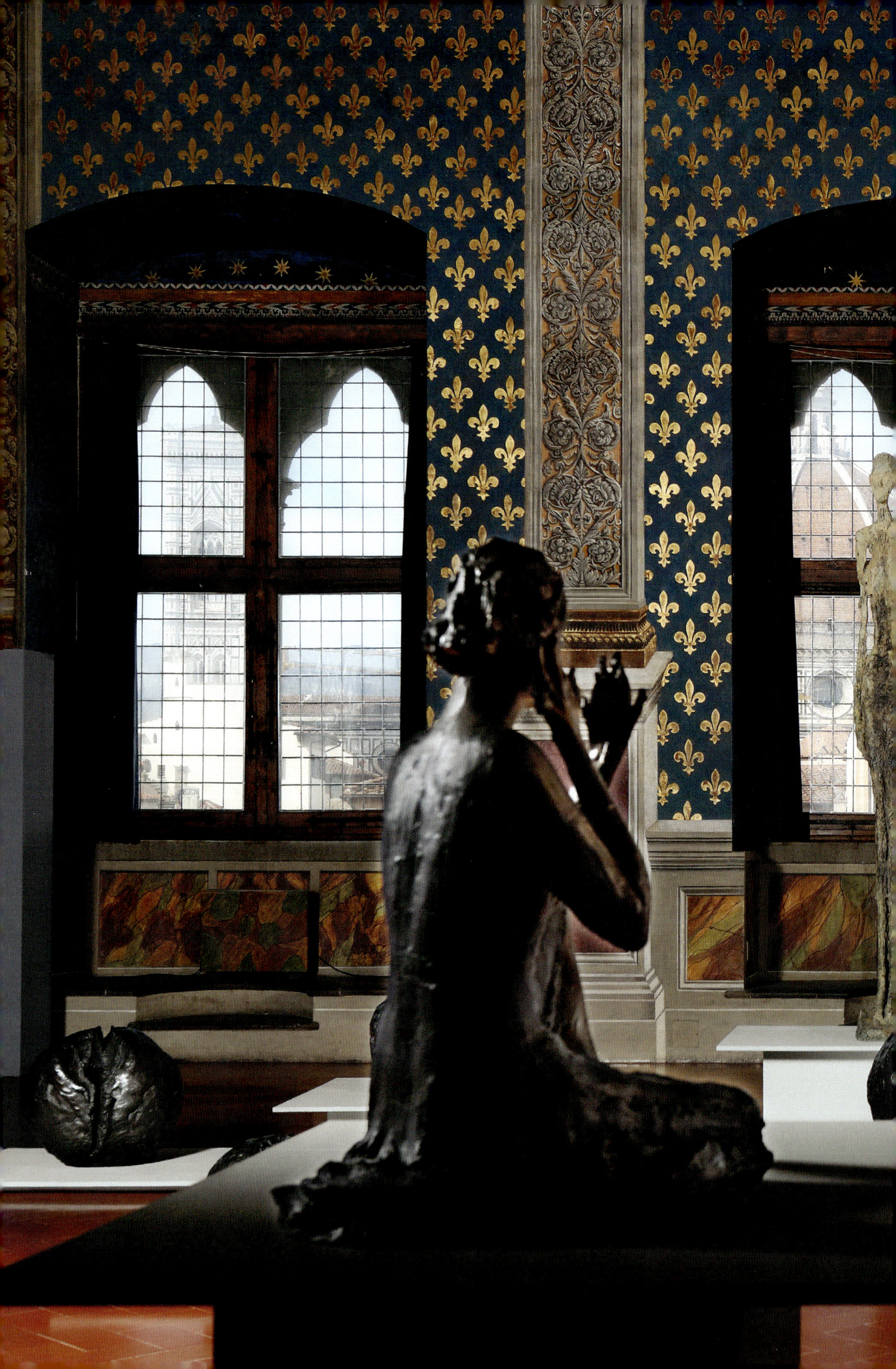

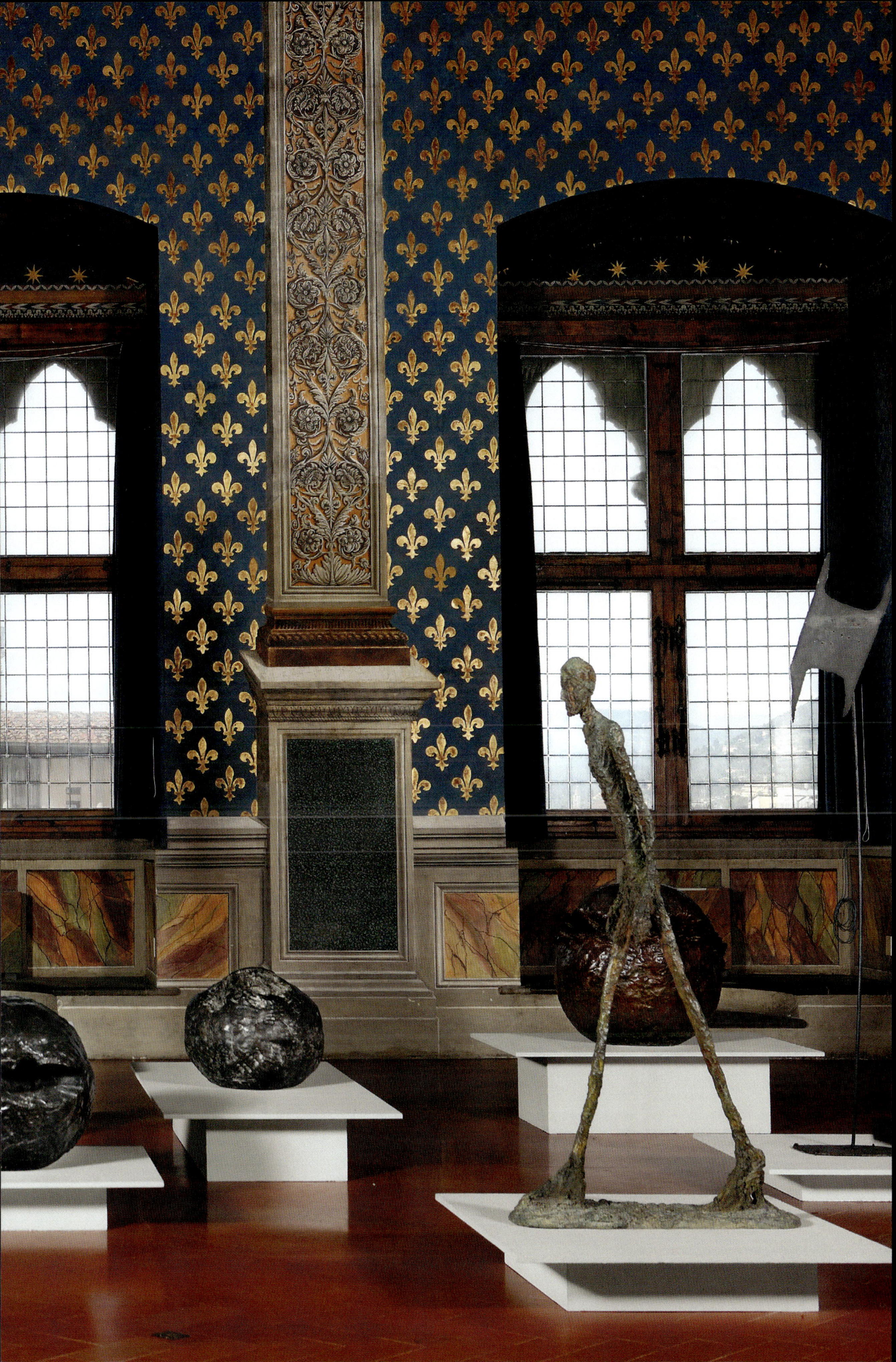

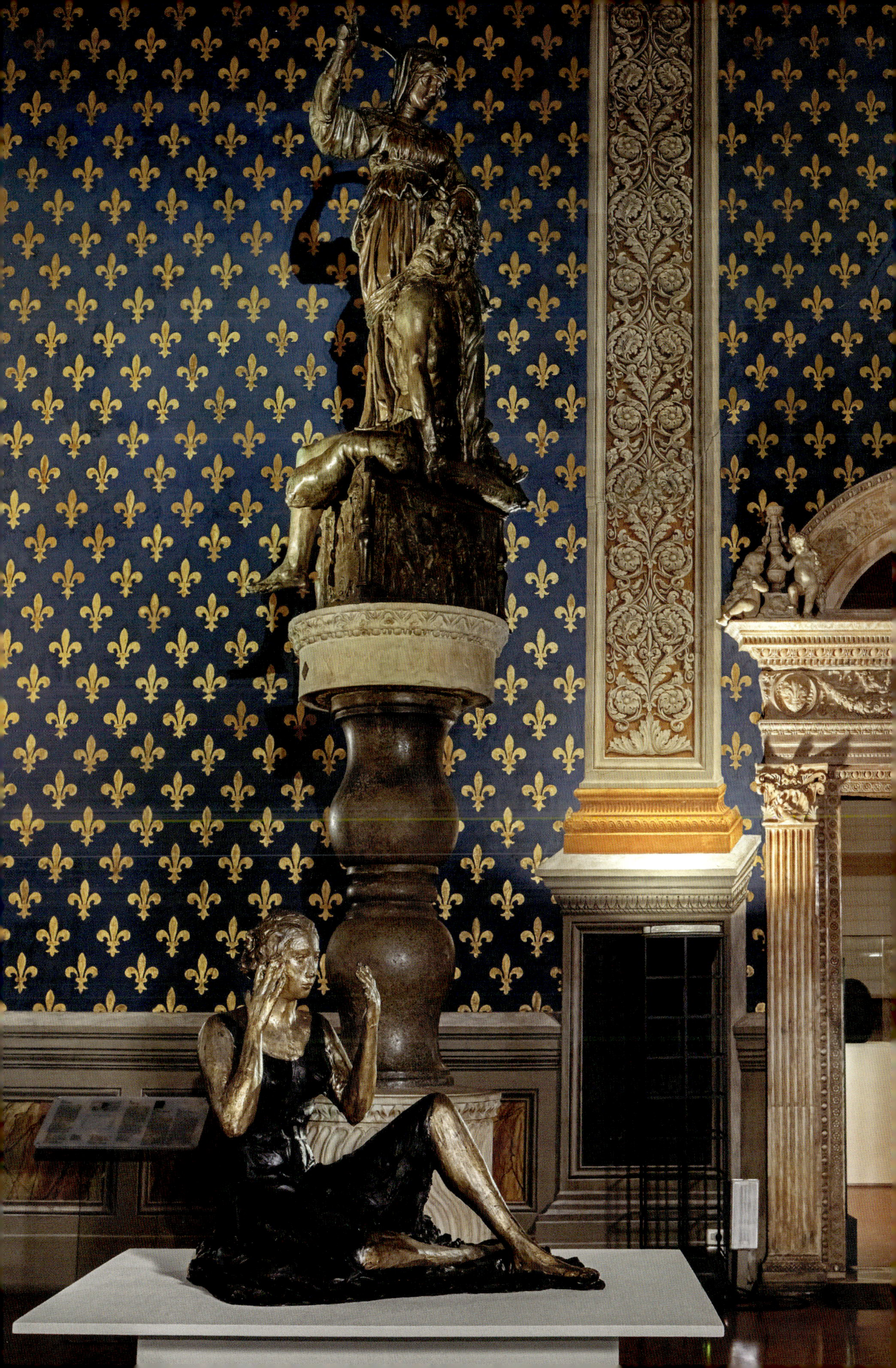

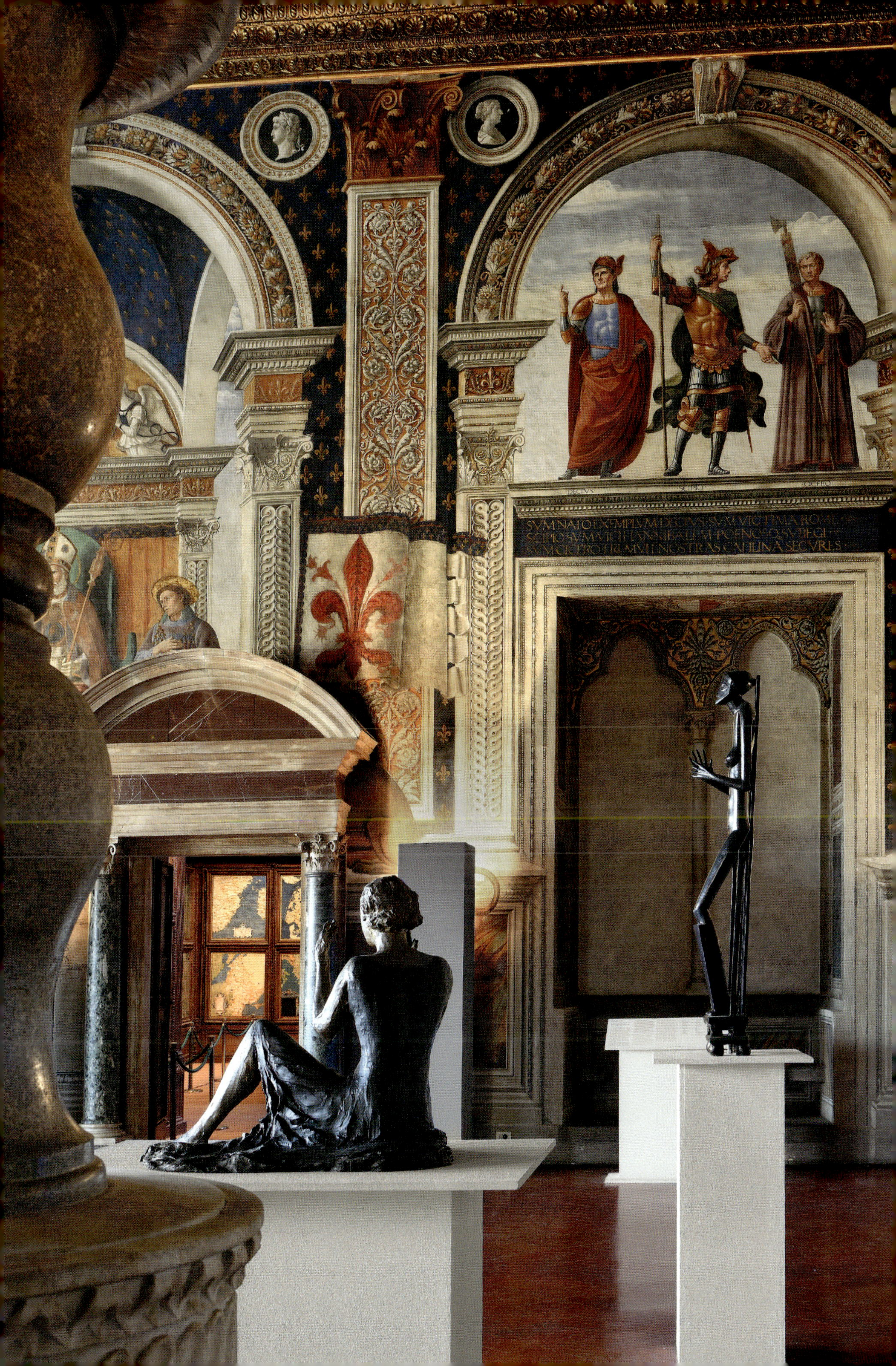
DECIUS
SCIPIO
CICERO

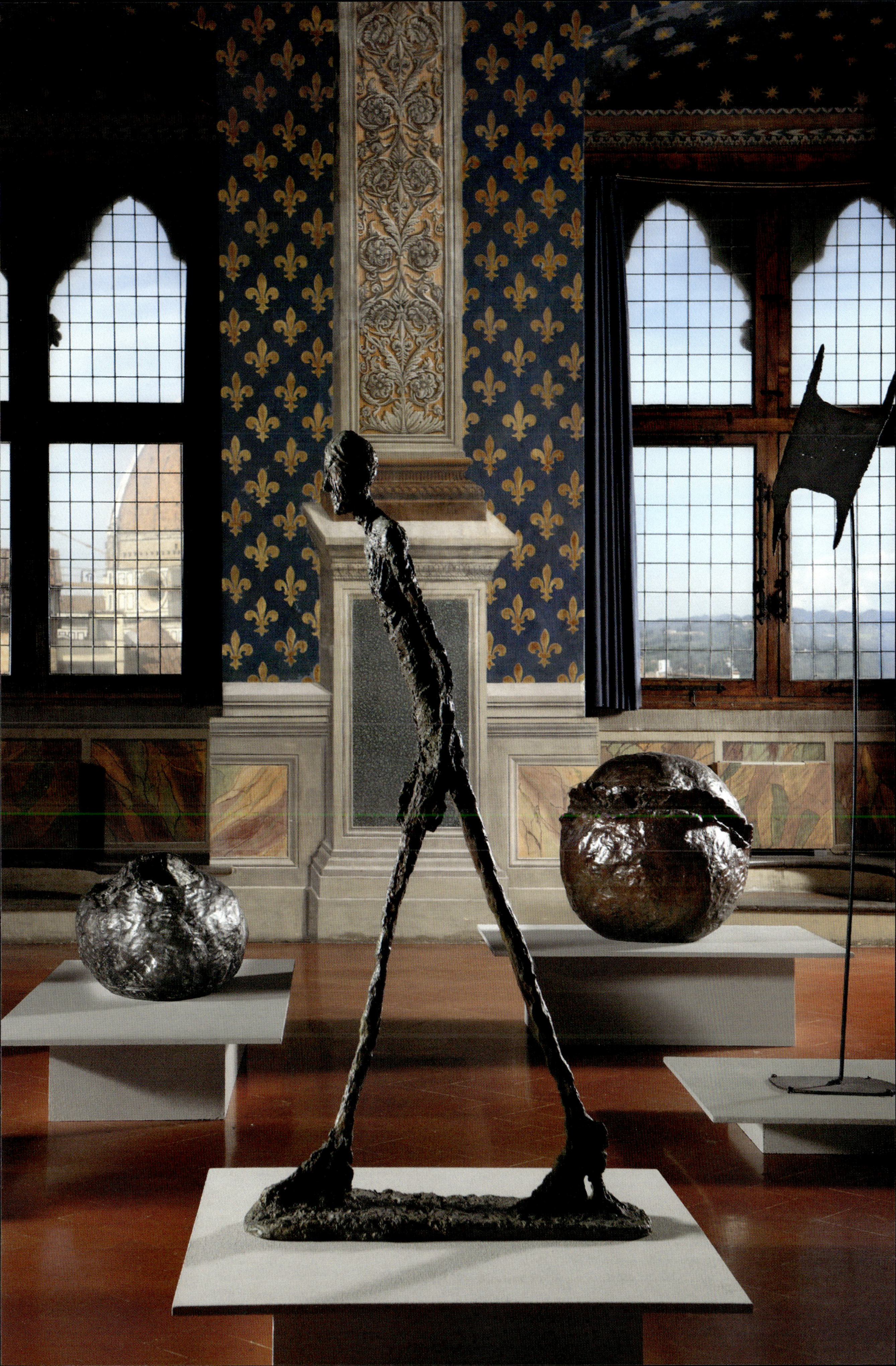

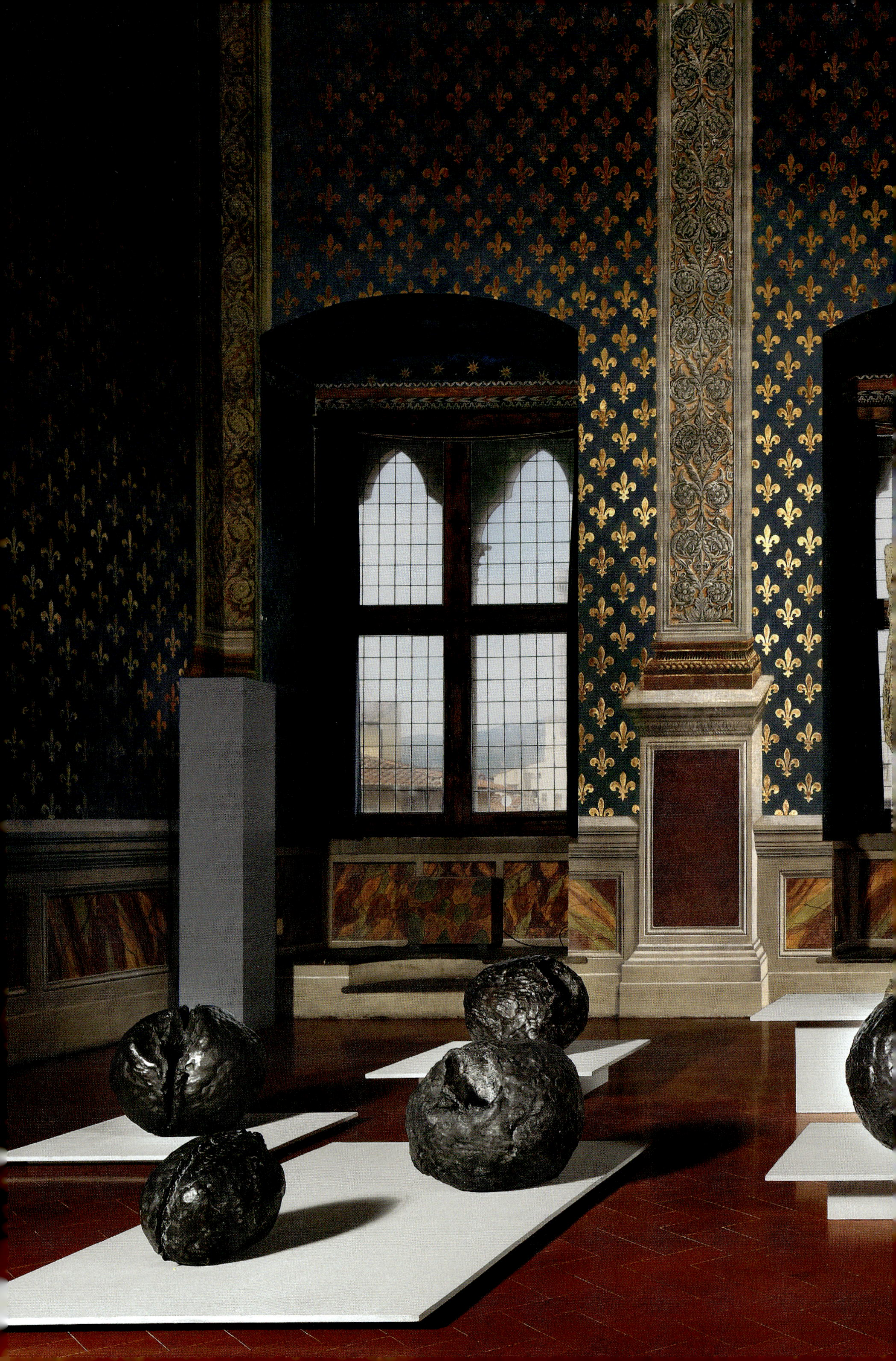

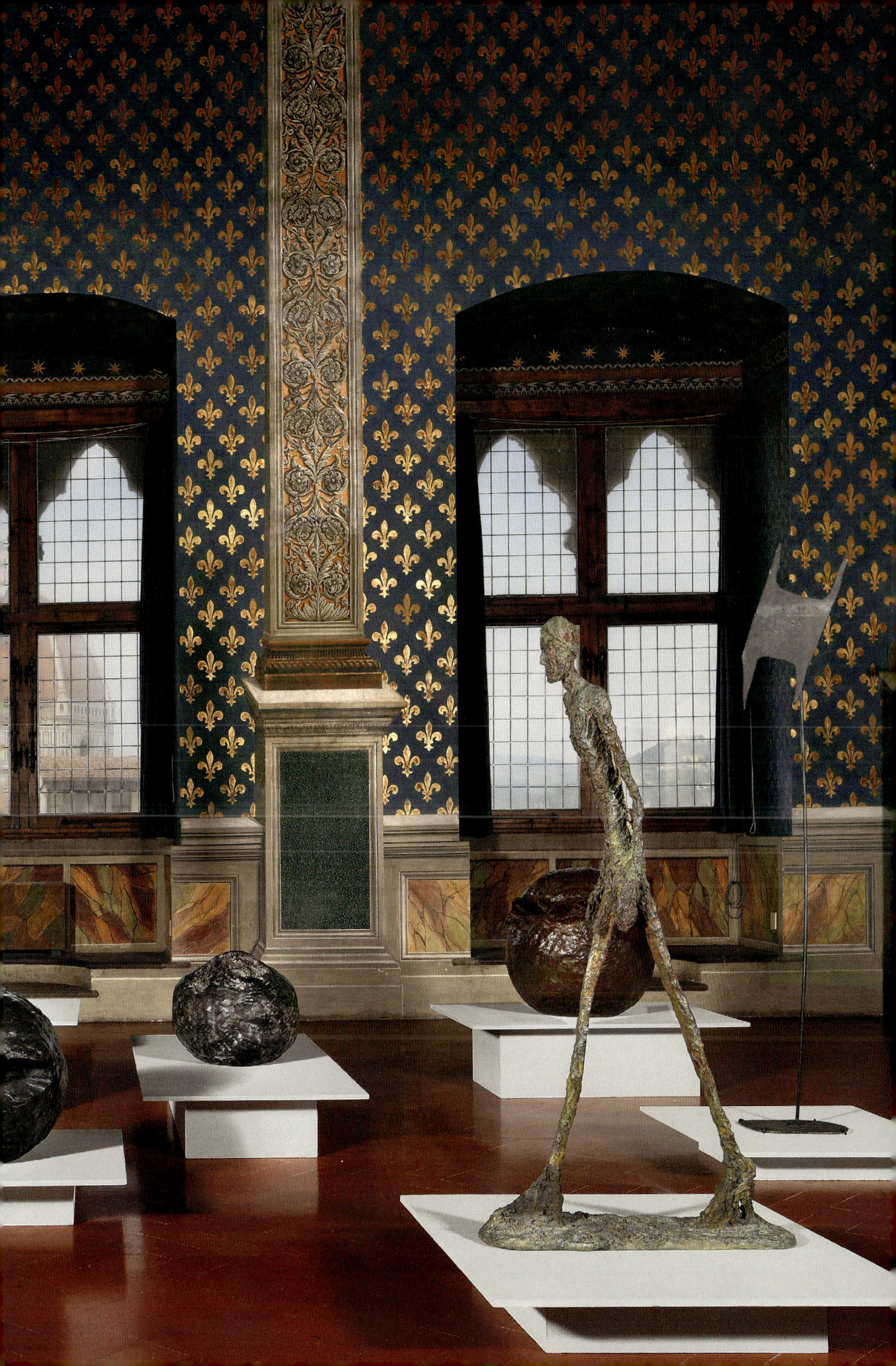

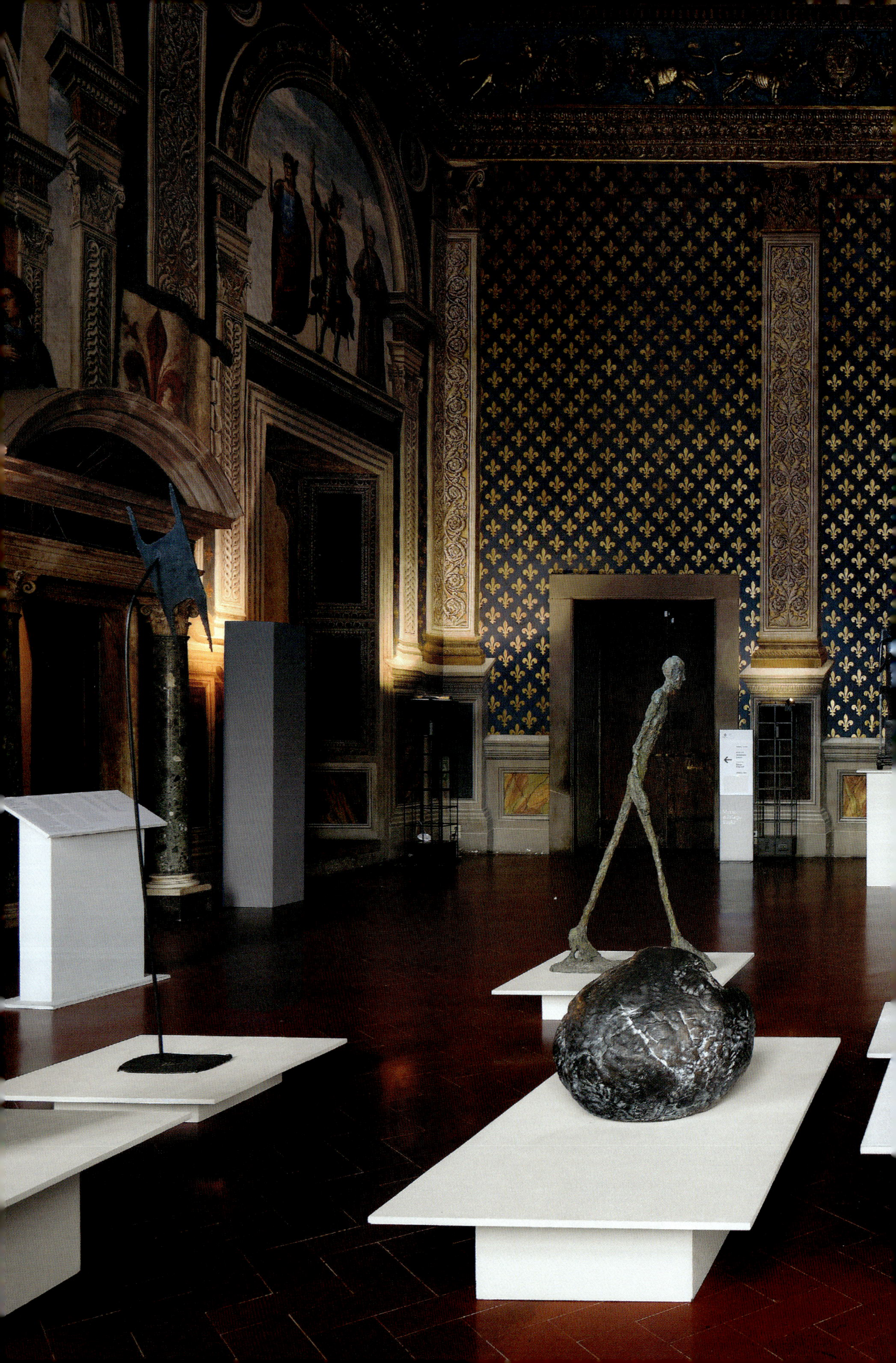

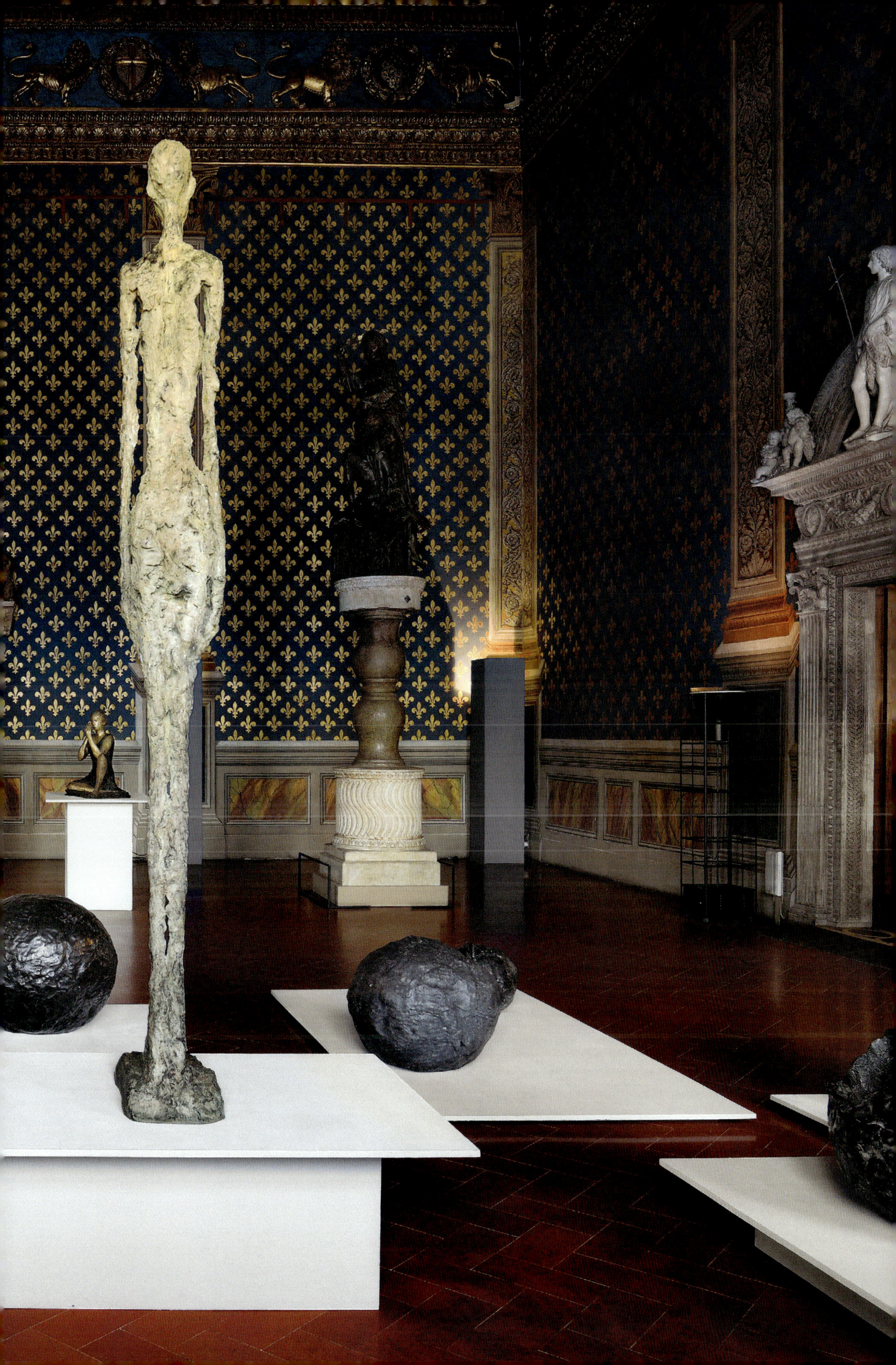

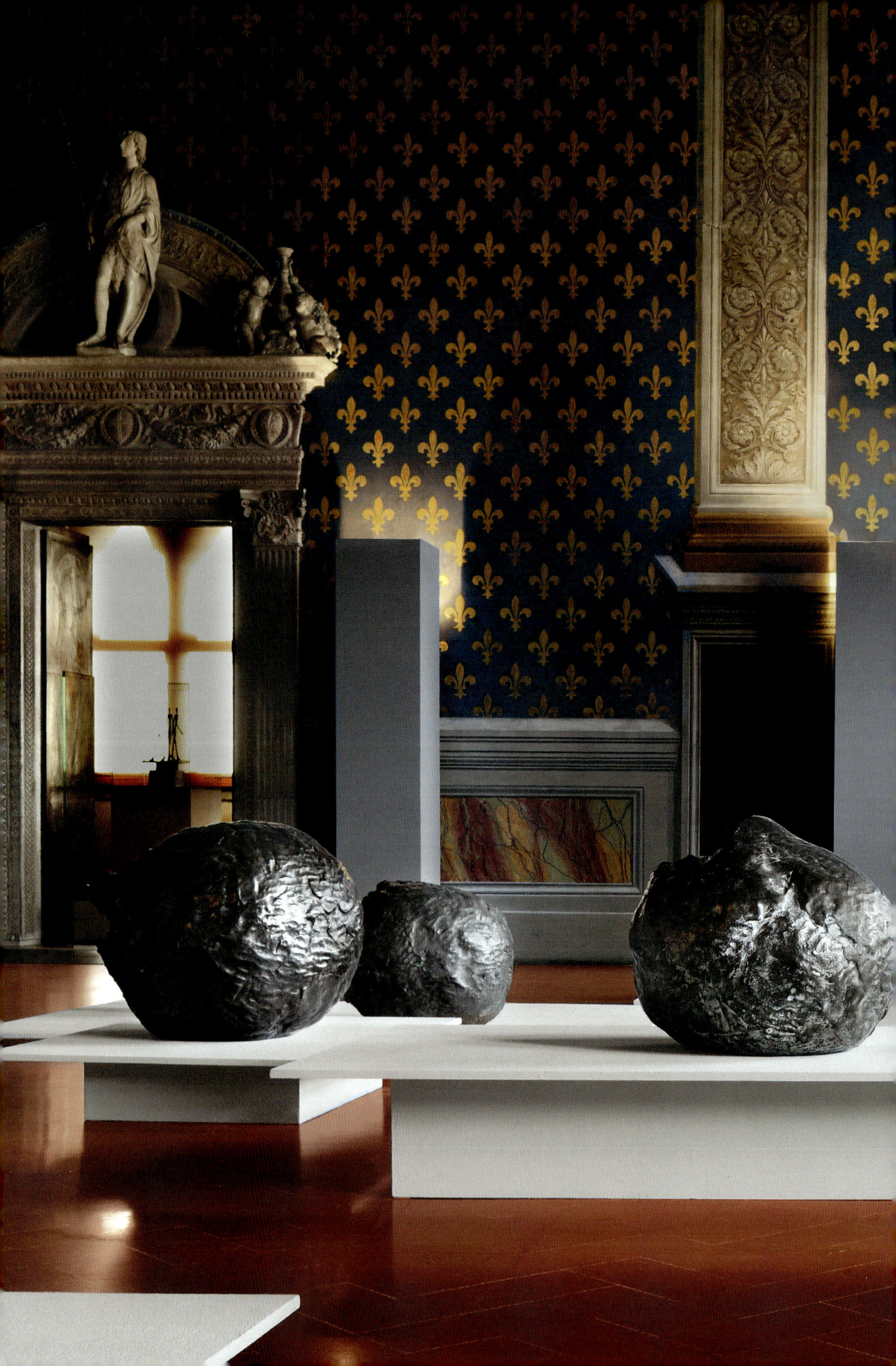

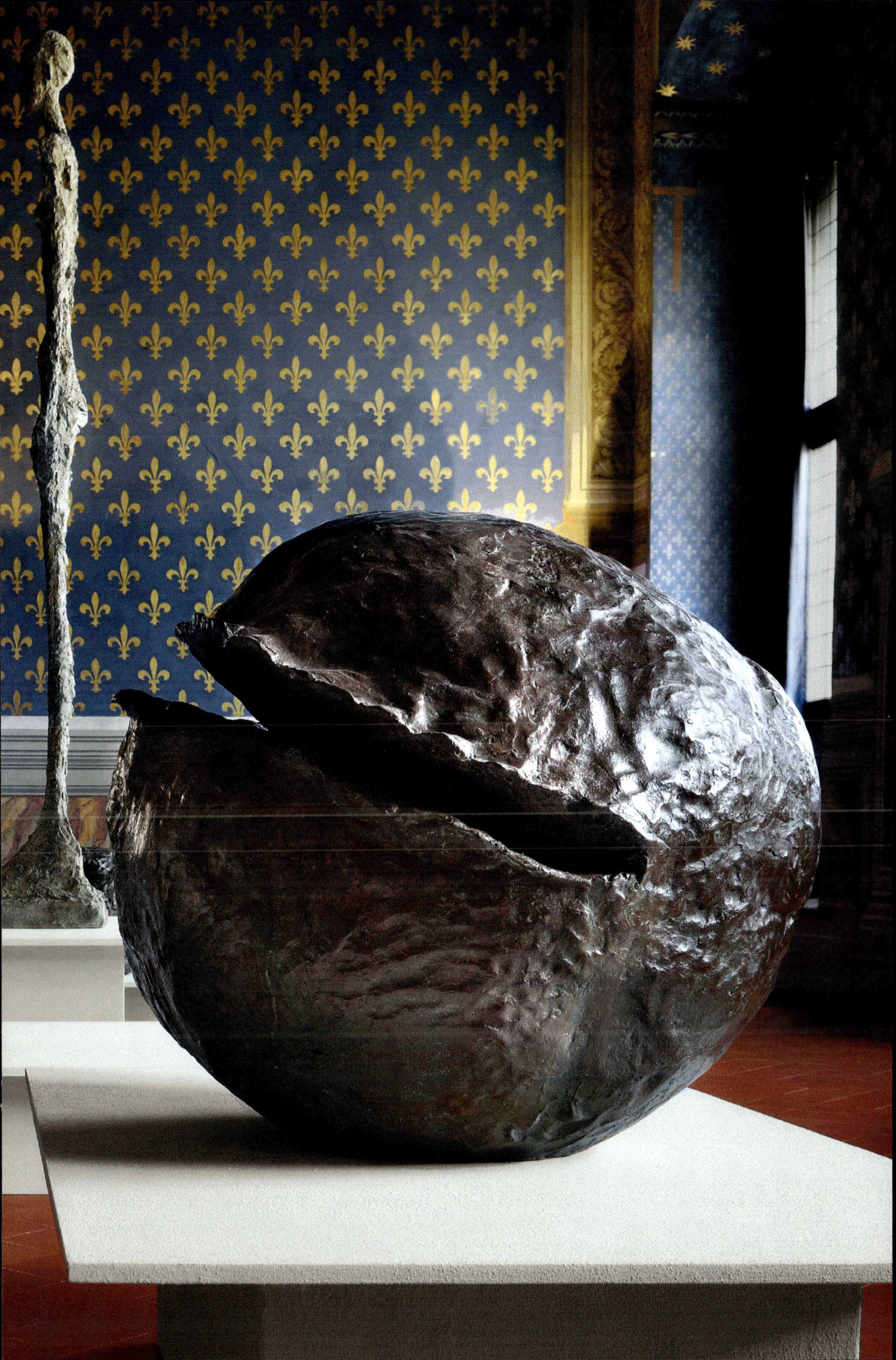

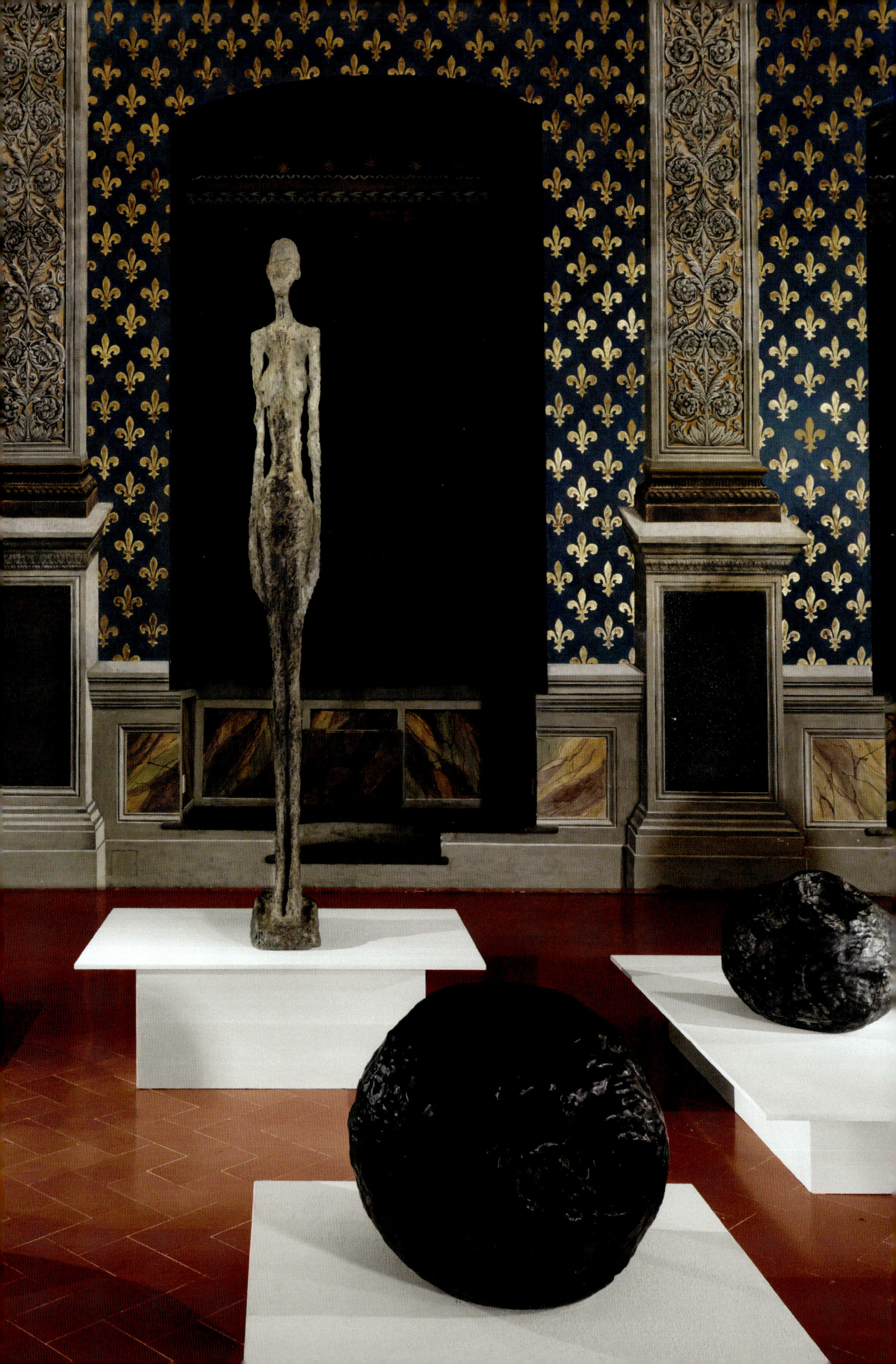

GIA
CO
MET
TI

FON
TA
NA

GIACOMETTI FONTANA

The Research for the Absolute

edited by
Sergio
Risaliti

SilvanaEditoriale

Like hand-to-hand combat. Without the gore but with extraordinary visual and sensorial value and impact.

The exhibition in the Sale dei Gigli and the Sale delle Udienze in Palazzo Vecchio is extraordinary: for the first time, it brings together two outstanding contemporary artists in a constant dialogue, and continual cross-referencing between them and rooms that host them.

This exhibition offers viewers a unique opportunity to try to understand the relationship between past and present, and the continuous dialogue within the world of art and artists. Everything is handed down and transformed. In the Sala dei Gigli, Giacometti's jagged humanity comes up against Donatello's humanism. The impressive Judith, which has just undergone restoration and cleaning, and the experience of the relationship between man and the cosmos as defined by Fontana, relates to the perfect geometry on the ceiling and the enormous globe in the Sala delle Carte Geografiche a little further on, the perfect summation of the Medici cosmogony.

Here, then, we are faced with a short-circuit of history, art, sensations and perceptions that makes this exhibition truly unprecedented, once again making Florence not only the natural cradle of art but also the perfect venue for the many renaissances that art has continually brought into play from the past to the present.

In fact, this exhibition takes place in a Florence that has chosen to invest heavily in contemporary art and culture in recent years: we have opened new spaces, mounted important exhibitions (Fabre, Koons, Penone, Fischer, Saville, Moore, just to mention a few of the many examples), relaunched events and shows, and promoted public art. All of this with a precise idea: not catwalks, not spontaneous initiatives, but projects that challenge us, asking questions about what direction art and Florence itself are taking now, and trying to indicate a new, visionary, dialectical path that pushes the sumptuous past into the future.

Dario
Nardella

**MAYOR
OF FLORENCE**

When I Model a Woman, then Motionless; a Man, always Walking

Sergio
Risaliti

In every work of art, the subject is primordial, whether the artist knows it or not. The measure of the formal qualities is only the sign of the measure of the artist's obsession with his subject; the form is always in proportion to the obsession. It is therefore the origin of the subject and of the obsession that needs to be investigated, and there is no saying that it is necessarily Freudian.

Alberto Giacometti

The man began to walk upright and his hands became available [...], the jaw freed the hand from its heaviest work [...], the snout became a face, the flint a tool, the hand became inventiveness, and intelligence has been seized by death.

Edgar Morin

I

L'homme qui marche (*Walking Man*), an imperious walker with monstrous feet, is one of Alberto Giacometti's most celebrated sculptures. The long, indistinct silhouette seems able to point the arrow of time in two directions, into the most distant past and into a future still foreign to us. As a prehistoric figure, this walking man gives the impression of having just raised himself up into an erect position, leaving the animal that he was behind him, in order to become aware of the world, and, soon after, of being-toward-death. The first of these figures, realised in 1947, just two years after the end of the Second World War and the dropping of the atomic bomb on Hiroshima, seems powerfully inspired by Egyptian art, given the two-dimensionality to which the sculptural form of a man in movement is reduced. This clue already tells us that Giacometti worked on the cusp of mortality and eternity. But this walking man seems consumed by toil and pain, eaten up and made thin by exterior and interior forces, as if he has been subjected to continual corporeal work, like a monolith washed and carved by the seasons and the elements. Modelled in plaster in the artist's studio, between grey walls and with ash on the floor, the figure was then cast in bronze under the watchful eye of Alberto's brother, Diego. He is a resilient figure and looks determined to march on to the very end. A passage opens in space, propelled by a strength of will the magnitude of which we do not yet know. His attitude and posture recall that of a man lost in a crowd, isolated from the rest of the world, "walking eternally towards completion", as Reinhold Hohl put it. And how can one not think of a hominid who has just emerged from a cave, and, driven by the instinct for survival, lengthens his stride to traverse a territory as vast as it is unknown – the open air. Photos taken inside Giacometti's studio show recently modelled preparatory models enveloped with white sheets, still damp to keep the material fresh. These clothes are very temporary, humble rags that look like shrouds. The figures are like resurrected beings who have emerged from a tomb, still swathed in bandages covering their wasted flesh, the stench of decomposition perceptible. Their appearance as living ghosts is also that of Lazarus who has returned to the light of day. Remaining for days on end in his studio, working day and night, Giacometti felt at ease with the afterlife, with the world of shadows and the dead; he experienced his environment of ascetic concentration as a tomb, to which he could retire for hours to converse with the people of the dead.

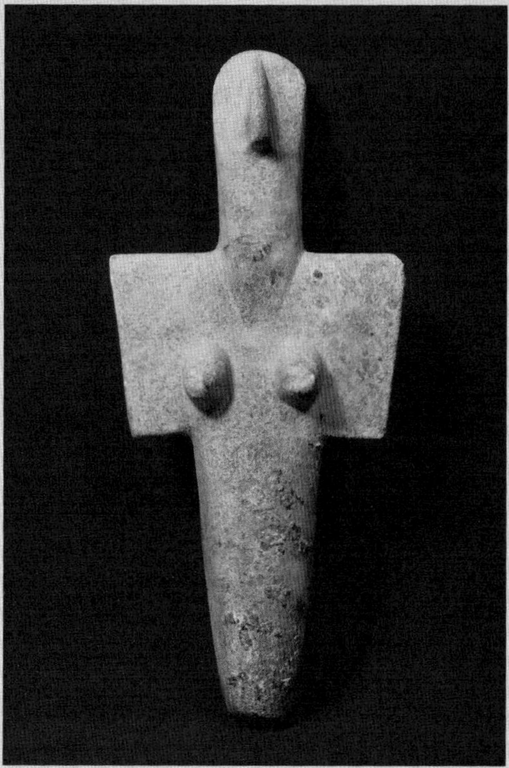

Dea Madre di Turriga da Senorbì, circa 4.000 – 3.300 a.C., Museo Archeologico Nazionale, Cagliari, inv. 135887

Giacometti liked caves a lot, finding inspiration in them and searching for the essence of movement in the Lascaux cave drawings, in the figures of animals and hunters: "I copied the bison, the mammoths, entire walls of Lascaux many times." And again: "Cave painting. Drawings in caves, caves, caves, caves. There, and only there, is the movement successful. Understand why, discover the possibilities, but I doubt it." In describing his childhood, Giacometti referred to the discovery of an enormous rock and a cave: "As a child (between four and seven years old) all I saw of the outside world were the things that might feed my pleasure. First and foremost, rocks and trees, and rarely more than one thing at a time. I remember that, for at least two summers, all I saw of what surrounded me was a large rock about eight hundred metres from the village, and beyond that rock, the objects that directly related to it. It was a gold-coloured monolith, with a cave opening at the base, the whole lower part carved out and eroded by water. The entrance was low and oblong, barely taller than we were at that time. The inside became deeper and deeper, until at the end it formed what looked like a second, small cave. It was my father who showed us the monolith one day. An enormous discovery. I immediately considered that large rock to be a friend, a creature animated by the best of intentions towards us; it called us, smiled at us, like someone already met and loved in the past, and found again with infinite amazement and joy... Our first thought after discovering the rock was to limit access. There had to be a fissure just wide enough for us to enter. But I was overjoyed when I could curl up in the small cave at the back; I could only just get in; my every desire was met." For Jean Clair this memory conceals, or reveals, elements useful for a psychoanalytic reading of some of the artist's obsessions. For example, that the double cave, the entrance obstructed by the monolith, should be related to a drawing from 1928–31 of a phallus and vagina.

There is something fascinating and terrible about Giacometti's sculptures. This is because they pose fundamental questions. They offer no answers. They throw out questions as heavy as rocks, demolishing aesthetic certitudes and constructing an oasis of silence. They are at once protected and isolated in a single place that has the size and function of a crypt or sacellum, a *dispositif* of eternalisation amidst a market of voices and rapid steps. Theirs is not the time of becoming, but of circularity; here the beginning coincides with the end, the remote past with the unknown yet to come. So, in what direction is the walking man heading, this nameless and ageless remnant of humanity? Is he coming towards us or going away from us, is he walking from left to right or vice versa? Is there a privileged point of view we are unable to access? Should we consider the sculpture to be a classic in-the-round work? Up close, one has the sensation of crashing against a cliff. Exterior and interior coincide, like a piece of clay that has been beaten up or stripped of its flesh to discover the essence of the human being, that scrap of eternity or truth which suffices to save us from nothingness, from the senselessness of life. The space it occupies is close to our own; it almost coincides with where we dwell, but we inexorably sense, or rather, recognise an unclosable distance between us and the figure of the walking man. It is this duality that attracts and disconcerts – of bodies and faces that are close and distant, similar and alien, of the living and the dead, inhabitants of an upper and lower world, of light and shadow. The form does not allow the gaze to slide gently across the bronze flesh, but breaks its flow, like what happens when you stroke a piece of lava with your fingers. From this alone we can see how, for Giacometti, sculpture is concerned not just with space, built from sculpture's coming into the world, but also with the gaze, which is prompted to rediscover and rethink itself. Giacometti, as we know, was unappreciative of smooth and reflective forms of the kind produced by Constantin Brancusi, regarding them as verging on design. In his figures the skin is rough, wrinkled, broken, painful to the touch. The surfaces are jagged, stony, cutting; they keep touch at a distance and are a form of negativity, like something repellent, traumatic and painful to the eye. Totally unlike the smoothness of certain minimal and even reflective surfaces, they are diametrically opposite to the transparency and the optical seductiveness of certain shiny, mirror-like metals. They are not delightful, enchanting or alluring. On the contrary, something terrible and fatal contaminated them before birth, condemning them to a certain abyssal melancholy. When we encounter them, we sense a wounded soul. The wound that Genet spoke about after being stimulated by the discovery of Giacometti's work: "Beauty has no other origin than the singular wound, different in every case, hidden or visible, which each man bears within himself, which he preserves, and into which he withdraws when he would quit the world for a temporary but authentic solitude." This wound is the limit and the threshold between life and death, between being and nothingness; it is the risk to be faced, about which R. M. Rilke spoke. In other words, Giacometti's figures are those of a humanity that dwells in the world of life in the moment of retreating from it, belonging to death for ever. Or revenants that reach the land of the living, of light, with the air of belonging to the world of the dead.

Going back to fix the model from real life, or the model in the studio, Giacometti passed over resemblance, pushing way beyond presence itself, in that his works elude it. They elude real presence, demonstrating that they already pertain to death and to nothingness. By doing so, he was able to rediscover the sublime in beauty, and in what is disturbing the logic of profound sensations. There is no doubt that Giacometti had fully understood what Cézanne meant when he affirmed the necessity to translate his sensations into painting. He too believed it was impossible to copy nature, though it was "the only thing to do, the only thing I am interested in", he said, convinced that it was an unachievable goal. He would often say: "I must open a hole for myself in nature and go through it. I have effectively opened this hole, but it is too small to pass through". Those cracks we recognise in the paintings of Cezanne, left to extend the gaze beyond the visible, those holes made by Lucio Fontana, with gestures as radical as they are irreversible, to penetrate the infinite.

And like other of his figures, elongated like cypresses, *L'homme qui marche* could also pass through a small crack or cut, and penetrate a different universe to our own, leapfrogging the dimensions of space and time known to us in order to live in a world of reminiscences, in a dream, in a before or after the collapse of the planet. In fact, I have no difficulty in seeing in this sculpture the stride of Adam expelled from earthly paradise as imagined and painted by Masaccio in the church of the Carmine in Florence around 1423–25. This figurative artist also interested Rodin, the father of modern sculpture. Indeed, how can we not see an echo of those Renaissance figures in the *Homme qui marche* that Rodin produced by assembling, around 1900, a study for the legs of a Saint John the Baptist and a torso, where the smooth lower section is in sharp contrast with the much more formless upper part. Giacometti must have had these illustrious precedents in mind, both the work by Masaccio and the one by the great French sculptor. All this is borne out by the existence of a drawing in which one can make out the two progenitors as they appear on one of the frescoed walls of the Brancacci Chapel. It may have been a recollection of his first trip to Florence in the 20s, which Giacometti visited when he was young after having gone to Venice and Padua. Alternatively, that memory may have arisen from Giacometti's lifetime practice of studying catalogues, volumes, photographs and prints. In a note from 1965 about the importance of copies, the sculptor wrote: "When I first saw reproductions of artworks, and this dates back to my earliest childhood and is mixed up with my most distant memories, I immediately wanted to copy everything that attracted me most, and in actual fact the pleasure of copying has never passed." Giacometti often spoke about simultaneity, about a kind of stratification of experiences and memories, of real images and emotions, all together like a millefeuille, with time and space compressing and combining before the subject: "all of a sudden I see myself at the Galleria Borghese in Rome while I'm copying Rubens, one of the great discoveries of that day, but in the same instant I see myself simultaneously along the whole trajectory of my past; near the window in Stampa in 1914, engrossed in copying a Japanese print, of which I could describe every detail; and in 1915, Durer and all the engravings of Rembrandt, and then comes a Pinturicchio and all the frescoes of the Quattrocento

Auguste Rodin,
L'Homme qui marche, 1907,
plaster, 219.2 x 124.2 x 151 cm,
Kunstmuseum, Basel, Inv. P 49

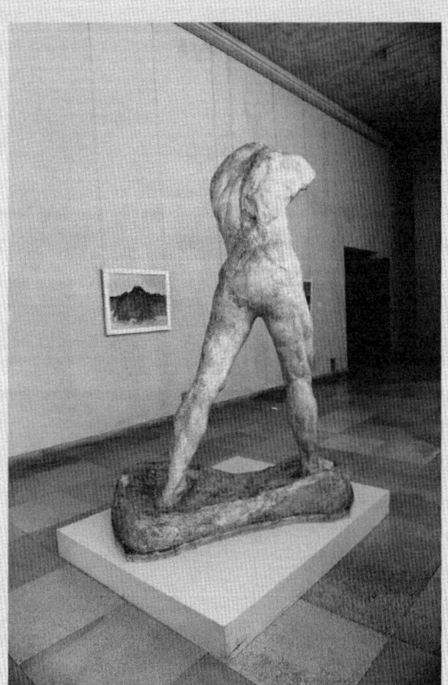

painters in the Sistine Chapel. But I also see myself forty years later as I return to my Paris studio in the evening, leaf through books and set about copying some Egyptian sculpture or another, or a Carolingian miniature, or even a Matisse. But how to say all this? Standing before me is all the art of the past, of every age and civilisation. Everything becomes simultaneous, as if space has taken the place of time. Memories of artworks blend together with affective memories, with my work, with my whole life." In another drawing Giacometti focused on Donatello's *Judith and Holofernes*, a statue with an intricate history in Renaissance Florence. Produced for the Palazzo Medici, it was expropriated from that context and displayed in the Piazza Signoria when the wealthy and powerful Medici family were expelled from Florence in 1494. The Republic was keen to shrug off the supremacy of that hegemonic group, which had grown weaker after the death of Lorenzo the Magnificent in 1492. The statue, realised by Donatello towards the end of his life, has an extremely violent subject, representing the young woman decapitating the Philistine general after having got him drunk. She is a disturbing and shocking figure, like one of the Erinyes re-emerging from the pagan past, a wild fury launched against the powerful male. The iconological drama combines joy and sorrow, pleasure and castration, the biblical text and mythology. Donatello's *Judith and Holofernes* is now in the Sala dei Gigli in the Palazzo Vecchio, where several of Giacometti's works, including *Object invisible*, *L'homme qui marche* and the great *Femme debout* are on display. Judith's frozen gesture enacts a theatre of the sublime, especially with the totemic figure of the *Object invisible* alongside, stemming from a mix of medieval and African sculpture. A Virgin Mary who seems to have had the divine son taken from her breast. An unviolated executioner who beheads the wine-addled male. And behind it the recondite allusion to political meanings, like those of interest to a republic in conflict with any form of tyranny, internal or otherwise. Also in the same room is the *L'homme qui marche*, moving through the space quite heedless of the apocalyptic sight; and the large standing woman, "tall, mysterious, inscrutable, like a tree" – a queen of the night surveying the scene, an oracular figure raised up on a tall pedestal, as if she inhabited the threshold between life and death.

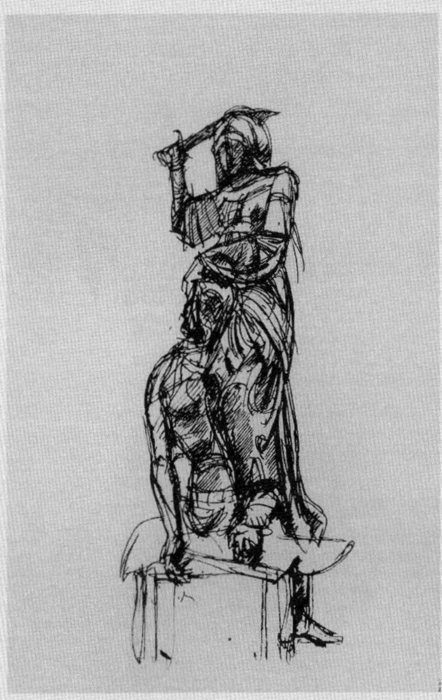

Alberto Giacometti, according to Donatello, *Judith and Holofernes*, 1935-1937 circa, pen and blue ink on paper. Fondation Giacometti, Paris

Just like *Adam* by Masaccio, *L'homme qui marche* has big feet, one firmly planted on the ground, the other already arched – as normally happens in the moment when the body thrusts forward to start another step. But the attitude and gesture (the hand covering the face) are totally different in the Renaissance figure. Chased by the angel with a drawn sword, the narrow door of Paradise behind him, Adam is leaving the Edenic state. He can feel the weight of his body, the cold, shame; he fears the judgment of God and, even more, that of men. On his shoulders he carries the weight of guilt of the original sin that has condemned the whole of humanity to toil and pain, destined to know being-toward-death. *L'homme qui marche* has no Paradise behind him, and there is no god condemning or redeeming him. Giacometti seems convinced by Nietzsche's thesis – God is dead – and knows that to reach the truth man must proceed to destroy every acquired value, every conviction and moral convention. All that exists is history without teleology and his own miserable, glorious existence, caught from the beginning between solitude and anguish, and subject to living in the cone of shadow of Death rather than in the light of Reason. We might say that man, from Giacometti's perspective, corresponds to the *Ens causa sui* spoken of by Sartre: "Every human reality is a passion in that it projects losing itself so as to found being and by the same stroke to constitute the In-itself which escapes contingency by being its own foundation, the *Ens causa sui*, which religions call God." This man, who is lengthening his stride and yet at the same time seems to be blocking time, could be the first or the last man to walk on earth, *Ens causa sui* who moves in this world without the protection or the threat of a Deus ex machina looming above his head, predictive surveyor of every human destiny. Here then is the explanation of the mystery of these sculptures: oracular figures of a new transcendence, man without qualities, master and victim of his own destiny, relegated to existing within the limits of his own world, which are the limits of language. Playing out between these two poles is Giacometti's investigation of form, his obsession: to pursue transcendence, at the cost of failure, within the limits of language, which for him is figurative language; coming to terms with death, that experience which seems to have opened its doors to the artist's nocturnal, unconscious life, ever since the day when he came face to face with the corpse of his friend T.

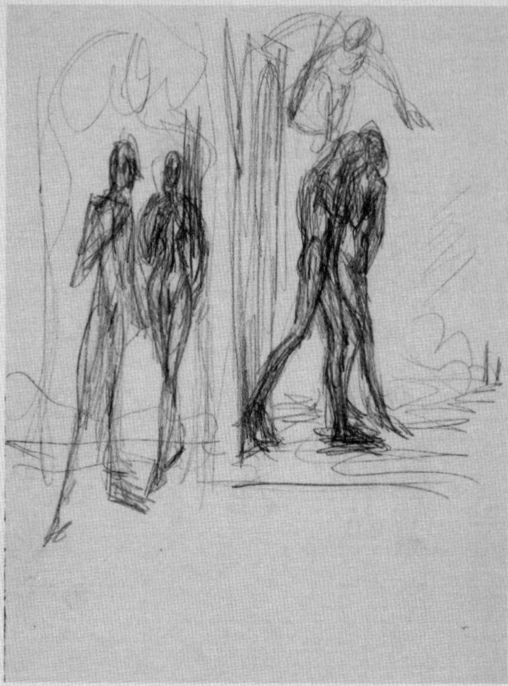

Dopo Masolino, Tentazione di Adamo ed Eva, La cacciata dal Giardino dell'Eden, pencil on paper, Alberto Giacometti, 34 x 25.8 cm, Paris, Fondation Giacometti

II

Jean Genet wrote that every figure by Giacometti is like a ghost of unlived life arising from the realm of the dead. Speaking with the sculptor, the writer, poet and playwright learnt that his friend had some strange intentions. Giacometti had confessed to him that he wanted to bury his sculptures so they could be exhumed by posterity. More than one conjecture could be made to explain this project, which lies somewhere between the archaeological and the necrophiliac. Giacometti might have wanted to reinforce the dependence of his art on civilisations that even predated the history of art, inscribed in a primordial world where art still had a cultic and magic function. In a distant future, those statues, already more than archaic today, would appear to modernity to be undatable and would instead be framed in an a-temporal structure, like the fossil precipitate of a simultaneity of eras, phenomena, models, experiences and even of raison d'êtres. As if those figures, already similar to corpses, were anticipating in their appearance a future reborn from the chthonic world. Something similar – namely, to bury a sculpture to antiquate it – had been asked of the young Michelangelo by his friend and patron Lorenzo di Pier Francesco de' Medici known as 'il Popolano'. In that case it was a subterfuge to give the sleeping Cupid in marble sculpted by the young Florentine artist the appearance of being an old object, in order to deceive would-be purchasers. The story was related by Ascanio Condivi, the biographer authorised by Michelangelo, and by Giorgio Vasari as well, who wrote: "He carved a little figure of Saint John in marble for Lorenzo di Pierfrancesco de' Medici, and then with another piece of marble he immediately began to carve a life-size figure of a sleeping Cupid. When this was completed, Baldassare del Milanese showed it as a beautiful piece of work to Pierfrancesco, who agreed with Baldassare's judgement and declared to Michelangelo: 'If you buried it, I am convinced it would pass as an ancient work, and if you sent it to Rome treated so that it appeared old, you would earn much more than by selling it here.'" The archaic rather than ancient appearance of an object belonging to a past civilisation seems, then, to have interested Giacometti as well. Once art had been pushed to the extreme boundaries of figurative language, Giacometti's intention was to force the work to assume the substance of a timeless object, older than any artistic culture, to the extent that it might be something from an as-yet undecipherable future; so as to rediscover a lost or re-emerged sacrality, that of the earliest beginnings and that of the future. It would seem then to be a question of time, a juncture and a tie linking the most remote past with the future. Those figures are already now as they will appear in millions of years' time when they could be disinterred by new inhabitants of planet earth. In other words, *L'homme qui marche* and *Femme debout* have risen from a primordial future and they are now in our midst without having lived in the historic time behind and before them. They are figures that straddle the modern age, an age in which art has been stripped of any aura and of any cultic or magical function, together with that of an apotropaic object.

The two figures do differ, however, in one aspect.. The legs of the large woman are completely sealed together, like almost all of Giacometti's figures from the 1940s on. This accentuates the archaic nature of the work. *L'homme qui marche* has thin legs, like dry tree sticks or insect legs, and hoof-feet that seem unable to detach themselves from the muddy ground – the clay from which, biblically speaking, Adam was made. In a text devoted to the myth of Isis and Osiris, Plutarch describes how Isis intervened on the body of Amon, who had been born with his legs joined together, a physical condition that prevented him from walking. Ashamed of his infirmity, he was forced to live in solitude. However, Isis separated his legs with a cut, enabling him to move normally. "On the plane of religious significance, this myth confirms Isis' role as a liberator and reviver", Jean Christophe Bailly writes, "and one can similarly note how there is a transition here from one to two, a transition from the inertia of the joined legs to the mobility of the legs able to walk normally." Bailly pursues this and points us to another issue: "It is hard not to read this myth in another way, supposing a direct interposition of the Greek gaze with respect to Egyptian matters. This different reading, which imposes itself immediately, is aesthetic in nature: the incision carried out by Isis on the inert body of the god may in fact represent to our eyes an allegory of *mimesis*." And here we touch on one of Giacometti's themes, or rather, obsessions: the move away from the tradition of imitation and the discovery of reality as the search for the absolute that situates figurative language at an ontological proximity with the truth of being. Bailly goes on to say: "Indeed, the body with stuck-together legs recalls an Egyptian statue, and Egyptian statues, as the Greeks themselves had noted, resemble the *choanon*, that is, the archaic statue of preclassical times, emblematised by the legendary figure of Daedalus. The *choanan*, the genuine effigy of magic, is exactly that from which it was necessary to be separated, what mimesis separated, like Isis, through an incision." We cannot help but think of the *Femme debout* here, motionless in her hieratic pose, and of the *L'homme qui marche*, who moves by separating one leg from another. "While the immobile body of the *choanon* was thought to possess a power, an authentic embodiment of the god, the 'resembling' statue of the classical epoch could no longer be, and above all, no longer wished to be, an idol. Abandoning the magic of presence it became more properly an image, an evocation that we know to be the evocation of an absence." In other words, imitating means simulating the presence of an absence, as Jean-Pierre Vernant claimed, going back to the original meaning of *mimesthai*. The *Femme debout* therefore seems to belong to a sacred time, to be the hieratic image of a woman who exceeds human nature as a sovereign and higher entity. She has the stature of an icon and exudes the unmoving and inexorable power of an idol who could be the embodiment of Mother Earth. If Giacometti rejected mimesis it is because he tried to grasp what remained of the thing stripped of any relative appearance, the coinciding truth of subject and object, of form and sensation. He approached the model by working on the memory of it, striving to escape the imperative of resemblance. He searched in absence for the presence of what is always and inexorably absent, that always goes beyond and disappears from the visual field, from the room in which the model poses nude in front of the artist. The great *Femme debout* now appears on the threshold, a mysterious idol, raised on a field populated by furrowed meteorites, very similar to ripe pomegranates, spherical bodies that have been shaped in a journey into infinity or which have emerged from the chthonic depths; opening on them, like wounds and lacerations, are breaches, genital fissures or obscene uncovered anuses. Lucio Fontana used the title *Nature* (Natures) for these uncertain forms, somewhere between base materialism and cosmology, enormous balls of bronze worked and penetrated with volcanic impetuosity, which the artist began to work on between 1959 and 1960.

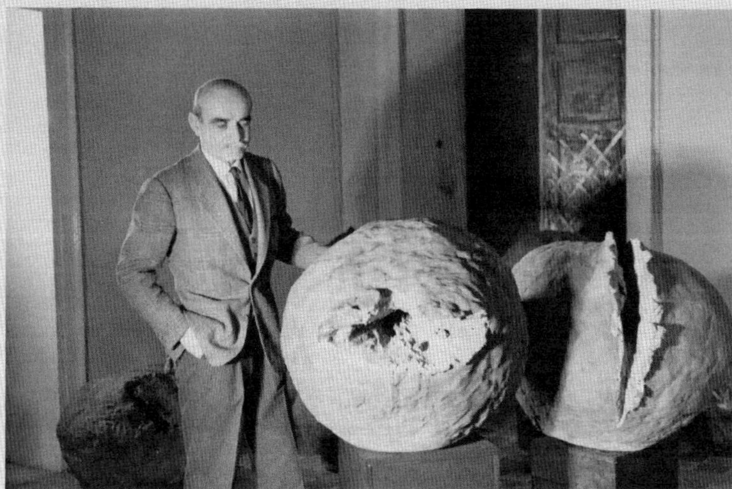

Lucio Fontana
with *Nature*, 1961

These two figures – *Femme debout* and *L'homme qui marche* – hardly resemble us at all, other than that they are erect or seem to be walking. The limbs can barely be distinguished, and they do not have an identifiable face. The head is more of a cranium, the face reduced to little more than a mortuary mask, where everything revolves around the eyes, transforming the gaze into a gravitational vortex. Take the walking man. Freed from any naturalistic frill or illusory feature, this primordial hominid is conceived as a small but not minimal structure. The title itself circumscribes and universalises in the walking man both man's being and the destiny of humanity, determining its essence and substance. It is nothing other than that. Everything comes down to this: walk, proceed, advance or move away. The whole of humanity is summed up in this action and in the coinciding of existence and destiny in a single action. This walking man does not speak with others if not with himself, yet he says many things about human nature and our destiny in the world. His transcendence dwells here in the limits of the space that he creates and inhabits; however, his solitude belongs to the whole cosmos, of which he has become aware with a feeling of amazement and horror. Defleshed and stripped of any superfluous element, and pared right down to the essential, this bronze figure embodies the extreme, ultimate anthropomorphic depiction in sculpture, the humanistic subject that has dominated Western art since the beginning of the twentieth century, between naturalism and Platonic idealisation. Giacometti always risked failure as he worked, finally reaching and exceeding the boundary of the visible without denying it, that is to say, considering that boundary from a reverse perspective: "I see the sculptures in front of me… a failure. Exactly that, a failure! But in each of them there is a trace of what I would really like to create one day … Whatever I'm looking at, I am surprised, amazed, and I don't recognise what I'm seeing. It is as if reality lies behind a screen – and behind this another one still, and then another. But I have the impression or the illusion of making progress. This stimulates me, as if in the end I should reach the point of discovering the secret of life. And so I carry on, knowing that the more I move closer to the 'thing' the more I am moving away from it. It is an endless search." It is as if Giacometti re-departed from where Michelangelo stopped with the *Pietà Rondanini*, to leave a new and unexplored space for manoeuvre for those wishing to engage with the human figure in sculpture. In this regard he wrote: "No sculpture ever displaces another one. A sculpture is not an object, it is a question, an answer. It can never be either finished or perfect. The question does not even arise. For Michelangelo, everything began again with the *Rondanini Pietà*, his last sculpture. Michelangelo could have carried on sculpting Pietàs for a thousand years without ever repeating himself, without going back, without ever finishing anything, pushing further and further on." Giacometti was fully conscious of this limit: man conceived from the point of view of eternity and the truth of the world after the death of God. Man ontologically free and at the same time a prisoner of his own solitude and finitude. Lucio Fontana also thought that modern man had freed himself from the immanent presence of God. Except that he addressed this reality with a spirit of optimism and attributed to science and technology primacy over life and consciousness. In the final years of his life, he produced his *Pillole* (Pills), smooth, shiny sculptural objects that encapsulate, in a form tending towards the minimal and abstract, the ultimate sense of the cosmic egg. Like his celebrated cut pictures, this ovoid has also been cut, opening its shell to an imagining of the infinity nestling within. The incommensurable, the mystery of life in relation not to terrestrial measures, but to those of infinity and eternity as revealed to the imagination, a conceptual leap into the invisible beyond form.

The body of the *L'homme qui marche* extends upwards from much larger-than-normal feet, gradually narrowing as it reaches the top, where the head buds like a flower at the top of its stem. The lower limbs are open like a pair of compasses and the arms seem to be hanging down along the axis of the torso. The walking man appears immobilised. Or, on the contrary, the sculpture seems to be setting into motion as if it wants to make us forget it is a bronze object, such is the truth of that walking man. It is the absurd logic of movement to which Giacometti gave the utmost attention. He declared on several occasions that movement was and remained his obsession. The same can be said of the head and the gaze. The head as the centre of life, as the fire of sight and imagination, a centre of gravity endowed with formidable energy. "I will never manage", Giacometti said to Jean Genet, "to put into a portrait all the force that there is in a head. The mere fact of living already requires so much will and so much energy." The master of his destiny without a supporting theology, *L'homme qui marche* is the image of a humanism that exceeds history and goes back to the most remote times of man's evolution. And it is also the symbol of a solipsistic dimension from which man cannot free himself, and which emerges in other works as well, such as *L'homme qui marche sous la pluie* (1948) and again in *Trois hommes qui marchent* from the same year. These figures, whether isolated in their world or in the presence of others, all have the air of living and moving on their own, alone, with their own thoughts and intentions, in a pose or direction that the others are unaware of; what they have in common is incommunicability, moving in that margin of reality that remains between being and nothingness, in the minimum portion of reality in which truth and form coincide. This is why we feel they are so close to us when all our feelings of omnipotence run up against the sense of life, death, nothingness. Indifferent to us, the two figures of the *Femme debout* and the *Homme qui marche* are aloof, unaware of our existence. All we can do is contemplate and perhaps experience the true function of art, become contemplators in order to gain access to the enclave of eternity that opens in the indistinct flow of life.

III

The road, or perhaps a square, is reduced to a small plate. And yet that portion of world seems boundless, and the three silhouettes intersect and brush up against each other; each one goes in its own direction without being the slightest bit aware of who or what is around them. As they move, their gaze is distant, giving a virtually infinite continuity to their march. Each moves on its own inside a bubble of incredible silence. For Giacometti movement equates with a succession of points of absolute immobility: "a succession of immobilities that are completely detached from each other, immobile moments that could last eternities, interrupted and followed by other immobilities." In an interview with Pierre Schneider subsequently entitled "Ma longue march" (My long walk), the artist referred to people in the street "who come and go… a bit like ants, each has the air of moving on their own account, all alone, in a direction unknown to the others. They intersect and overtake… without seeing or looking at each other. Or they move around a woman." He then said something definitive: "It occurred to me that I can never make a woman in any other way than motionless, and a man always striding; when I model a woman, then motionless; a man, always walking." Simple, isn't it? A totemic, immobile woman, a man walking like Adam.

With the figure of the walking man, Giacometti wants to tell us that this is our destiny: to walk and never rest, when alive and perhaps also when dead. To be walking should also be interpreted in the sense of being so with respect to the axis of eternity, in which every movement, ever step borders on immobility. The step of the walking man eternalises the fact of moving by discharging weight on the sole of the feet. Capturing the instant in which a just-lifted foot moves away from the other negates the oscillation of the pendulum (one step after another), that situation which conveys the impression of a succession of moments, instants suspended from each other in a line of apparent continuity. Movement, though remaining such, thus appears blocked in a space and time that is unlimited and separate from reality. According to Simone de Beauvoir, Giacometti's intention was to carve, for instance, a face inside a concrete situation, keeping it at a distance and managing to overcome the claims of both subjective idealism and false objectivity. When the work is complete, what remains of resemblance is a residue of vision whose origin lies at the intersection of memory and imagination. Grasp everything by detaching oneself from reality, to give life to an illusionary and absolute space. The same happens with the sculptures, an outstretched arm, a truncated leg, or rather, a leg like a trunk detached from the tree, a woman seen from in front, a walking man. Each of these gestures, moves, actions pertain to the body and to a part of it. Together they might reconstruct the entire figure of an ideal man, at least for Giacometti. That is, his image of humanity in man. A piece of youthful thinking conveys his version of artistic humanism: "Body and mind form a unity. The body is matter, it is a part of that great matter of which the earth and all the other planets are formed. The mind is a particle of the spirit, which, combined with matter, forms the universe. The universe is the most complete oneness that the human spirit can co-conceive. It is the complete fusion of matter and spirit. It is the greatest and most enduring oneness that exists. From his very first breath, man is a miniscule and very short-lived universe. From the first through to the last instant of life, this small oneness or universe does nothing other than search for union with the first, complete universe. Continually, without a moment's pause, the body looks for the point of attachment, for the fusion with the earth; the mind pursues fusion with the great spirit."

IV

So *L'homme qui marche* is effectively immobile, even though he seems to be walking. Observed carefully, it appears dominated by an inner fury, and this moving forward is his strength, something like a primordial instinct to tenaciously resist falling, to resist an opposing force that might send him plummeting flat on the ground. *L'homme qui chavire* is another masterpiece by Giacometti, where an enormous force is needed to stay upright. The figure is off-balance, projecting forwards in the moment in which the man is losing his equilibrium, losing control of his body, defeated by his own weight and by gravity. This sculpture breaks with the ideal verticality and stability as established in art history from the classical age onwards. The walking man raises one foot after another from the earth's surface: he lifts it for a moment from the ground from which he comes and to which he will return. Instant after instant, day after day, we detach ourselves from the earth before falling for the last time. For Giacometti, existing means moving, walking in towards one's destiny while avoiding falling. This holds true for the artist as well, engaged every day in resisting nothingness in the face of the inevitability of failure. It takes great strength to remain on one's feet and not fall. But it requires even more determination to move by breaking inertia, to walk and move forward, shrugging off immobility. Giacometti places the beginning of humanity at the moment in which man began to walk. Where he started from, how long he has been walking for and how long his walk will last are not known. But we do know that it started early. The scene has something sacred and primitive about it; it points to an epoch in which the sacred sphere and the everyday sphere could belong to the same place, with the threshold marked by the presence of an idol or totem. The woman is standing upright. Motionless, like a deity. She seems so distant and indifferent to the walking man. She seems to belong to a different time and space. That of matriarchy. As if that goddess, shamanic and regal, has always remained in position, appearing eternal. While the man is forced to move through open space, with everything that entails. As if the woman were still at the beginning of history, on the threshold separating human time from that of eternity, between our earth and the Edenic world from which Adam was banished. The scene therefore projects us into a time and a space secluded to us, supressed by us. The scene is archetypal, a reminiscence. We return to the beginning of history and of art.

V

In Giacometti's work the woman is often associated with a divinity. When he drew a nude standing woman – arms hanging down at her side, stomach slightly swollen, sagging breasts, fixed gaze staring at nothing, at no one, helpless and powerful in her insuppressible distance (the aura) – the space she occupies seems to be inaccessible, beyond a screen, very distant, to the extent that the figure appears to get smaller as we look at it, as if she wants to protect herself from our profane gaze. "Around her is a void, so the divine power can generate the space that is hers."

It is well known that Giacometti adored prostitutes. Brothels, which he frequented assiduously, were marvellous places for him, somewhere he could take refuge and rediscover himself. Marco Belpoliti wrote that for Giacometti the woman is a goddess, "but also a whore: with all probability, a goddess because she is a whore. The bond is inextricable." Genet had grasped a lot of things about his friend Giacometti. Above all, how much he adored whores. Genet also regarded women as divinities, and the same thing happened for him with prostitutes; indeed, they both proved to be one and the same thing. It depended on the space, on the place of encounter. He confessed: "When I walk along the street and see a girl at a distance, fully dressed, I see a chick. When she is in front of me in the bedroom, completely naked, I see a goddess." Ultimately, modern art was born in whorehouses. Just think of Manet's *Olympia*, of the *Demoiselles d'Avignon*. The two friends often talked about this. Genet recalled that the sculptor mourned the closure of brothels like the Sphinx, a house of pleasure with a significant name and the protagonist of a dream by Giacometti about which much has been written. Alberto was almost like a worshipper when he visited. "He saw himself kneeling before some divinity, implacable and distant. Between every naked whore and him there was perhaps the distance that all statues establish between themselves and us. Every statue seems to step backwards – or return – in a night so dense and distant as to be confused with death. In this way, every whore should reach a mysterious night where she would be sovereign. And he is abandoned on a shore, from which he sees her get smaller and bigger at the same time." Distance, of things, faces and bodies that move away and return until they are near, is one of the central themes in Giacometti's art. He returned to it frequently, and critics have sought to explain it. Distance transforms women-whores into regal apparitions, into divinities. When they are close, they become threatening, even aggressive. The naked women seen at the Sphinx, while Giacometti sat at the end of the room, seemed unreachable to him, as distant as the immense, uncrossable space of the establishment. "At the Sphinx a vast expanse of shiny floor relegated nudity into an almost sacred distance."

VI

Giacometti would return to the theme of the walking man on other occasions on paper, through until 1958–60, when he produced some large figures for a public monument project in the plaza in front of the Chase Manhattan Bank in New York. *L'homme qui marche* was to have appeared together with a large *Grande femme debout* and a very big head – vaguely reminiscent of the monumental head of Constantine, an older forebear of the great totemic stones on Easter Island. In that New York context – a square conceived as a Roman forum, the child of a new modernist imperialism – that triptych of sculptures, born outside of time, would have seemed like a dramatic and destabilising tribal scene. One of Giacometti's obsessions, besides the gaze, was unquestionably movement in opposition to immobility. In fact, *L'homme qui marche* dialectically plays its match for eternity with the *Femme debout*, which, with its hieratic pose, corresponds to a sacred and divine imagination of woman, with its mystery and its enchanting power. Much has been written about this, with critics searching in the artist's biography for the deep causes of his complex relationship with women and with female sexuality. The theme of maternity is unknown to Giacometti. The fertile woman associated with the moon is not part of his imagination, as it would be for Lucio Fontana, who, in producing his *Nature* and his *Tagli* (Cuts), thought of sexuality and eros as vital, generative forces on earth and in the cosmos. Fontana's language is ultimately of Platonic origin in this sense too, given that for the Greek philosopher, drawing on concepts expressed in Hesiod's *Theogony*, Eros is the oldest and most powerful of the gods, born from primordial Chaos at the same time as Gaia. Giacometti's *Femme debout* (or *Femme de Venise*) sculptures have nothing of the palaeolithic Venuses with large breasts and voluptuous hips that embodied the fecund and formless organic principle. The Mother Goddess. Life against death. Giacometti's female figures evoke other relations. They are a cross between priestesses, shamans and mummified regal bodies, not too far removed from Donatello's *Mary Magdalene*, saint and prostitute, a "wizened, gap-toothed crone" draped in a stringy mop of hair reaching down to her animal-like feet. She is frozen and praying, consumed by anguish and by ardour. Camille Paglia describes Donatello's *Mary Magdalene* in these terms: "Her staring eyes are sunk in deep hollows, while her mouth gapes in dementia or shock. Her nasal muscles constrict and retract, as if she were stifling sobs or repulsed by a bad smell, the stench of mortality which similarly afflicts Hamlet. Her skull, like a memento mori, is surfacing through her sunken cheeks. Fasting has stripped away her female curves… Mary is a pariah, both feeling and causing disgust. She has been reduced to near-animal existence, shown by her foot gripping the rock edge like a bear claw." I would have no hesitation in supporting the notion that Giacometti saw Donatello's wooden sculpture first-hand during his visit to Florence – in other words, not just a Grand Tour to the Archaeology Museum or the Medici Chapels, to San Marco or the church of the Carmine. It is worth pausing to consider the face, reduced to little more than a skull, of the Renaissance woman, with a radically different beauty to certain refined and lyrical Madonnas by the Della Robbias or Desiderio da Settignano. The spectral mutism of the *Femme debout* makes one think of a Sibyl and a Sphinx, due to the attraction and repulsion of the female body. Something very similar is conveyed by Donatello's *Mary Magdalene*, which instead of vain beauty prefers the opposite, a sublime beauty that is more ugly than beautiful, more mystical and closer to God than to men.

According to a substantial proportion of critics, beginning with Jean Paul Sartre, *L'homme qui marche* is at the origin of space and time from an existential point of view. But the *Femme debout* defines space and time from a transcendental perspective; it dialogues with the metaphysical nature of one and the other. It lies on the threshold of reality and eternity, of everyday life and the afterlife. Both appear to be hermetic figures, descendants of Hermes, the god with the gift of passing through the realm of the living and the dead, and recognised as a psychopomp, the guide for souls in the afterlife. In this sense, one can speak of a connection with archaic art and especially with the Etruscan world. Moving in opposite and irreconcilable directions, the one and the other – standing woman and moving man – seem to filter through the porous wall of the kingdom of shadows and walk our streets. That is how it appeared to Jean Genet, according to whom they were at once familiar and traumatic. Over and above any existential consideration, there is however an anthropological background that characterises them and relates them to a lot of early twentieth-century art. They live, they exist at the bottom of time, at the origin of everything. They approach and move away in a sovereign immobility. Giacometti does not use the archaic, the primitive or the primordial to leapfrog academic art and free himself from tradition. He searches for the most sincere and radical way of giving body to his obsessions, to his vision of the exterior world, "especially of the face and of the human being as a whole". Artistically speaking, he behaves like a cave artist, perfectly at ease with a form of artistic expression which, in the age of mechanical reproducibility, pertains to a cultic, magical and apotropaic dimension – which is why we are profoundly attracted to it.

THE NATURE SCULPTURES OF LUCIO FONTANA BASE MATERIALISM AND COSMOGONY

At the feet of *L'homme qui marche* and *Femme debout* are seven *Nature* or *Concetti spaziali* (Spatial Concepts) by Lucio Fontana. They are large earthy, formless objects, spheroids similar to meteorites, to cosmic asteroids. Or rather, they are boluses, large balls made up of apparently organic matter. Or again, pregnant, incubating balls from which a life form was born or has yet to be generated, turgid and ripe fruits, open like erogenous zones, like split pomegranates, symbols of death and rebirth in ancient iconography. Something between the botanical and the geological, between the genital and the anal, which conveys a fecund nature and a need for evacuation. The artist used penetrating instruments and gestures to cut through, break or thrust into the material, nothing at all like a soft, delicate and gentle practice of striving for fluid, sensitive curves and planes. The surfaces are in fact coarse and earthy, and are in this sense primordial, at the extreme opposite point to the history of figurative art and of the biblical tradition; in other words, this lies outside the horizon of a modelling God who shaped man from clay in his own image and resemblance. There is no idealism here. Form, like life, is generated from energy and impulses on earth or in the cosmos, in the absence of a theological schematism. After all, Fontana himself wrote in his Spatialist manifesto of 1948: "We look to matter and its evolution, generating sources of existence." Others have seen in them something very similar to dung, which however has still rained from the sky onto the Lombard countryside. An image to bring a soaring poetic impulse down to earth, to lower to ground level a revelatory imagination, something that in many respects may recall a metaphysical yearning in Fontana's sought-after other-worldly spatiality. This is the view of Rosalind Krauss, who believes the Italo-Argentine artist to be an officially recognised exponent of "bad taste", immersed in kitsch from the start of his career and ready to take delight in the obscene and the supressed in his polychrome work. According to the well-known American critic the notion of base materialism as Bataille understood it is required to understand Fontana's formlessness and kitsch, that is, a materialism not founded on concepts, in which matter is not subject to any ontology but is the agent for lowering anything that is high. From this materialism lowered to the scatological, Krauss argues, come certain works like the *Nature*, which look like amorphous piles of mud and seem to evoke the possibility of the *informe*, that is, of the material manifestation of what Bataille called such. From here on in Fontana's polychrome sculpture was no longer the essential medium for his scatological cry, but one of the ways with which his base materialism lowered even further. As an example of all this, Krauss cites the *Ceramica spaziale* of 1949, a polychrome ceramic work that transforms the mass-produced, industrialised cube that has emerged from a metal press into a muddy object, the product of the intestine, worked in the open air with the instinct and irresponsibility of a child. It is something that appears mangled, ingested and regurgitated, the American critic wrote, "a mess of blackened matter – gleaming and iridescent, with an agitated surface – which seems to have fallen there on the ground like a massive turd. ... Geometry (form, the Platonic idea) is not suppressed but mapped onto what until then it had had the task of 'suppressing by overcoming' (*aufheben*, to use the Hegelian verb)." Krauss concludes by saying that, with Fontana, reason suffered a "low blow": "No dialectical synthesis, but the simple interjection of an obscenity into the aesthetic house of cards", threatening to bring it down. In contrast to such readings, in recent years many critics have tried to reduce Fontana's adventure to a strictly conceptual and minimalist idiom, cleansing it of any expressionistic or *informale* emphasis, of any sinking into spheres of indecency or irrationality. They have looked for formal, epistemological or phenomenological toeholds to join together the opposing directions taken by an academic, eclectic, baroque, metaphysical, even gestural and obviously astrophysical Fontana. In this regard, writes Luca Massimo Barbero: "With his perfect geometric form, the *Fine di Dio* works are in the place in which Fontana developes the various strands of his previous work, sustained by the firm conviction of promoting an idea beyond and through matter. In these works, the artist created some of his most complete and complex masterpieces, intervening with a light, etched – almost drawn – mark around the perimeter and inside the initially smoothed surface, before then pressing on plastically through matter and support in an increasingly agitated and rich fashion, as if to evoke an asteroid. Mother Earth, the satellite planets, the monumental depth of lunar craters enter into a dialogue in this subject and in this new way of working."

At this point, with respect to the relationship with matter, it is worth stressing what has rightly been pointed out by Maria Grazia Messina: "Despite Fontana having clearly stated in the 1948 *Spatial* manifesto that "art will remain eternal as a gesture, but will die as matter", he was unaware that he was establishing the contiguity between the intentional and archetypal spheres of his work. Most critics, agreeing to frame Fontana's work in terms of a spatial question, understood this spatiality as the result of a vitalism, circumscribed in the trajectory and calibration of the gesture, but they only investigated the holes and cuts as a sculptural problem, in the results, and a logical-conceptual one, in the motivations, necessarily relegating the gesture to a secondary, operational function. While, on the other hand, the hallmark of Fontana's art is the gesture, and not a graphic one, but one performed with total transport in the material – the films that portray him are enough to convey this -, it is precisely the imaginary, with its essence, that emerges overbearingly. It is the archetypal and symbolic images that recur in it that must be investigated. Taking advantage of Bachelard's intuitions, later systematised by Durand, Fontana's gesture corresponds to the pattern of descent, of penetration, a load-bearing matrix of the so-called "nocturnal regime" of the imaginary, which includes the archetypes of the containing-contained binomial, of the cavity, and the ultimate meaning of womb or uterus, and insularity". Maria Grazia Messina further reminds us that "The comparative study of the archetypes, in light of their structures and constellations, involves a very different connotation for the so-called sexual allusion of Fontana's gesture. Holes and cuts appear to be part of the first and vital woman-mother-earth-principle nexus, distinguished, as Durand points out, by an isomorphism between the symbolism of sharp or pointed weapons and ploughing implements, so that the gesture of cutting is mirrored in that of penetrating and fertilising, and the vagina is likened to the furrow, as the access to a generating womb. In Italy, this path was explored at an early stage only by Giulio Carlo Argan, in a text with no great results in 1960, the same year as Durand's study. This at least suggests a horizon of shared interpretations. For the spheres of *Nature*, Argan cites the Chthonian myths, right down to the steatopygian female effigies of Neolithic agricultural cultures, while for the cuts in the *Attese [Expectations]* he writes that 'that cut is a furrow, of the earth and of the woman, the same one that connects the surface, be it earthly or human, with the profound, inscrutable spatiality of the creativity of the cosmos [...] the artist turns back, because now the space that attracts him is no longer the sky but the deep'".

The different positions can therefore be understood within the same cultural horizon, once high and low do not reciprocally exclude each other. Argan wrote at length about this in 1960: "That cut or those cuts always fall in the right point; they comply with the necessity to break the perfect plane, as if matter, taken to the furthermost limit of rarefaction, wished to recover, in that incident, the sense of the reality of its own existence. In fact, that cut is a furrow, of the earth and of the woman, the same one that puts the surface, whether terrestrial or human, in communication with the deep, inscrutable spatiality of the creativity of the cosmos. From the final boundary of space and time, of the determinate and indeterminate, the artist turns round, because the space that attracts him now is no longer the sky but the deep. Fontana's most recent, disturbing images are *Nature*, large irregular-shaped balls, like swollen, burst seeds, and cruelly split, almost violated, by huge cracks, by chasm-like holes. We are at the chthonic myth, at the origins, where the steatopygic form of the first woman is confused with that of the seed."

This is the point: the origin of the world, where there is woman and moon, faeces and female nudity, the vaginal crack and the birth of galaxies. Fontana would appear to move in a dimension of creativity and of drives that does not distinguish between the playful and the metaphysical, between eros and primary creativity, playing without modesty or inhibition on the different but not antithetical fields of idealism and base materialism, on the excrementitious, sacred symbolism and cosmological imagination. As Alessandro Del Puppo aptly stresses: "Here he is at last, the Fontana that few really expected. It is a chthonic Fontana, and it was the unsuspected rationalist, Cartesian and Marxist Argan who recognised this. It is the prodigious offering of a different image. Something primeval and humid, between the botanical and geological, a fertile thalamus, a seminal receptacle. Cut or cleft, it is not only a symbolic opening, but an opening to different hypotheses regarding meaning. Not everyone, however, understood it in the same way".

These *Nature* – as they are commonly called and known – these balls, asteroids, giant turds that have fallen from the sky, can therefore belong to a dimension that is at once chthonic and cosmological, mythological and psychological. On the one hand the imagination goes back to cosmological myths, on the other to the origin of life and of artistic creation, between childish impulses and sculptural elaboration. These forms, of brutally primary, telluric matter shaped with a Promethean gesture and impulse, of a beginning-of-the-world sculpture, bear the signs of a cosmic journey. Like that of an eternal return to the beginning of life on our planet before light and lands became distinguished, and in the cosmos when energy produced space, time and matter. Rolling forms, split open by gashes and holes that appear coarsely characterised by mouths and orifices, like vaginas or anuses, fertile and disgusting forms of life. Formless masses shaped in the palm of a demiurge artist who acts by translating the excremental and the mud of biblical origin into docile clay matter, following primordial and infantile instincts. In this sense the conceptual or abused philological readings that seek to relate these things to Futurism appear highly reductive. Instead, they pertain to a creative experience conditioned by both a sexual-erotic and by an anthropological-cosmological dimension. As Andrea Bruciati rightly stresses: "From the *Uomo Nero* (*Black Man*, 1929) to the contemporary unicellular scratched tablets, the geological beginning and start of human history coincide in the artist's work, almost as if the universe's physical Big Ben were inseparable from the biological origin of the world. Using a scale that goes from amoebic structure to sidereal representation, and so where the beginning forms a whole with the end, Fontana unfurls the most innovative ideas of the manifestos through signs and an apparently basic, archaic language. Almost prehistoric forms, floating in para-Surrealist amniotic liquids, are inevitably partnered with geographic cosmographies, in accordance with a vitalistic anthropophagous approach in some ways similar, in terms of the richness of linguistic results, to that of Picasso. [...] The Nature evoke both the cosmic imagination of the manifestos and the primary anthropological act, represented by the abyss of the hole, so often mentioned by Fontana. As Marcello Venturoli observed: 'The key to the sculpture lies in their threatening vitality, part vegetable, part animal: these inflated, blind fruits, full of a lymph that stretches their surface like a skin, the solids and voids on the also round body of which almost seem to make them breathe, were attacked and in a certain way profaned by the artist. Palm-length marks made with a piece of wood, he inflicted gashes and wounds on these lives, longitudinal tears that seem to have been made with a giant tin opener. What remain are eyes and throat, fissures and lips open in the blindness of this living matter, so helpless and terrible in its protest. On the one hand, a kind of Dionysian explosion; on the other, an almost Jungian search for the origin of everything, towards a path that seeks to return to the origin and thus found a new metaphysics".

And at a cosmological level, beginning and end are on the same axis, in a single dimension which is that of infinity and eternity. While at a terrestrial, horizontal level, we can say that before form there was only matter, for the most part formless. The meaning was added later. There is therefore a need for a hermeneutic ascent or descent towards base materialism or the cosmological imagination, without making the two dimensions antithetical. Fontana seems to have wanted to introduce us to the origin of the world and to that of creative instinct, the fecund energy that coincides with drives and instincts as much as it does with cosmic forces and intensities. At the beginning it is energy. Immediately after matter there is the formless modelling that may arise as a response to the first drives of childhood or of primates in the phase of moving beyond the animal state. These obscene spheres lie in fact between pure original matter and the erect human figure, between the animal body and human consciousness, in a moment in which it is hard to distinguish between dejection and fertility, evacuation and procreation, anal and vaginal eroticism. In Fontana's universe the cosmological and the scatological seem to yield primordial forms, the outcome of a primitive creativity even preceding life on earth.

Alberto Giacometti and Lucio Fontana

The Form of the Void

Chiara Gatti

"Life is form, and form is the modality of life. [...] In order to exist at all, a work of art must be tangible. It must renounce thought, must become dimensional, must both measure and qualify space. It is in this very turning outward that its inmost principle resides"[1].

Henri Focillon

It was 1933 when Alberto Giacometti transcribed a memory from his childhood. As a child, playing with his friends on the Bregaglia trails, attracted by gorges and caves, he came across an enormous block of black stone. The darkness and power of that atavistic and magnetic presence unsettled him so much that it both attracted and distressed him. "The stone immediately struck me as a living, hostile, threatening being. [...] I approached it anyway, but with the feeling sof surrendering to something shameful, secret and sinister. I barely touched it with my hand, with revulsion and fear. [...] I ran away from that black stone. I didn't mention it to the other children. I ignored it and never went back to see it"[2]. And yet the overpowering image of that dark and impenetrable monolith remained etched in his memory. It reappeared like an obsession during the years of his artistic training and his youthful years in the ranks of the Surrealists.

In the stream of consciousness involving the mental, hallucinatory and psychotic experiences preached by André Breton and his followers, Giacometti was actually re-awakened by that childhood experience, by a sensitive child's encounter/clash with the otherness of a mysterious element. The ambiguity of an obscure object was destined to become an obsession, an irremediable torment, a knot to be untied, but at the same time, the miraculous source of a formal and also existential inspiration that fed his imagination and every one of his artistic representations even in his later years. He was always and constantly hounded by the enigma of a present life and a life beyond the visible.

The "stone", lodged in the hard ground of Maloja, had fallen from an inexplicable elsewhere, straight into the path of a boy unlike any other. It had shown itself to him in all its compressed strength, its blind volume, condensed in the implosion of the form, in a solid and solemn nucleus, a grandeur that was both archaic and alien. In Albert's eyes, it manifested itself as the embodiment of every question about the meaning of things. "Where do we come from? I haven't the slightest idea. Nowhere, everywhere, the air, the fire", he later wrote between the disjointed lines of his feverish notes[3]. The answer to any doubts about the origin of life showed itself like this; it took the form of a figurative, symbolic element, a mute

---

1 H. Focillon, *Vita delle forme seguito da Elogio della mano*, Einaudi, Turin 2002.

2 M. Leiris and J. Dupin (presented by), *Alberto Giacometti. Scritti*, Milan 2001, p. 36.

3 Ibid, p. 219.

and majestic monolith, the materialisation of an invisible knowledge, of another world that man aspires to and of which the "stone" itself could be interpreted as a gateway, an opening, a passage; the gateway to the stars.

This explains why Giacometti already in the "torsos" of 1925 - beyond the classic reference to all the Cubist literature and influence of non-European cultures - had begun to carve at the volumes with sharp edges and irregular profiles. They were like splintered boulders violently collapsed in on themselves, "a narrow and pointed pyramid whose walls fell almost vertically" he continued in the account of his childhood discovery.

The invaluable 1934 analysis of *Le Cube [The Cubes]* by critics like Reinhold Hohl, Jean Soldini and George Didi-Huberman, uncovered every possible antecedent or reference to art masterpieces that might have influenced its genesis, along with the sylvan vision of that day of troubled play[4]. The clear derivation from the rhomboidal polyhedron of Albrecht Dürer's *Melencolia*, an allegory of the human intellect meditating on the fate of the cosmos, can be seen in his ink drawings of the 1930s, *La table surréaliste*, *Figure* or *Lunaire* of 1935, where the mysterious object lies on planes that accommodate it like a relic and a trinket, something a woman-mannequin with closed eyes searches for in the dark, moving her long fingers in the void to grasp it. This marvellous device contains an occult energy that returns in other, but formally more abstract, surrealist sculptures of his. Critics have often traced these back conceptually to the physiognomy of archaic ritual objects, revelatory oracles, such as the *Fegato di Piacenza*, the small Etruscan votive bronze preserved in the Museo di Piacenza, a magical tool for the haruspices' practices. In these, Carola Giedion-Welcker, Hohl himself and later Rosalind Krauss glimpsed, and not by chance, a model for *La vie continue* of 1932, a horizontal Surrealist sculpture, innovative for the ninety-degree twisting of the figure. Or that *Testa/paesaggio* in which the features seem to evoke the reliefs of the "liver", a mirror of the division of the celestial vault from which the haruspices drew auspices and prophecies[5]. The *Objet désagréable à jeter*, another oneiric bronze from 1933 in the Kunsthaus Zurich, with its geometric protuberances – small solids that seem to allude to the cusp of his ancient "black stone" in a small format – also conceals undercurrents of an affinity with the Etruscan artefact and its

---

4 See J. Soldini, *Alberto Giacometti. Lo spazio e la forza*, Mimesis, Milan-Udine, 2016; G. Didi-Huberman, Il cubo e il volto. A proposito di una scultura di Alberto Giacometti, Electa, Milan 2008; J. Soldini, *Il colossale, la madre, il sacro. L'opera di Alberto Giacometti*, Bergamo, 1998; R. Hohl, *Alberto Giacometti*, Hatje, Stuttgart 1971; J. Genet, *L'atelier d'Alberto Giacometti, Les bonnes, L'enfant criminel, Le funambule*, L'Arbalète, Décines (Rhône) 1958.

5 See Carola Giedon Welcker, *Contemporary Sculpture, an Evolution in Volume and Space*, New York, 1960; Welcker 1960; Reinhold Hohl, Alberto Giacometti, London, 1972; Rosalind E. Krauss, The originality of the avant-garde and other modernist myths, Cambridge MA, 1985, as well as Casimiro Di Crescenzo (edited by), Alberto Giacometti. Sculture, dipinti, disegni, (exhibition catalogue, Milan, Palazzo Reale 26 January-2 April 1995), Florence, 1995, which emphasises here the relationship between Giacometti's "small panels" of the late 1920s and certain solutions of Etruscan art, which he came to know thanks to his close relationship with the Italian artists of the Gruppo dei Sette.

sculptural effect played out on triangular peaks not far from the idea of the errant boulder of the Grigioni ("narrow and pointed pyramid...").

Connecting the dots on this map between Giacometti's works, the "objects", the "cube" and their putative fathers, there emerges a clear picture of research strongly conditioned by this adolescent episode and the mental impression left by the enigmatic silhouette of a sidereal boulder that re-emerged in both his flat table sculptures and in the cosmic solitude of the dark cube. In view of the reasons expressed, this work gathers astral themes within itself, swallows up space and even time in matter, "the amassing of time in a single point" Paulo Barone wrote, commenting on the coincidence between the proximity of the object and the immensity of space[6]. To close the circle, this "amassing" of time in space is expressed, not for nothing, by the symbol of the meteorite, a duel icon of gravity and, at the same time, of the ether. Similar to Lucio Fontana's *Nature* – and this brings us closer to the dialogue between the giants – it pulses with incandescent matter, vivid and heavy, but comes from a spatial elsewhere; a vestige of a remote place but, also, a concretisation of a stony genesis[7]. At the point in which space and time coagulate into a solid, the finite nature of the geometry circumscribes the infinite nature of the universe and reveals it analogously to Martin Heidegger's concept of *aletheia*, namely, the unveiling, the unfolding of an instrumental-epiphanic casing that contains and "in-forms" the immaterial[8]. To use a medical metaphor, the form of the cube-meteorite acts as a means of contrast to increase the density of the void, emphasising the space occupied by the invisible and the time that shaped it. The meteorite, whether it be *cube* or *nature*, is the very form of the invisible that has plummeted to the ground. It is the cosmos on earth, the sky in our hands.

Observing the evolution of Giacometti's cube, one understands how it defines a tangible skeleton of being and its ineffable soul. It is not surprising that just as it appeared, it can disappear. Exactly like a stargate, it has its visible manifestation and its invisible nature. And here lies the transition - well described by Soldini - between *La table surréaliste* and *L'objet invisible*, where the subtraction of the cube from the hands of the queen-woman-mother is not a loss at all, but the exaltation of the essence, the sublimation of the physical presence in a diuturnal dimension[9]. The conceptual comparison with Fontana, already prompted by the symbolism of the meteorite and semantically similar in the research of the

---

6 P. Barone, *Età della polvere. Giacometti, Heidegger, Kant, Hegel, Schopenhauer e lo spazio estetico della caducità*, Saggi Marsilio, Venice, 1999, p. 24. Also see L. Sacco, *Alberto Giacometti e Maurice Merleau-Ponty, un dialogo sulla percezione. Fenomenologia dell'esperienza artistica*, Gangemi Editore, Rome, 2917.

7 For greater detail, M. Gounelle, *Météorites. A la recherche de nos origines*, Flammarion, Paris, 2013.

8 See op. cit. Barone, 1999, p. 85.

9 See op. cit. Soldini, 2016, pp. 37-43.

two masters although distant in its formal rendering, is intensified when speaking of creation by subtraction. Fontana's famous remark regarding the reason for his cuts ("Everyone believed that I wanted to destroy: but it is untrue, I have constructed", constructed a space with a cut, constructed a place with a chasm) coincides with Giacometti's need for expansion when he draws a force field between his fingers and digs its core deep into the ground, letting the hands emphasise it like a gap. Herodotus of Halicarnassus maintained that architecture was the act of building by removing, eroding by removing material. But if it is true that, again architecturally speaking, space needs a perimeter in order to represent itself, Fontana and Giacometti are architects of the incorporeal and know how to translate it into transparent geometries, even though they are aware that, once erosion has taken place, between inside and outside, on the edges, in the borderline places of architecture, all the mystery of the transition unfolds, the *expectation* of the beyond (to quote Fontana himself).

Returning to Giacometti's *Lunaire*, the figure protruding from the back of a piece of furniture in the shape of a protruding or sucking truncated cone (an optical trick to create another cavity) grasps the polyhedron with the same posture of the arms and hands that can be seen later in *L'objet invisible*, with the difference that the object is no longer there. The stone of Albert the child has been taken away, but the void it has left is full of its memory, because it has built the hole. It has expanded and pulsates between the palms of those who, attempting to poke at it, draw its bulk in space, lap against its substance. Fontana's *Signorina seduta* raises her thin, bare arms into the void in the same way. Her face is reflected in an evanescent surface. She stares into a liquid gash; she is attracted, magnetised, ensnared by it. She sees what we do not see. She moves the air as if it were a sphere. And it is this sphere that qualifies the entire composition; it is the balance point, the heart, the keystone as in the structural and at the same time allegorical secret of the Pantheon's round umbilicus. More solid than a rock. The void of the *Signorina seduta* generated by the expansion of the centre is, as Fontana said, "pure intelligence". It is energy that radiates everywhere[10]. This is quantum physics: between the phalanxes, an invisible network of tensions blazes, splitting space like a fault line. Both dated 1934, Giacometti's *Oracolo nero* and Fontana's *Donna d'oro* are clearly the spontaneous products of the complex era in which they were created. At the dawn of the age of catastrophe, while classicism consoled and surrealism moved away from the dramas of contingency, they nurtured in their wombs the desire for an elsewhere, fleeing from conflict and totalitarianism, projected with a simple gesture towards the realm of dreams and the unconscious. But, above all, of the absolute and the divine.

Alberto's *Cubo*, as a reconsidered projection of the youthful experience of the "stone", ended up shaping all of his later work with its

10 Letter from Lucio Fontana to Charles Damiano of 7 August 1960, in G. Gaggiotti, *La visione verticale*, Morlacchi editore, Perugia 2019, pp. 132-133.

mystical nature: he made it the module on which to base his obsession, to which he returned, tormented, to question the meaning of things and explore them in a material way, arriving at the reduction of sculptural forms to a radical and powerful synthesis, to the rarefaction of the image, and disappearance of the body. Miraculous. Again, Soldini mentioned that *L'objet invisible* may have been derived from Dali's *L'homme invisible* of 1929[11]. But Giacometti responded to the Surrealist game with an existential truth, which he resolved in the extraordinary formal invention of the void-fullness. The void as a place of happening, of *aletheia*, of the revelation of the eternal, rendered figurative by that handful of air circumscribed by a mass that defines its boundaries. Once again, the removal of the object becomes an epiphany, while the directives woven by the gesture define indefiniteness, the infinite in the boundary. The fingers of the oracle and the *signorina* trace a sort of *hortus conclusus*, the precious garden of love, the place where a luminous spirituality is shored up by an enclosure that guards it like a sacellum.

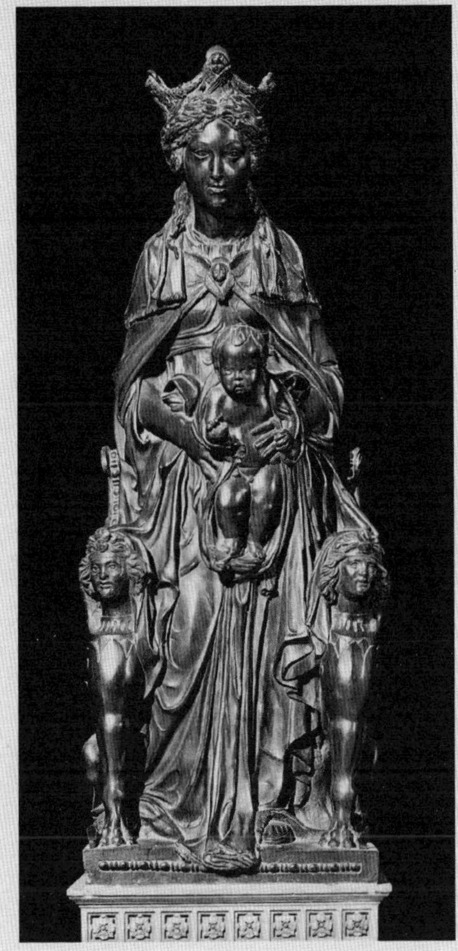

Donatello, *Madonna col Bambino*, bronze, 1446-1453. Padova, altar of the basilica di Sant'Antonio

It is not surprising that in regard to *L'objet invisible* there was a reference to Donatello's *Madonna and Child* on the altar of Sant'Antonio in the Basilica in Padua, which Giacometti is said to have seen on his first trip through Italy in 1920-21. The coincidence of the sculpture's posture with the upright, frontal position of the Virgin's upper body, the symmetrical position of the proffered arms, the legs blocked by the vertical draping of the garments and, above all, the jutting gesture of the hands holding the Child, which Giacometti nevertheless removes to paradoxically enhance the Child's presence. The invention of such a removal was probably inspired by other ancient insights, such as Cimabue's *Madonna in Majesty* or the statuette of *Isis nursing Horus* admired in the Louvre Museum during the endless Sunday visits of his youth in search of figural references. Italian primitives and archaeology, no holds barred.

The archaic artefacts of the Musée de l'Homme, the ethnographic museum on the *rive droit*, where he gazed at length at the axe-carved woodwork of the bushmen of southern Africa, provided him with inexhaustible ancestral references, including that of the carved statues worshipped by the Asmat peoples of New Guinea, embodiments of ancestral spirits governing the universe. Their ceremonial gesture, with arms raised straight up and elbows joined at the knees is an act that simulates birth (the foetal posture or *wenet*) and at the same time death,

---

11 J. Soldini, *Conoscenza, attrazione e temporalità nell'opera di Alberto Giacometti*, in *Giacometti. Dialoghi con l'arte*, exhibition catalogue, edited by Casimiro Di Crescenzo and Simone Soldini (Mendrisio, Museo d'arte, 17 September - 12 November 2000) Mendrisio, 2000.

in the continuous cycle of life and an otherworldly destiny. Here is another wonderful example of a sidereal portal that anthropology explains as man's eagerness to cast his heart beyond matter and its finitude[12]. The sacred meaning of these sculptures, the spirit of the ancestors, the celestial perspective yearned for in the synthetic gesture of a hand that opens a gateway to the beyond, help us to understand how that conceptual chain that spans the globe, and even time, generated the extensive array of offerors from different cultures holding liturgical offerings in their hands as a sign of oblation, like the small bronzes with the focaccia typical of the Italic, Nuragic or Etruscan peoples (which Alberto loved...) to the point of uniting the immortal gesture of two modern sculptures in their anthropological motives. From the postures of ritual weeping, expressed in different nuances of latitude, to the Christian iconography of the Virgin Annunciate, the motifs that rise behind Giacometti's idol, and behind Fontana's *Signorina*, unravel the enigma of their attitude, of their being poised on the threshold that separates the perishable dimension from the infinite. That pose of the hand that represents a contact, the sign of a volitional connection, punctuates the history of art from Antonello's *Annunciation*, which crystallises the moment and frames the invisible, to Lorenzo Lotto's frightened Madonna, whose hands (also symmetrical) draw a void in the air that already contains the fruit of her womb.

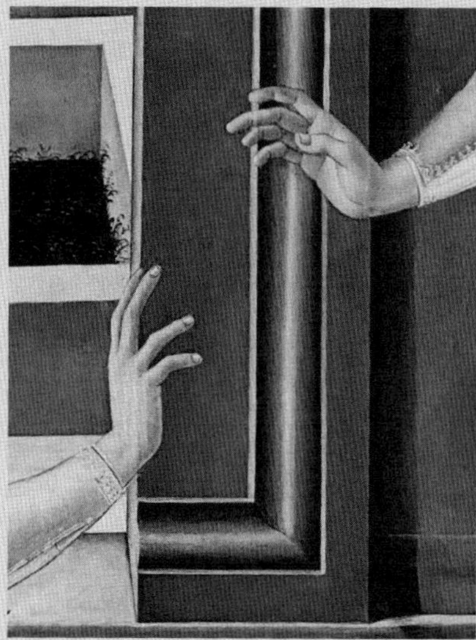

Sandro Botticelli,
Annunciazione, detail,
tempera on panel, 1489-1490.
Firenze, Gallerie degli Uffizi

It goes without saying that, formally speaking, in Botticelli's *Annunciation* in the Uffizi, the magnetic sphere, the keystone of the entire architecture of the painting, is condensed between the angel's right hand and that of Mary, against the backdrop of the door panel. It circumscribes a bubble in space, the place where the divine is manifested, the site of the famous *unfolding* of contact with God. Therefore, it is not unreasonable to grasp this today in Giacometti and Fontana's parallel reflection on the osmosis between the visible and invisible, earth and cosmos, immanence and transcendence[13]. As Jacques Dupin theorised when analysing Giacometti's diaries: "the void, the opening, the black space, the hole filled with air ... [...] the void is the life force, the effervescence in everyone, the establishing principle... eroding ancient and tenacious opaqueness, it opens the space to the irruption of the outside and the future, to the emancipation of hidden germs, to light..."[14]. The void is an active presence, in short, and here Dupin rightly

---

12 For a more detailed discussion of the significance of the work in Giacometti's research and reflection on the iconography and symbolism of gesture and step in *L'objet invisible*, see R. Hohl, *Alberto Giacometti*, Hatje, Stuttgart 1971; C. Gatti, *L'assoluto nel gesto. Pose, sguardi e passi di sculture immutabili, in A un passo dal tempo. Giacometti e l'arcaico*, exhibition catalogue edited by Pietro Bellasi and Chiara Gatti (Nuoro, Museo MAN, 24 October 2014 - 25 January 2015) Silvana, Milan, 2014.

13 Recommended reading: G. Mazza, *La liminalità come dinamica di passaggio. La rivelazione come struttura osmotico performativa dell'interesse trinitario*, Pontificia Univ. Gregoriana, 2005

14 C. Dupin, *Una scrittura senza fine*, in M. Leiris and J. Dupin (introduced by), *Alberto Giacometti. Scritti*, Milan, 2001, p. 28.

adds the phenomenon of light. The figural references to the classical and Italian primitives, which are still a suture between Giacometti and Fontana, both devotees of Giotto and, before that, of Byzantine icons, fuel their investigation of space and the theme of limits and boundaries as explored in depth by Pavel Florensky in his *Le porte regali* (The Royal Doors). As a means of reaching towards the abstract, towards the sacred, for the great Russian philosopher "the royal doors" of the iconostasis represented the glimpse between the visible world and the invisible world, "a place where a sublime painting is manifested and in which things are "products of light", he said[15]. In the *Madonna* of Borgo San Lorenzo and that of San Giorgio alla Costa or the later *Ognissanti Madonna*, the metaphysical sky is no longer infinite and therefore undefined, but physical and real. The figures are as robust as sculptures and in the background, though gilded, the air circulates. It is light that brings truth into the painting of icons, where Giotto always identifies a light source that shapes volumes and invades space, making it plausible and natural. Inhabitable.

"The fundamental conditions in modern art", wrote Lucio Fontana in his *Manifiesto Blanco*, "are clearly evident in the 13th century, when the representation of space begins". Giotto's new and illusory space is in fact transformed into a truly three-dimensional space. It irrupts into a mental perimeter, making it suddenly accessible. The light in the form of gold that passes through it makes the principle of the threshold palpable, illuminates the threshold. This is why Fontana also drenches his *Signorina* in a golden patina, heightening the dimensional projection already exerted by the radical synthesis of her gesture. The gold of the skin in turn becomes a threshold. It is she who is the regal door. And her hands help to open it. If critics have speculated that she might originally (or conceptually) have held a mirror between her fingers, the presence of the object would still have had value as a multiplier of space, however didactic, and perhaps it was left out for this reason. The passage opened by the hands, here as in *L'objet invisible*, sucks reality in at this point and ferries it towards the absolute. "I try gropingly to grasp in the void the invisible white thread of the wondrous, which vibrates and from which events and dreams escape, with the roar of a stream over small, precious, living pebbles", Giacometti confessed in his notebooks, as he was captivated by his black Madonna who ensnared him in her hypnotic vortex. "She stared at me so intensely that I felt on the verge of being caught in a spider's web from which I could no longer escape"[16]. It was as if the force field generated by the tension of the palms had turned into a cage for him, a motif destined to return in *La cage* of 1950 (arms raised as if in a resurrection, similar to Fontana's *Paulette*...) but also to qualify his contemporary painting, the paintings and drawings that frame bodies and faces against the backdrop of rooms enclosed in geometric

15 P. Florenskij, *Le porte regali. Saggio sull'icona*, Adelphi, Milan, 2021.

16 See op. cit. Soldini, 2016, p. 46.

perspectives, cubes within cubes, perimeters imposed to demarcate a living space. "Space? An illusion, a fantasy. Everything sinks, everything is alive, everything moves, everything returns", he repeated maniacally in 1934 at the sight of his fetish[17].

Contructing the space in the gesture of the sculpture that enveloped him eventually compelled him to construct it all around. His studio portrayed as through a window, seen from the outside. A ribbon unfurled around easels, heads and busts. The line of a square to delineate portraits of Diego or Jean Genet. The same line drawn in the open air, a frame for the *boulevards* of Paris, for men walking like atoms following diagonal trajectories within the cropped edge of a landscape. They are boxes, dioramas, where life flows and space is dense. Giacometti's *Personnages*, which punctuate a protracted landscape defined by a pencil line, date from 1950. And also dating to 1950 are the *spatial concepts* that Fontana created by puncturing paper with aligned holes and small tears that were in turn enclosed in the line of a circumference. Storytelling and abstraction, figure and synthesis, share the intuition and need to give form to that same void that, years earlier, both had placed in the hands of their sculptures. At the time it was sealed in a transparent object, but now it is sealed in a patch of horizon. "In the first trials on paper, in fact, Fontana makes use of a light hole", Luca Massimo Barbero wrote, "still close to the image of a dot and often arranged as a vortex or as a composition closed by a line symbolising space. Already in these trials, the stroke etches the paper in scratches or tears that drag parts of the material into a sort of felicitous slippage"[18]. The affinity between the giants was deepened. There was the entropy of the material and, at the same time, the urgent need to anchor it in the void, to capture it in a space-time tunnel. They both eroded but preserved. They scanned the sky but ploughed the earth. They dreamed of air but set boundaries.

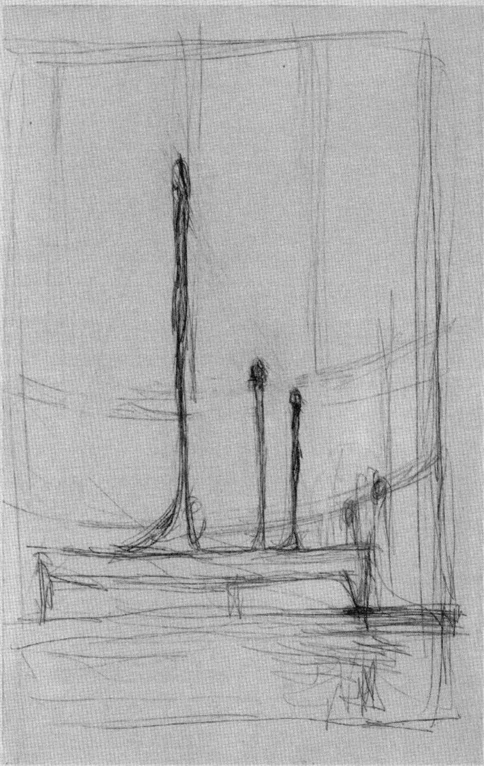

Alberto Giacometti, *La Place*, pencil on paper, 1950. Saint-Paul de Vence, Archives Fondation Maeght

Georges Didi-Huberman, who for a long time dedicated himself to the exegesis of Giacometti's *Cubo*, broadened his investigation from the device of the cage-object to the irradiation generated by the solid itself, providing an interpretation inspired by Dürer's stereometric figures and Leonardo's Vitruvian man as a principle for measuring space on the scale of the body, now bent in a more tormented, existentialist and fragile vision, where the cage is made of crystal, slender and diaphanous. The

17 Cfr. Giacometti, *Scritti* cit., p. 219.

18 L. M. Barbero, *Lucio Fontana: il segno come diagramma del Concetto Spaziale*, in *Lucio Fontana 1946-1960. Il disegno all'origine della nuova dimensione*, exhibition catalogue, edited by Simone Soldini and Luca Massimo Barbero (Mendrisio, Museo d'arte, 20 September – 14 December 2008), Mendrisio, 2008, p. 43.

same cage that the hands draw in the void and within which the void is qualified. “But what void? In what form? Certainly it is part of the strategy of the work to bring each of our gazes towards a phantasmatic and vain filling of this void surrounded by ten fingers”, Didi-Huberman insisted[19]. And, in fact, looking at *L’objet invisible* or Fontana’s *Signorina*, our eyes instinctively drift to where a part is missing, to the gap, to the sculpture orphaned of visible substance. Hunting for a presence.

But it is still the hands that find it and give meaning to the whole. Touching to shape it. Pointing to construct it. The phalanxes orchestrated in the air caress the mystery of life that wore Alberto down to the end of his days and inspired Lucio at the height of his quest. United in vision, distant in temperament. Giacometti was swallowed up by the same breach he had opened. “His real preoccupation”, said Simone de Beauvoir, “was defending himself against the infinite and terrifying emptiness of space. For a long time, walking the streets, he needed to touch the solid wall in order to endure the abyss that opened up next to him”[20]. Like a blind man groping in the dark, he needed references (cages...) but, at the same time, he wanted matter to live a life of its own. Like his men marching in the rain. “I don’t want to engage in anything, but always keep my hands completely free in the air, not enter into any scrapes, not touch anything, at least directly, but let things come with mute steps, entering by themselves without me hearing any slamming of doors opening and closing, no straight lines, no wounds, I won’t touch them”[≠]. In contrast, Fontana could have hovered in the air like the light forms of his spatial environments, papier-mâché, light and wire. “I used to follow his drawings”, Raffaele Carrieri recalled, thinking about his method. “Fontana’s ideas can be touched like bones [...]. When he came to talk to me about Spatial Art he began to shape the air: the air in his hands became a glowing body. He told me he was tired of clay, of static forms, of skill, of nobility. He wanted to do it another way. To blend with the air, to compose his sculptures in the air”[21]. And in this, believing in space as form and air as a demiurge capable of modelling life, Fontana converged with Giacometti. “Space”, he said, “becomes the pure form of intuition that anticipates every representation of sensitively determined objects”. Words that, once again, explain how the gesture of *L’objet invisible* and *Signorina seduta* hold the same secret. The object - just like the cube, the stone, the meteorite, *nature* - only occupies a vestibule that existed before it. It reifies the void and highlights it. But the void has its own form. It is architecture. It is an invisible volume with precise contours.

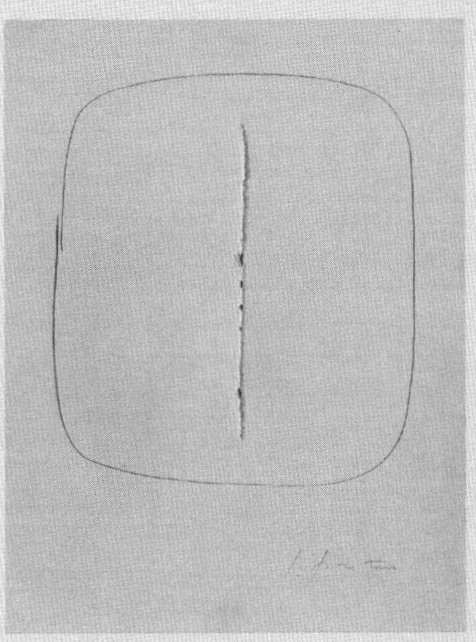

Lucio Fontana,
Concetto spaziale, 1950.
Private collection

19 See op. cit. Didi-Huberman, 2008, p. 56.

20 Cf. Giacometti, *Scritti* cit., p. 219.

21 R. Carrieri, *Pittura e scultura d’avanguardia in Italia 1899-1950*, Ed. della Conchiglia, Milan, 1950, p. 288.

The Obstinate Search for the Gaze

Francesco
Paolo
Campione

As underlined by many critics,[1] Giacometti harboured a smouldering dissatisfaction for the solutions he had found and experimented during his first fifteen years in Paris. The main reason for his constant and restless frustration stemmed from the central role he assigned in his research to memory and then to imagination and subconsciousness, which gradually steered him, perhaps inevitably, towards a symbolic use of forms. His stepping into the realm of surrealism, with its endless discussions regarding the impossibility of directly translating an artist's visual experience and the dangers of all realistic, "objective", and middle-class deviations, led him, in the second half of the 1930s to a strenuous reaction and to resolve to embark on a lonely journey towards a reconciliation with the figure, as he himself wrote in a famous passage of his 1947 letter to Pierre Matisse:[2]

> I saw afresh the bodies that attracted me in life and the abstract forms which I felt were true in sculpture. But I wanted the one without losing the other [...] And then the desire to make compositions with figures, for this, I had to make (quickly I thought) one or two studies from nature, just enough to understand the construction of a head, of a whole figure, and in 1935 I took a model. This study should take me (I thought) two weeks, and then I could realize my compositions.I worked with the model all day from 1935 to 1940.Nothing turned out as I had imagined. A head (I quickly left aside figures, it was too much) became for me a completely unknown object, one with no dimensions. Twice a year I began two heads, always the same without ever ending. I worked with the model every day from 1935 to 1940. Noting was as I had imagined. A head (I quickly abandoned figures, that would have been too much) would become for me a completely unknown object, with no dimension. Twice a year I would begin two heads, always the same ones, never completing them.[3]

The transcriptions of the conversation between Giacometti and Dupin (see note 62) and the Italian translations of all the original sources are by author.

1 Dupin Jacques, *Alberto Giacometti* (Paris: Maeght Éditeur, 1962), 18 and following; Hohl Reinhold, *Alberto Giacometti*, French trans. (Lausanne: Éditions Clairefontaine, 1971), 106 and following.; Lord James, *Giacometti. Una biografia*, Italian trans., (Turin: Umberto Allemandi & C., 1988), 166. Original edition, *Giacometti. A Biography* (New York: Farrar, Straus and Giroux, 1985); Megged Matti, *Dialogo nel vuoto. Beckett e Giacometti*, Italian trans. (Cernusco Lombardone, Como: Hestia, 1993) 39. Original edition, *Dialogue in the Void. Beckett & Giacometti* (New York: Lumen Books, 1985); Yves Bonnefoy, *Alberto Giacometti. Biographie d'une œuvre* (Paris: Flammarion, 1991), 269 and following; Jean Soldini, *Il colossale, la madre, il "sacro". L'opera di Alberto Giacometti* (Bergamo: Pierluigi Lubrina, 1991), 97 and following.

2 The third son of Henri Matisse, Pierre Matisse (1900-1989) was an art dealer and collector who owned a famous art gallery on the 17th floor of the Fuller Building on 57th Street in New York. See Griswold William M. & Tonkovich Jennifer (eds.), *Pierre Matisse and his Artists* (New York: Pierpont Morgan Library, 2002).

3 First published in an anastatic edition as an insert in the catalogue of the temporary exhibition entitled *Alberto Giacometti. Exhibition of Sculptures Paintings, Drawings*, held at the Pierre Matisse

Simplifying the matter to its essence, we might affirm that Giacometti's journey towards a reconciliation with the figure unfolded along three coinciding directions.

The first direction aimed at reflections on the subject of the visible and on the value of objectivity, a question many times discussed – if not even agreed upon – even with Jean-Paul Sartre and Simone de Beauvoir.[4] The second direction was that of mastering his own expressive means, starting from his (initially very troubled[5]) restored practice of figure studies with models. The third and last direction, had to do with his artistic culture and was, in particular, marked by a prolonged meditation on the expressive characters of artworks of the past, a matter that had been deeply preoccupying him since 1922.[6] Along this last direction a relevant role was played by his copies, a practice which derived from his study years, that for Giacometti became a preferential method to better observe and understand; copies that most of the time came from a meticulous observation of illustrations in books or art magazines rather than from seeing the original artworks.[7]

Along all three of these directions, as Jacques Dupin wrote, for the artist it was always about

> Discovering new mediums and tools that had to be reinvented each time, each moment. The old gesture, the obsolete tool had to be set aside in order to relearn everything, to step closer, to make corrections, to pare down, to destroy, and to endlessly start over. Helplessly. In order to define reality the way he can finally see it, as it emerges in its searing distance, the sculptor cannot but try, paradoxically, to catch it with the fine net of a live duration, and to draw gradually closer to it through an alarming and tedious sequence of progressions and regressions, with the painful awareness that his works are only nearing reality, and the artworks nothing more than approximations.[8]

Gallery in New York from 19 January to 14 February 1948. The quoted passage is on pp. 42 and 44. The introduction to the catalogue ("The Search for Absolute", 2-22) is by Jean-Paul Sartre. The letter was later republished in several volumes, either in an anastatic version or as a transcription.

4 On the consonance of Giacometti's and Sartre's views on the synthetic truth of reality, see for example what Simone de Beauvoir writes in *La force de l'âge* (Paris: Gallimard, 1960), 502.

5 See for instance what Giacometti confided to Pierre Schneider (1925-2013) in the beautiful conversation entitled "Ma longue marche", L'Express, Paris: Éditions de "L'Express" (8 June 1961): 48-50.

6 Radrizzani Dominique, "Alberto Giacometti nel paese di Fidia", *k+a. Kunst + Architektur in der Schweiz*, monographic issue entitled *Griechenland und Moderne*, Bern, Gesellschaft für Schweizerische Kunstgeschichte, no. 1 (1999): 57-65.

7 The expression "copies of the past" coined by Luigi Carluccio in connection with Giacometti's works, refers not only to ancient works of art, but to a diverse set of sources to which ethnic artworks and works of art from medieval and modern Europe also belong. See Carluccio Luigi, *Alberto Giacometti. Le copie del passato* (Turin: Edizioni Botero, 1967); Koepplin Dieter, *Warum kopierte Alberto Giacometti ältere Kunst. Zu einigen Zeichnungen hauptsächlich im Kupferstichkabinett Basel* (Basel: Wiese Verlag, 1995); Wiesinger Véronique (ed.), *Alberto Giacometti. Les copies du passé*, (Lyon: Éditions Fage, 2012).

8 Dupin, *Alberto Giacometti* (1962), 23 (translation ours).

On the other hand, it is also true that considering his artistic evolution as a whole, Giacometti's centre of gravity was and remained the tangible reality of existence. As Sartre wrote:

> He shows us men and women already seen. But not already seen by him alone. [...]. Each one of them reveals man as one sees him to be, as he is for other men, as he appears in an intersubjective world, not, as I said above, to entangle himself at ten or twenty paces, but at a proper human distance; each shows us that man is not there first and to be seen afterwards, but that he is the being whose essence is to exist for others.[9]

Human beings: human beings that Giacometti either observed and represented in art through a psychological lens and the irrational side of human nature, or approached through realism, attracted by the unstoppable desire to confront matter, despite being aware that every effort to represent reality was inevitably destined to fail.

THE THEME OF THE HEAD

The head theme, mentioned in his letter to Pierre Matisse, wasn't a novelty in Giacometti's work. It could be said that this subject was for him a matter of continuous reflection, almost a torment – as the artist wrote in an article in 1945 – caused by the feeling of not being able to step close to a sculpture, because

> There always persists an indefinite dimension that separates us from it, a space that is around the sculpture and that is already the sculpture itself [...] And this is the same feeling I have often felt in front of living beings, above all in front of human heads, that sense of a space-atmosphere which immediately surrounds beings, that pervades them, as if that sense were already a being itself; the exact limits, the dimensions of this being are indefinable. An arm is as vast as the Milky Way, without this phrase having nothing mystical about it.[10]

Without considering his early works prior to when he moved to Paris, we can identify a first specific interest in the elaboration of the theme

---

9 Sartre, *Alberto Giacometti* (1948), 14. The article was later published under the title *The Quest for the Absolute*, in the collection of Sartre's writings, edited by Wade Baskin, entitled *Essays in Aesthetics* (New York: Citadel Press, 1963), 82-92 (translation ours). The original French version appeared under the title "La Recherche de l'absolu", *Les Temps Modernes*, Paris Gallimard no. 3 (28 January 1948): 1153-1163, and soon afterwards in Sartre's collection of writings entitled *Situations III* (Paris: Gallimard, no. 3), 289-305. A negative assessment of Giacometti's relationship with existentialism is presented by Tobia Bezzola in the article "Phenomenon and Imagination. Giacometti's Concept of Vision", in *Alberto Giacometti*, eds. Klemm Christian, Lachner Carolyn, Bezzola Tobia & Umland Anne (New York: The Museum of Modern Art, 2001), 30-39.

10 Alberto Giacometti, "Un sculpteur vu par un sculpteur. Henri Laurens par Alberto Giacometti", *Labyrinthe. Journal mensuel des lettres et des arts*, Genève Pierre Cailler, no. 4 (15 January 1945): 3 (translation ours).

of the head in the 1923 oil painting (and in its preparatory sketch) depicting a cranium placed on the green cover of a book[11]. This is a captivating small-size work whose expressive research seems directed to establish between the subject and the observer a dialogue based on the attempt to represent the cranium in its entirety, delivering its living presence. As Giacometti himself confessed thirty years later to Georges Charbonnier,[12] due to his tormented incapability to represent a comprehensive vision of his subject, his attempt failed, forcing him to shift his attention to one particular aspect of the head. That was how the eye sockets became the centre of a meticulous representation agglutinating the other parts of the drawing, capturing attention as if they were alive.

The same magnetic quality of the small cranium painting can be found in two pencil self-portraits of that same period that schematise the subject with a series of close fine lines dividing the head in sections, at the centre of which the eyes stand out[13].

From 1924 to 1929 Giacometti made a series of heads using different materials portraying his father, his mother,[14] Flora Mayo,[15] Josef Müller,[16] and other subjects. Among these works there is also the half plaster mask entitled *Tête du père*, made between 1927 and 1929[17] (fig. 4). This piece, also due to its size, recalls a Japanese half mask of the happy old man, like those used by actors during the *okina* ritual, prelude to *nō* theatre performances[18].

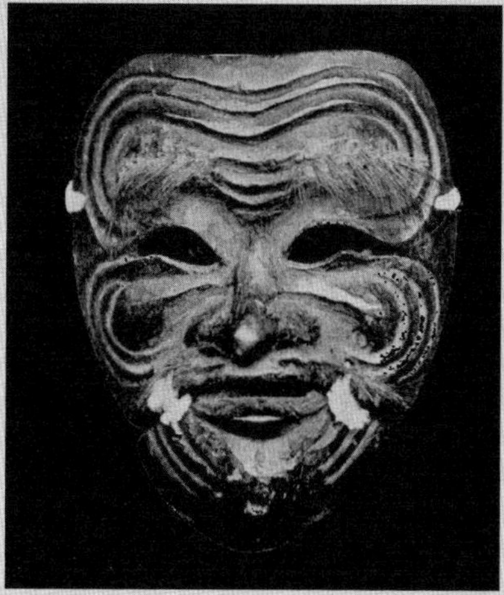

Wooden half mask from the Nanbokuchō period (1336-1392), the work of the master mask-maker Nikkō, used for the Kokushikijō (Okina) dance of the nō theatre.
The work belonged to the famous nō theater actor Kongō Kinnosuke (1854-1923), 19 × 14 × 7 cm.
Private collection

---

11 *Le crâne*, 1923, oil on canvas, 30×24 cm. Private collection, Paris. *Le crâne*, 1923, pencil drawing on paper, 23×21 cm. University of East Anglia, Norwich, Sainsbury Collection, inv. 39. See Bonnefoy, *Alberto Giacometti* (1991), figg. 111-112, pp. 122-123.

12 Georges Charbonnier, *Le monologue du peintre*, 2 voll., (Paris: René Julliard Éditeur, 1959) I vol. (*Entretiens avec Braque – Singier – Ernst – Coutaud – Dewasne – Hartung – Lapicque – Villon – Bazaine – Prassinos – Miró – Picabia – Marchand – Soulages – Giacometti – Masson*), 165. The whole periodical is on p. 159-170. The text was also published in *Les Lettres Nouvelles*, Paris Éditions Julliard, n.s., no. 6 (8 April 1959): 20-27.

13 *Autoportrait*, 1922-1924, 23×21.5 cm, Alberto Giacometti-Stiftung, Zürich currently at Kunsthaus Zurich, inv. GS 096; *Autoportrait*, 1922-1924, 50×32.4/32.7 cm, Kunstmuseum Basel, inv. 1964.47. See Bonnefoy, *Alberto Giacometti* (1991), figg. 65,109, pp. 68,119.

14 See Dupin, *Alberto Giacometti*, 190-191; Bonnefoy, *Alberto Giacometti* (1991), 156-160; Beye Peter, Honisch Dieter & Schneider Angela (eds.), *Alberto Giacometti* (München: Prestel, 1987), 158-161.

15 *Tête de femme – Portait de Flora Mayo*, 1926, painted plaster, 31.2×23.2×8.4 cm, Fondation Giacometti, Paris, inv. AGD 439. In 1990, the work was reproduced in bronze in eight copies. Born in Denver in 1899, Flora Mayo met Giacometti in 1925 at Bourdelle's sculpture classes at the Académie de la Grande Chaumière, and after a while became involved in a sentimental relationship with him that lasted until 1929. See Lord, *Giacometti. Una biografia*, 83-100.

16 *Tête de Josef Müller*, 1927, plaster, h. 34 cm, private collection. See Bonnefoy, *Alberto Giacometti* (1991), fig. 152, p. 160. Originally from Solothurn, Switzerland, after studying engineering at the Zurich Polytechnic and a two-year trip to the United States (1912-1914), Josef Müller (1887-1977) decided to devote himself to art, moving first to Geneva and then to Paris in 1922, where he also collected modern, antique, ethnic, and Oriental art. He returned to Solothurn in 1942 and was curator of the local Kunstmuseum (1943-1967). Part of his collections are today held at the Kunstmuseum Solothurn and the Musée Barbier-Mueller in Geneva.

17 Fondation Giacometti, Paris, 15×10.5×3.7 cm, inv. AGD 457.

18 See Perzyński Friedrich, *Japanische Masken. Nō und Kyōgen*, 2 voll (Berlin: Walter de Gruyter & Co.,1925), vol I, 20-36.

This series is offset by the schematic ovoidal head with a large nose at Beaubourg[19], *Tête qui regarde*[20], and the other congener works (*plaque*), where faces are reduced to a combination of horizontal and vertical elements, carved into the surface of a quadrangular vertical plaque with rounded corners.[21]

Despite their great formal differences, these two types of works seem to equally reflect the artist's attempt to experiment new expressive solutions and effective tools to translate the uninterrupted flow of impressions that, as Pietro Bellas wrote, brought him to endlessly expose himself to

> [...] Prehistoric industries, Sumerian, Egyptian, Etruscan, and Nuragic antiquities, or African, Oceanic, and pre-Columbian "tribal art" pieces. With his frenetic production of copies and by metabolising them in his own evolving "style", he dwelled on the essence, on the stylistic root of those works, in their dual quality of archetypes and stereotypes. The penetrating and constant quality of their presence is also due to that distance, that temporal and cultural "alterity" that endows them with their meta-historic presence, ultimately bearing witness to the non-temporal essence of an artwork; that "simultaneousness" of artistic research and present experience that Giacometti was so keen to affirm.[22]

An actual hinge between these two artwork typologies might be represented by the marble statue entitled *Tête du père*[23] which seems to operate a synthesis between the flattened engraved heads, remindful of first and second century BCE Celtic sculptures and the schematic and abstract works in which the influence of non-western figurative codes is more evident, in particular those of traditional African art[24].

We find a further synthesis between the two genres in a very significant drawing of 1927, entitled *Nature morte dans l'atelier*, that juxtaposes an abstract head of 1926[25] and the plaster cast of the head of the diorite

---

19 *Tête*, *ca.*1929, plaster, 28.8×30×8.5 cm, Centre national d'art et de culture Georges-Pompidou, inv. AM 1981-509.

20 A work of which there exist plaster casts, some bronzes and a marble version by Diego Giacometti (1902-1985), now on display at the Kunst Museum Winterthur, on deposit at the Alberto Giacometti-Stiftung, Zürich, 41×37×8 cm, inv. GS012.

21 See Bonnefoy, *Alberto Giacometti* (1991), 153-155 and 162-163 (figg. 145-147, 154-155).

22 Pietro Bellasi, "Vaghi crinali di realtà. Alberto Giacometti e la simultaneità dell'arcaico" in Bellasi Pietro & Gatti Chiara, *Alberto Giacometti e l'arcaico. A un passo dal tempo* (Cinisello Balsamo – Milan: Silvana Editoriale 2014), 39 (translation ours).

23 *Tête du père*, 1927, honed marble, 30×23×21 cm, private collection, Geneva. See Fiduccia Joanna Marie, *Hollow Man. Alberto Giacometti and the Crisis of the Monument, 1935-45*, doctoral thesis in art history, University of California, Los Angeles (CA) 2017, 299.

24 See Krauss Rosalind Epstein, "Giacometti" in Rubin William (ed.), *Primitivism in 20th Century Art. Affinity of the Tribal and the Modern*, 2 voll. (New York: The Museum of Modern Art, 1984) II vol., 503-533.

25 *Tête* [*Autoportrait*], 1926, plaster and wood, 42.5×16×10,5 cm, private collection, (AGD 3589).

Sumerian statue representing Gudea, ruler of the state of Lagash,[26] that Giacometti bought during one of his visits to the Louvre.[27]

The third period that characterizes this interest for heads was approximately between 1933 and 1935 when Giacometti made several of his so-called "head-skulls": at least two terracotta ones, five or six in plaster and two in marble[28] consisting of an abstract block made by superimposing and interlocking geometric volumes. Thanks to a masterful handling of distances between adjacent volumes, the figure presents a prominent chin, an open mouth, a chiselled nose, and a thick jawline ending at one extremity in a pointed cheekbone. The eyes are shaped as circular cavities and recall the *plaque* of the previous decade and the powerful extrusion of the 1923 small skull painting. In any case, even if this is not the philological manifestation of an expressive continuity, it is clear that once again the eyes are at the centre of the construction of Giacometti's figure and determine its perception from the different angles from which the work itself can be observed.

Closely connected to the head-skulls, of which it seems to offer a bidimensional vision is the etching entitled *Tête*[29] that Agnès Angliviel de la Beaumelle believes is related to the transparent quartz sculpture representing a cranium, which for a long time was displayed at the Musée du Trocadéro,[30] where Giacometti most probably saw it. [31]

From the same period of the cranium-heads, and under many respects rather akin to them, are *The Cube*, a large irregular dodecahedron that

---

26 Inv. AO 12. From the excavations conducted in 1881 by Ernest de Sarzec (1832-1901) in ancient Girsu (today Telloh, in the Iraqi province of Dhi Qar), the work measures 26.5×19×25 cm, and is dated between 2125 and 2110 BCE.

27 *Nature mort dans l'atelier*, 1927, charcoal on paper, 49.5×32 cm, Graphische Sammlung der Eidgenössische Technische Hochschule, Zürich, inv. 1990.117. See Hohl Reinhold, *Giacometti. A Biography in Pictures*, (Ostfildern: Hatje, 1998), 45; Angliviel de la Beaumelle Agnès (ed.), *Alberto Giacometti. Le dessin à l'œuvre* (Paris: Gallimard, 2001), 87, 219.

28 Angliviel de la Beaumelle Agnès (ed.), *Alberto Giacometti. La collection du Centre Georges Pompidou, Musée national d'art modern* (Paris: Réunion des musées nationaux, 1999), 108-111. The name *tête-crâne* was given to this genre by Giacometti himself in his letter to Pierre Matisse in 1947. Head-skulls are also known as "cubist heads".

29 *Tête [cubiste]*, 1933, etching, 30.6×25.4 cm, The Museum of Modern Art, New York, inv. 42.1968. See Angliviel de la Beaumelle *Alberto Giacometti* (2001), 105, 223-224.

30 Established in 1878 by the Ministry of Education as the Muséum ethnographique des missions scientifiques, the Musée d'ethnographie du Trocadéro (the "Troca"), named after the building that housed it, was the first ethnological museum in Paris and the venue par excellence where artists of the time went to discover the so-called "primitive arts". While its first director Ernest Hamy (1842-1908) was in office the museum grew steadily until 1906, only to gradually die out due to a lack of funds, inadequate space and, not least, the massive mobilisation of its staff during World War I. Starting in 1928, under the leadership of Paul Rivet (1876-1958), the museum experienced a phase of recovery, until, in 1935, the old building was demolished to build Palais de Chaillot, where the museum reopened in 1937 renamed Musée de l'Homme.

31 Purchased by Alphonse Louis Pinart (1852-1911) in the Parisian workshop of Eugène Boban (1834-1908), and later donated to the Musée du Trocadéro, the work is 11 cm high and weighs over two and a half kilos. Considered Aztec for a long time, it is actually a fake that was artfully made in Germany in the last quarter of the nineteenth century. See Walsh Jane MacLaren & Topping Brett, *The Man Who Invented Aztec Crystal Skulls. The Adventures of Eugène Boban* (Oxford: Berghahn Books, 2018).

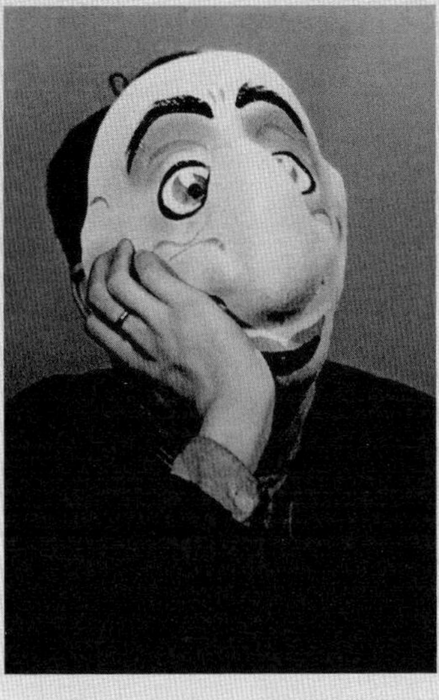

Detail of a photograph by Jacques-André Boiffard published in the article by Georges Limbour, *Eschyle, le carnaval et les civilisée*, in "Documents. Doctrines, archéologie, beaux-arts, ethnographie", n. 2, Jean-Michel Place, Paris 1930, pp. 97-102

Giacometti himself described as a monumental head,[32] and the today no-longer existing plaster head of 1934 of which we have a beautiful photo by Marc Vaux.[33] These two sculptures, close in their style to the cranium-heads, must be also related to the *L'Objet invisible*[34] head and *Grande tête,*[35] both from the surrealist phase of Giacometti's research. These are actual masks that, inspired by different formal solutions, try to resolve the matter of representation in essentially evocative terms, giving shape to a particular latent energy residing inside the face. For Rosalind Krauss, the *Grande tête*, clearly inspired by a carnival mask photographed by Jacques-André Boiffard[36], could be the original project of the *L'Objet invisible* head, that in the final version was replaced by Giacometti – as Breton wrote – with a "flee market mask".[37]

The transformation of Giacometti's approach and language in the mid-1930s is also manifested in a piece that significantly concludes his surrealist adventure. In the pen drawing entitled *Lunaire*[38], the top left head of a human figure (almost a mask) faces the bottom right shape of the sculpture entitled *Cube*. Between the two figures, frontally illuminated from the two opposite sides, a thick hatching creates a dark screen that nullifies physical space and excludes any possible reference to natural reality – almost as if the artist, as Reinhold Hohl[39] correctly pointed out, wanted to express his inner conflict between a self-sufficient art form and a metaphoric human form that despite being open to the future is destined to remain essentially uncertain.

---

32 On the significance of the *Cube* as head and face, see Didi-Hubermann, *Le Cube et le visage. Autour d'une sculpture d'Alberto Giacometti* (Paris: Éditions Macula, 1993).

33 See Dupin, *Alberto Giacometti* (1962), 224. Marc Vaux (1895-1971) was a photographer of Normandy origin. Active in Paris since 1915, in the 1920s he specialised in reproducing works of art and reporting on temporary exhibitions. A personal friend of many avant-garde artists, collector and philanthropist, he directed the magazine *Paris-Montparnasse* and founded the Musée de Montparnasse in 1951.

34 *Mains tenant le vide*, plaster, 1934, 156.2×34.3×29.2 cm, Yale University Art Gallery, New Haven (CT), inv. 1950.730. There are several bronze castings of the work and a second plaster head from 1934 preserved at the Ny Carlsberg Glyptotek in Copenhagen (37.7×33 cm). The title *L'Objet invisible* was later assigned to the work by André Breton. See Hugotte Valéry, "'La présence active du vide' Objet invisible de Giacometti", *Esprit*, no. 189, Éditions Esprit (Paris, February 1993): 56-68.

35 *Grande tête*, 1934, painted and engraved plaster, 37.7×33×42 cm, Kunsthaus Zürich, inv. GS 299.

36 Limbour Georges, "Eschyle, le carnaval et les civilisée", in *Documents. Doctrines, archéologie, beaux-arts, ethnographie*, no. 2, (Paris: Jean-Michel Place, 1930):7-102.

37 Breton André, "Equation de l'objet trouvé", in *Intervention surréaliste*, monographic issue of the magazine *Documents 34*, n.s., no. 1 (Bruxelles/Brussels: Imprimerie Jean Malvaux, June 1934): 20. Republished as the third chapter in the volume *L'amor fou* (Paris: Gallimard, 1937).

38 *Lunaire*, 1935, Indian ink drawing on paper, 27.5×20 cm, private collection, Paris. See Hohl, *Alberto Giacometti* (1971), 87.

39 *Ibidem*, 102.

The period that goes from 1935 to the early 1940s – the same period that, as previously mentioned, marked Giacometti's return to realism – is characterised by the creation of heads that seem to be wanting to question their own nature, just as much as Giacometti meditated day in day out on the value of human features, going back under many respects to the portrait style he adopted during the first half of the 1920s.

These are works that in bidimensional or three-dimensional form present marked traits, highlighting a selective investigation pertaining a specific part of the figure; works that do not express thoughts or emotions, but that lend themselves to a research aiming at extrapolating from the head the vital subject of the artist's laborious research.

This expressive modality characterizes the many self-portraits Giacometti made from 1935 to 1937,[40] a certain number of other drawings – like the portraits of Isabel Rawsthorne[41] and Paul Éluard[42] for instance – and the sketches of the copies of antique works that explore with particular clarity the traits of faces and heads of Egyptian and Sumerian sculptures that seemed at that time to captivate the artist's attention.[43]

The process of reacquisition of the value of human features characterising the reality of the head is even more evident in Giacometti's sculptures, such as the heads that portray his brother Diego, Rita Gueffier[44], and Isabel Rawsthorne, dating from the 1935-1937 period;[45] or other later portraits, which underwent a gradual process of simplification of their traits and a miniaturization of their size.

---

40 Angliviel de la Beaumelle, *Alberto Giacometti* (2001), 18-114. Among the most significant are the two self-portraits of 1935, drawn in pencil on paper, from the Alberto Giacometti Stiftung in Zurich (49×31 cm, inv. GS 246, on deposit at the Kunsthaus Zurich) and the University of East Anglia in Norwich (Sainsbury Collection, 29.7×24 cm, inv. 60).

41 *Portrait d'Isabel*, 1935, charcoal on paper, 49×32, private collection, London. See Angliviel de la Beaumelle, *Alberto Giacometti* (2001), 105, 226. Isabel Rawsthorne (born Isabel Nicholas, 1912-1992), was a British painter, set and costume designer who had a long and complex relationship with Giacometti from 1934 until his death. The correspondence between the two was published by Véronique Wiesinger for Éditions Fage in Lyon in 2007.

42 *Portrait de Paul Éluard*, 1935, charcoal on paper, 29,7×24 cm, Musée d'Art et Histoire, Saint-Denis. Paul Éluard (Eugène Émile Paul Grindel, 1895-1952) was a French poet and collector, one of the leading exponents of the Surrealist movement.

43 *Ibidem*, 111-114.

44 See Dupin, *Alberto Giacometti* (1962), 226-230; Bonnefoy, *Alberto Giacometti* (1991), 247 and following. Born in Jersey to an English mother and a French father, Margaret (Rita) Gueffier lived in Paris from the 1920s onwards, posing as a model and occasionally painting and working with ceramics. After the war, she moved with her companion, Julienne (Lili) Jaumary, to Entremont (Haute-Savoie) to devote themselves both to ceramics. Starting in the winter of 1934, Rita posed for Giacometti almost every afternoon for several years. See Fiduccia, *Hollow Man*, 47, 104.

45 *Isabel I (l'Égyptienne)*, 1936, plaster, 27.6×20.7×22.9 cm, Fondation Giacometti, Paris, inv. AGD 400; *Isabel I (l'Égyptienne)*, 1936, terracotta, 27.6×20.7×22.9 cm, Fondation Giacometti, Paris, inv. AGD 1850; *Isabel II (Tête d'Isabel)*, 1937-1938, bronze, 21.3×16×17.2 cm, Fondation Giacometti, Paris, inv. AGD 299.

In both cases the volumes are first roughly outlined in a sort of basic shape, then sculpted and carved in detail by the artist using a penknife or his nails. The greatest attention is given to lips, nose, and above all to eye sockets and the eyelid line, while ears and hair are usually just outlined. These works draw power from their concretion: these works seem to encourage the observer to engage in a tactile experience to discover the secret of a fixity only just interrupted by subtle rhythms, as if the artist were in search of a way of expressing their hidden and ancestral energy. Works – like Giacometti himself wrote in the conclusion of his article on Jacques Callot – that are the subject of an obsession that finds its roots in a deeply intimate dimension.

> [...] In every artwork the subject is primordial, no matter if the artist is aware of it or not. The greater or lesser plastic quality is nothing else than the mark of a corresponding obsession of the artists for his subject; the form is always related to such obsession. What one needs to seek is therefore the origin of the subject and of the original obsession that does not necessarily have to be Freudian.[46]

The true watershed, and under certain respects the authentic accomplishment of Giacometti's sustained research on the head subject, came about in the second half of the 1940s, and consisted in the inner revelation the artist had about the difference between the representation of an eye and of a gaze. On the one hand a very polished practice, that of the representation of the eye, falling under the category of realistic depiction of a human being and his or her feelings; on the other, the gaze, a necessary and preliminary quality, an ever-becoming tension, in other words, the potential energy that for a long time he had obstinately searched in the construction of his works without ever really grasping its secret.

To understand the substance and the origin of Giacometti's discovery it is crucial to read with attention the comments he made during a radio conversation with George Charbonnier[47] aired 3 March 1951 on Radiodiffusion-télévision française:[48]

> The sculptures from the New Hebrides[49] are true, are more than true, because they have a gaze. Not an imitation of the eyes,

---

46 Giacometti Alberto, "À propos de Jacques Callot", *Labyrinthe. Journal mensuel des lettres et des arts*, no. 7, Pierre Cailler (Genève, 15 April 1945): 3 (translation ours).

47 Georges Charbonnier (1921-1990) was for a long time executive producer of Radiodiffusion-télévision française. Professor at the Sorbonne, art critic, translator and man of letters, he was the author of a large number of interviews with personalities from French cultural life, always conducted with great acumen and rigorous documentary care.

48 The conversation was republished in Charbonnier, *Le monologue du peintre* (1959), 166-167 (translation ours).

49 The New Hebrides (now called Vanuatu) are an archipelago of over eighty islands at the south-eastern tip of Melanesia. A series of elaborate and heterogeneous sculptural styles originated there, characterised overall by a strong expressionistic tension, the use of stylised forms, elongated figures and a decisive use of colour. For a first introduction to the art of the Vanuatu, see Kaufmann Christian, *Vanuatu. Kunst aus der Südsee. Eine Einführung* (Basel: Christoph Merian Verlag, 1997); Bonnemaison Joël, Huffman Kirk, Kaufmann Christian & Tryon

but an authentic gaze. Everything else is only moving around the gaze. Greek sculptures, on the contrary, have no gaze: it's the body that attracts my attention and my analysis. It's strange if you think about it.

In Egyptian sculpture, which has always equally disturbed and attracted me[50] we find *The Scribe*[51], whose eyes are made of glass or with stones, to provide the best possible imitation of a real eye. But *The Scribe* is not looking at us. He just has a glass eye, that's all. And this bothers me, despite all the admiration I have for *The Scribe*. It really bothers me. The Egyptian who sculpted *The Scribe*, is clearly infinitely stronger, knows countless more things, masters countless more things than the man who made the New Hebrides sculptures. However, he who made the New Hebrides sculptures succeeded in giving them a gaze without imitating an eye. The gaze is all that matters. The New Hebrides sculptor is way closer to reality, way closer to what we should be doing. He is more penetrating than the Egyptian. In other words, there is a contradiction between the knowledge made apparent by the *Scribe* and that sort of naivety – or stupidity – that is revealed by his glass eye. In the New Hebrides sculptures on the other hand there is no trace of this contradiction: there is nothing but the sensibility, the intelligence of the fact of having realised a gaze. Even when the sculpture – that is the physical aspect of the character – seems to have an uncontrollable and naif side to it.

From Giacometti's words we can't exactly tell if he was referring to a specific work in particular or to the style in general. Among the most impactful Vanuatu sculptures displayed in the 1930s in the Musée de l'Homme there were the fern wood *mage ne sagran* sign of rank from the island of Ambrym with its great round eyes, brought to France by John Higginson[52] (in full display at the centre of the Oceanic Hall of the Musée du Trocadéro as early as 1895)[53], and the large *trrou körrou* sign of rank in wood painted in pink and green-blue from the village of Sakavas on the island of Malo, sent to France from the members of

Darrell (eds.), *Vanuatu. Océanie. Arts des îles de cendre et de corail* (Paris: Réunion des musées nationaux, 1996).

50 Giacometti's relationship with Egyptian art is addressed in Wildung Christian & Klemm Dietrich, *Giacometti. Der Ägypter* (München/Berlin: Deutscher Kunstverlag, 2009).

51 The *Seated Scribe* is a painted limestone statue of a scribe at work, dating from around 2620-2350 BCE. The sculpture was discovered north of the Corridor of Sphinxes in the Serapeum of Saqqara in November 1850 by the Egyptologist Auguste Mariette (1821-1881) and became part of the Louvre's collection of Egyptian antiquities four years later (53.7×44×135 cm, inv. E3023).

52 John Higginson (1839-1904) was a French entrepreneur and adventurer of Anglo-Irish origin, founder in 1882 of the Caledonian Company of the New Hebrides, a trading company for the colonisation of Vanuatu.

53 Today at the Musée du quai Branly, 261×45×42 cm, inv. 71.1890.27.4.

the "Korrigane" brigantine expedition in early 1935.[54] Two very expressive works capable of exerting on the observer a strong visual attraction. We also know that Giacometti knew well the monographic issue of *Cahier d'Art* dedicated to Ocanic Art edited by Christian Zervos[55] which contained an important article by Felix Speiser,[56] whose illustrations he had used as a model for one of the "copies of the past" indexed by Carluccio[57]. His visits to the Museum für Völkerkunde in Basel,[58] with its extraordinary Melanesian collections, finally allowed him to become familiar with an expressive grammar that he probably felt intimately resonating with him, and which he could use to finally release the tension he had built up in twenty years of efforts aimed at the vivification of heads. Melanesian works, not only those from Vanuatu, but also from New Ireland and the Sepik area,[59] in which the combination of sculpture and human body generated an inseparable system, were perfect examples of a whole expressing a gaze regardless of the eye, directly relating to what is most radical in reality, i.e. the manifestation of being. The influence of ethnic art, therefore, decisively surpassed the affinities that had emerged during Giacometti's interactions with surrealism,[60] revealing the very substance of an artwork and its power to express the artist's and in general man's phenomenal world.

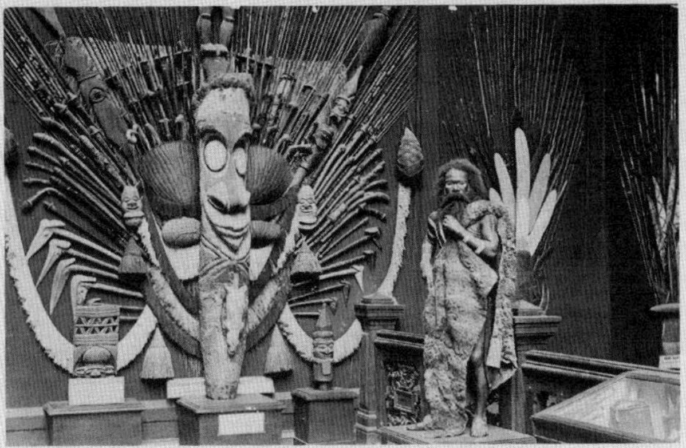

The Oceania Room of the Musée du Trocadéro in 1895. In the center of the image stands the mage ne sagran degree sign, carved in the arborescent fern in the second half of the 19th century. (see note 53)

Giacometti's awareness of this power surfaces in certain passages of the conversation he had with Jacques Dupin in his Parisian atelier in the autumn of 1965, for the film-interview by Ernst Scheidegger and Peter Münger:[61]

---

54 Today displayed at the Louvre (Pavillon des Sessions), h. 300 cm, inv. MH 38.42.8. See Coiffier Christian, "Sculpture de l'Île de Malo", Kerchache Jacques & Bouloré Vincent (eds.), *Sculptures. Afrique. Asie. Océanie. Amériques* (Paris: Réunion des musées nationaux, 2000), 274-278.

55 Christian Zervos (Chrístos Zervós, 1889-1970) was a French naturalised Greek art critic and publisher, founder of the magazine *Cahiers d'art* in February 1926.

56 Speiser Felix, "L'art plastique des Nouvelles Hébrides" in Zervos Christian (ed.), *Fascicule consacré à l'art des Océaniens*, monographic issue of the magazine *Cahiers d'art. Bulletin mensuel d'actualité artistique*, IV year, nn. 2-3, Éditions "Cahiers d'Art" (Paris, March 1929): 91.94. Felix Speiser (1880-1949) was a Swiss ethnologist, a great connoisseur of the cultures of Oceania and director of the Museum für Völkerkunde (today Museum der Kulturen) in Basel from 1942 to 1949.

57 Carluccio, *Alberto Giacometti* (1967), 10-11, fig. 5. Wiesinger, *Alberto Giacometti* (2012), 62-63.

58 Clair Jean, *Le nez de Giacometti - Faces de carême - Figures de carnaval* (Paris: Gallimard, 1992) 67.

59 Located in the northern part of New Guinea, the island of New Ireland and the vast river basin of the Sepik River were among the most important stylistic areas of the traditional cultures of Oceania. Works from the two regions were primary sources for the elaboration of primitivist art languages in the first half of the twentieth century.

60 Klemm Christian, "Influence of Tribal Art" in Klemm Christian, Lachner Carolyn, Bezzola Tobia & Umland Anne (eds.), *Alberto Giacometti* (New York: The Museum of Modern Art, 2001), 62.

61 Ernst Scheidegger (1923-2016) was a Swiss photographer, artist and publisher, author of

> In the end, if we look at a human face, we always look at the eyes. And the same happens when we stare at a cat looking back at us or when we look at a blind man: we look at where the eyes are, as if we could feel them behind. [...] There is a kind of gaze, but the strange thing is that if you define the eye with precision, you risk precluding the very thing you are looking for, which is the gaze. As far as I know, there are very few eyes where the gaze exists. In the Egyptian Scribe, for example, who has glassy, polished eyes, exactly the opposite happens. [...] The funniest thing is that in wild, or rather "exotic" sculpture – the work of a sculptor from Africa or Oceania – a head with eyes made of shells is incredibly alive. It is a work of wood, a highly transformed or I would say interpreted work, and the eyes are two shells. It almost seems to be made from a real skull to which the shells that make up the eye have been added. [...] It is incredibly alive, almost making us uncomfortable. [...] After the war I did not make one sculpture whose eyes are defined. There is the socket, and often there is almost only a vertical line where the pupil would be, and there is the orbit, there where we look when we sense the impression of a gaze. This is one of the aspects I base my work on, because now, what matters the most to me is to make the curve of the eye, because it seems to me the hardest thing. If I get the curve of the eye right, I'll get the orbit too; if I get the orbit, I'll get the root of the nose, the point of the nose, the nostrils, and the mouth. So, in the end everything could convey a gaze, without necessarily having to define the eye."[62]

An emblematic work representative of Giacometti's achieved mastery in the expression of the gaze is the *Tête sur tige*[63] a sculpture that seems to have been directly inspired by the remodelled skull collected in New Ireland in 1904-1905 by Albert Neisser,[64] purchased by Arthur Speyer[65] in 1920 and later resold to the Museum für Völkerkunde in Basel[66].

---

several publications on Giacometti and a great friend of his. Scheidegger's best publications on Giacometti include the illustrated volume *Alberto Giacometti. Spuren einer Freundschaft* (Zürich: Scheidegger und Spiess, 1991), translated into several languages.

62 Scheidegger Ernst & Münger Peter, *Alberto Giacometti*, 35 mm, Studio Scheidegger Zürich 1966, 17'40" et seq. Reissue on DVD, Künstler - Video Dokumentation, Zürich 2001. Colour film made in autumn 1965. Edited by Cinégram (Genève). Music by Armin Schibler (1920-1986). The quoted passages of the conversation can be found from 18'50" to 22'40" (translation ours).

63 *Tête sur tige*, 1947, painted plaster on metal rod and plaster base, 50×12.5×17 cm, Alberto Giacometti-Stiftung, Zürich, on permanent loan to the Kunstmuseum Basel, inv. GS033. See Bonnefoy, *Alberto Giacometti*, fig. 269, p. 294. There is a second plaster cast of the work (at the Fondation Giacometti in Paris, 54×19×15 cm, inv. AGD 461) and eight bronze castings: one from 1952, six from 1957 and one from 1954.

64 Albert Ludwig Sigesmund Neisser (1855-1916) was a German physician and art collector who discovered the pathogen of gonorrhoea.

65 Arthur Karl Hans Friedrich August Speyer (1858-1923) was the progenitor of a German family of collectors and dealers in ethnographic works, long-time suppliers to numerous European museums. See Schultz Martin, "Arthur Speyer - drei Generationen Sammler und Händler", *kunst&kontext*, no. 2, Berlin Vereinigung der Freunde afrikanischer Kultur (2016): 5-7.

66 overmodeled with vegetal paste and lime, decorated with plant fibers, shells and red

It is a rough-hewn piece with a tilted-back head, hollow blind eye sockets, and a gaping mouth as if it were screaming without being able to emit a sound. Strung on a thin rod, stuck in a bare plaster parallelepiped, this work seems to suggest to the observer the heinous practice of decapitating enemies and impaling their heads on a spear. A head that has been ripped off its body, but that is still alive and agonising,[67] to show without a shadow of a doubt that man's destiny is to become a disembodied skull, to be permanently extinguished, transformed into a simulacrum of death. Perhaps this is the reason why it is painted in blood red on all the parts defining its profile: the chin, the mouth, the nose, the cheeks, the forehead, and most importantly the eyes. Traces of colour like shreds of life glued to bodily parts voicing the wheezing quality of existence; traces soon destined to dry out in the silence of encumbering time.

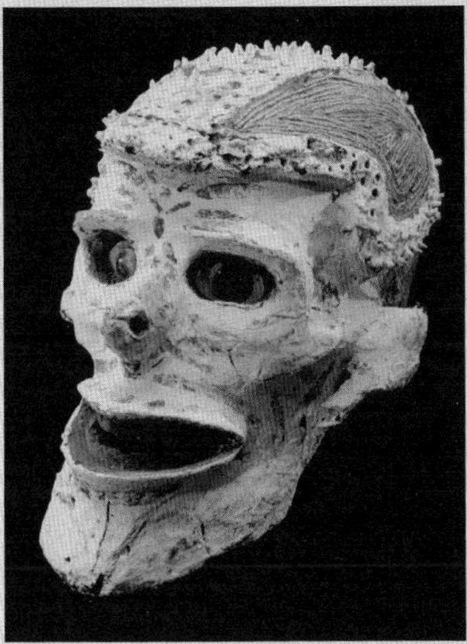

Overmodeled human skull from New Ireland (New Guinea). (see note 66)

A fully accomplished head capable of expressing a boundary between life and death through a gaze, capable of going beyond contingent reality to speak directly to being. A head that is finally animated by a well-executed gaze, although atrociously affiliated to the final instant of life.

Upon reaching the end of a long research, having finally resolved the matter of the gaze, Giacometti could step into the season during which he considered the entire human body and the human need to march along the pathways of the world gradually opening up to the experience of light.

---

and ochre pigments, 26×26×18 cm, inv. Vb 5009. Cf. Coiffier Christian, "Visage reliquiaires. Crâne surmodelés", in Le Fur Yves (ed.), *La mort n'en saura rien. Reliques d'Europe et d'Océanie* (Paris: Réunion des musées nationaux, 1999, (162-168); Gunn Michael & Peltier Philippe (eds.), Nouvelle-Irlande. *Arts du Pacifique Sud* (Milan: Five Continents, 2007): 180-185; Leicht Bernd, "Zeremonialschädel aus Neuirland" in Wieczorek Alfried & Rosendahl Wilfried (eds.), *Schädelkult. Kopf und Schädel in der Kulturgeschichte des Menschen* (Regensburg: Schnell und Steiner, 2011), 159-161. The identification of the relationship between Giacometti's work and New Ireland sculpture is by Jean Clair, *Le nez de Giacometti* (1992), 67-69.

67 The theme of agony (real or metaphorical) with regard to *Tête sur tige* has been addressed by more than one critic of Giacometti's work. See, for example: Meyer Franz, *Alberto Giacometti. Eine Kunst existentieller Wirklichkeit* (Frauenfeld: Verlag Huber, 1968), 121-123; Huber Carlo, *Alberto Giacometti* (Lausanne: Éditions Rencontre, 1970), 90 and following; Hohl, *Alberto Giacometti* (1971), 190-191.

The Chthonic Fontana

Alessandro
Del Puppo

The fate of great men (and women, it goes without saying) is to accumulate epithets. By turns, there seemed to have been a figurative Lucio Fontana, a surrealist Fontana, a spatialist Fontana, a Byzantine Fontana, a Baroque Fontana, an abstract Fontana, and a conceptual Fontana. No one would take offence, then, if here, faced with those magnificent and obscene craters of his, we were to speak of a chthonic Fontana. There do seem to be some traces of this.

In his first *Manifiesto Bianco* ('We are continuing the evolution of art', he dared to write in Buenos Aires in the year in question, 1946), initially, Fontana approached it in a somewhat roundabout way.

> "The new art takes its elements from nature. Existence, nature and matter are a perfect unity. They develop in time and space. Change is an essential property of existence. Movement, the capacity to evolve and to develop, is a basic property of matter. The latter exists solely in movement, not in any other manner. Its development is eternal. Colour and sound, bound together in matter, come together in nature. Matter, colour and sound in motion, are the phenomena whose simultaneous development makes up the new art. We present the substance, not the marginal nature of things. We represent neither man nor other animals nor other forms."[1]

The period cited is a rather long one, and for that I apologise, but I would like to emphasise two points that I think are important. First and foremost, the synaesthetic condition of artistic creation: matter, colour and sound coexisting simultaneously. And then the consequent kinaesthetic condition of form, meaning the insistence on movement and its processes. In other words, the property of evolving and developing is the basic condition of matter.

These words would be unthinkable without the precedent of the theoretical texts of Italian Futurism. As we know, Fontana openly declared that he was acting on the continuity of these texts.

But let us then try to read another page by Fontana. This time we are looking at the 'technical manifesto' of Spatialism, without too much hypocrisy and with some legitimate pride. Here, then:

> "A change in essence and form is necessary. It is necessary to go beyond painting, sculpture, poetry. What we need now is an art based on the need for this new vision. The Baroque has guided us in this sense. It is represented as grandiosity that has

---

1 L. Fontana, *Manifesto bianco* (1946), in G. Celant, *L'infermo dell'arte italiana. Materiali 1946-1964*, Costa&Nolan, Genova 1990, p. 79.

not yet been surpassed, where the notion of time is united with plasticity. The figures seem to abandon the plane and continue their portrayed movements in space."[2]

Here Fontana says three things, all of which are important. Above all, 'Baroque' is not a stylistic concept, let alone a historicist or antiquarian, retrospective throwback. Instead, it is a way of seeing that surpasses the purely optical experience and implies an action in space.

And how is this done? This is the second thing that Fontana says here. It is done by adopting an idea of the temporality of form. Forms must be set in motion, so that they leave the pictorial plane and invade real space. This approach of making the form an environment is an experience that takes place in time, that is, in the succession of instants: not in the simultaneity of an isolated object.

This leads to the third important thing and that is the highly sought-after transcendence of painting. But for Fontana, who was too shrewd an artist to fall for ploys or tricks, it was not at all a question of moving from the painted surface to the real object, succumbing to the ready-made shortcuts.

At one point, he explained this very clearly to Carla Lonzi: for him, it was enough to make the holes and call them 'Concepts'. This is where Fontana really dug in his heels, and it is worth listening to him: "I didn't call them objects because it seemed too materialistic."[3]

In short, this means that every extra-pictorial material used by Fontana (starting with the *Pietre*, which preceded the *Nature* by a few years) is not based on the *object trouvé*, that is, on the finding, somewhere between the prodigious and the ritualistic, of a random and aleatory object, but rather on what we could then define as an *object cherché* – an object, or extra-pictorial materials, sought-after, intentional.

In short, it is not the magical and heteroclite object (or matter), – and for this reason, that which destroys common sense – so highly cherished by the Surrealists; but rather a constructive matter that has compositional and expressive significance, that is part of the design of the work and not of its destitution of meaning. *Mater, Matter*: this is his very unique way of referring back to Boccioni. 'Conceptual', in short, is to be understood in this sense: as conceivable, generative.

And this is why it is necessary to return for a moment to the term "spatial concept".

---

2 *Manifesto tecnico dello spazialismo* (1951), ibid., p. 193.

3 C. Lonzi, *Autoritratto*, De Donato, Bari, 1969, p. 138. Cfr. G. Zanchetti, *"Un futuro c'è stato..." Anacronismo e suggestioni iconografiche in Fontana*, "L'uomo nero", no. 1, 2003, p. 93.

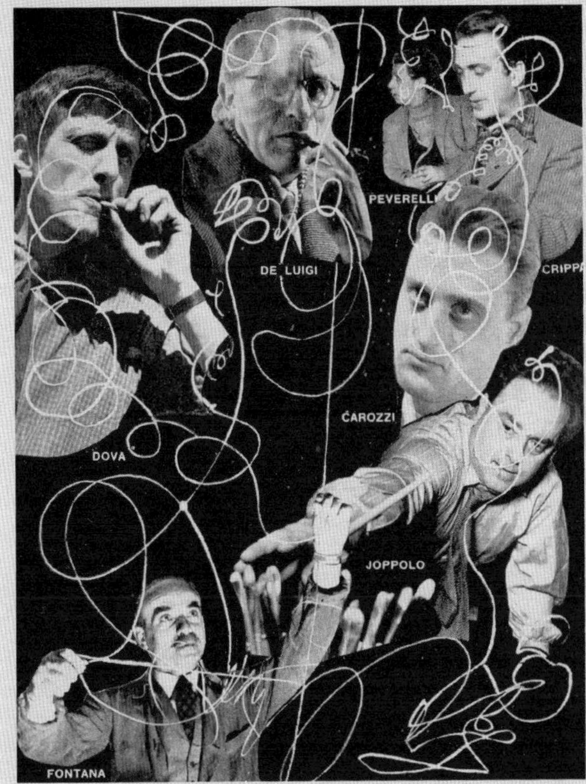

Photomontage from "Arte Spaziale", Galleria del Naviglio, February 1952

It is not a term that can be easily dismissed. Nor is it, as has sometimes been suggested, that concession to a semantics that is as misleading as it is inconclusive, if not for market purposes – that is, to align the most indigestible abstract experimentation with the far more popular fascination with the space age, and thereby generate a group and a label, that of 'spatialism', more useful to the interests of a gallery owner like Carlo Cardazzo than to those of the artists he collected under this heading.[4]

The term "spatial concept" brings together an abstract noun and an elusive adjective. Its sense of completeness lies in its complete independence, free of any external references. It does not describe an object, nor does it convey states of mind – apart from the transcendence of immateriality it instead suggests a possibility, or if you like, a flow.

Here, I intend first of all to interpret Fontana as a serial artist. In other words, an artist who one can really only try to fully understand by inspecting a vast range of works – as, for example, we see in Milan on the walls of the Boschi Di Stefano house – piled up one next to the other, in the knowledge that they are not merely the result of their irreducible individuality, but rather that each of these works is the result of being part of a discourse.

This is ultimately what happened at the 1954 Biennale. On that occasion, Fontana had landed an anthological exhibition and wanted to be introduced by one of his favourite critics: his name was Giampiero Giani. Fontana carefully prepared the exhibition. He designed a room with green walls and black bases for the sculptures, and set up a studied cross-section of his works from the beginning to the present. First of all, he wished to narrate the continuity of his research from the 1930s (with the graffiti panels of 1931 and the abstract sculptures of 1934) to his last works in 1952, with the *Concetti spaziali* on paper and perforated canvas. Some of the works (such as the disconcerting *Concetto spaziale*, namely that sort of black plaster coprolith presented at the 1948 Biennale) were already quite well-known. For the ordinary visitor the overt, uninhibited, even brazen experimental nature of the narrative displayed this way was less predictable. Fontana let his work speak for itself by piling up plaster casts, terra-cottas, bas-reliefs, ironwork, works on paper and canvas, one after the other, trusting in the inexhaustible continuity of

---

4 *Also see Carlo Cardazzo. Una nuova visione dell'arte*, exhibition catalogue, curated by L.M. Barbero (Venice, Peggy Guggenheim Collection, 1 November 2008 – 9 February 2009), Electa, Milan 2008.

his research over no fewer than three decades and with a sovereign disregard for the distinctions – at the time still well established and defined – between painting, sculpture and graphics. When Leoncillo, not just anyone, saw these things, he immediately realised how wrong he had been with his "post-cubist" fricassee.[5]

There is something irresistibly Giacometti-like in all of this. The idea of the exhibition not as the fulfilment of a process or, God forbid, the ostentation of the "masterpiece", but rather as a somewhat irksome moment when it was necessary to bring the game of forms and research to a halt, to pander to demands, to satisfy the market and the critics. In short: to be modern integrated artists instead of ancient ungrateful ones; to leave aside, at least for a moment, doubts and obsessions; to pretend to believe that the elaboration of the material leads to its completion. Anyway, the artists know that it's back to the studio the next day, *nulla dies sine linea* [no day without a line].

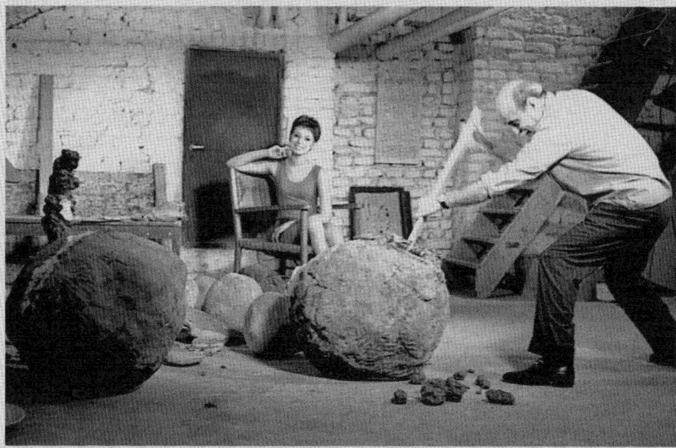

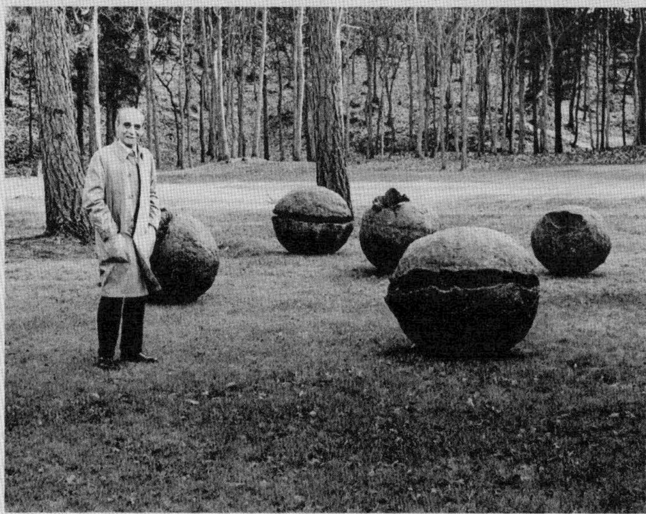

Giancolombo, Lucio Fontana at work on *Natura*, 1960

Lucio Fontana, *Nature*, Kröller Müller Museum Otterlo, 1962–1963

And here Fontana's 'line' plunges into the *Nature*. Who knows how or why?

These are few things, but all crucial, that greatly undermine the credibility of an artist who is not hard to find barely credible. And fortunately Argan stumbled upon those things, and wrote something about it that is still memorable today, or so I believe. Here it is.

> "That cut or those cuts always fall in the right point. They obey the need to break the perfect plane as if the material, the matter, brought to the ultimate limit of rarefaction, in that incident, wanted to recover the sense of the reality of its own existence: and in fact, that cut is a furrow, of the earth or of woman, the same one that connects the surface, whether earthly or human, with the profound, inscrutable spatiality of the creativity of the cosmos. The artist turns back from the ultimate limit of space and time, from the determinate and the indeterminate, because now the space that attracts him is no longer the sky but the depths. Fontana's most recent, disturbing images are

5 Also see my *Leoncillo 1954: l'antologica alla Biennale e la crisi del "realismo"* in *Leoncillo. Natura ed espressione*, edited by A. Leonardi, S. Petrillo, Electa, Milan 2021, pp. 78–87.

> 'Nature', large irregular balls, like inflated burst seeds, cruelly gashed, almost violated by immense fissures, by holes like chasms. We have arrived at the chthonic myth, at the origins, where the steatopygian form of the first woman is blended with that of the seed."[6]

Here he is at last, the Fontana that few really expected. It is a chthonic Fontana, and it was the unsuspected rationalist, Cartesian and Marxist Argan who recognised this. It is the prodigious offering of a different image. Something primeval and humid, between the botanical and geological, a fertile thalamus, a seminal receptacle. Cut or cleft, it is not only a symbolic opening, but an opening to different hypotheses regarding meaning. Not everyone, however, understood it in the same way.

A few years later, Crispolti thought that Fontana was still tied to the resolution of the informal – that is, the thing that had generated many more problems than it was then able to solve. "The limit that informal poetics has reached", wrote Crispolti in *Ipotesi attuali*,[7]

> "a limit that is nevertheless of course its own reason and historical justification, seems to be something that a young painter recently called the 'wall of anguish'. Anguish that resolves itself into cynical irony (Dubuffet), or into the exaltation of a modern activist myth (Fontana, or otherwise Kline)".

Who knows if this was really the case. Once again, however, Fontana's dual role appears crucial here: the author of the rarefied *Ambienti Spaziali*, on the one hand, and the visceral sculptor of the *Nature*, on the other. Argan again confirmed in 1960 that

> "The way of this unconscious recovery of the fabulous myths of Mediterranean prehistory is still craftsmanship, or rather that primordial craftsmanship directly related to terrestrial and celestial nature that is agriculture: so that the marks that determine the image are those that are dug in the furrow by the spade and the ploughshare." It is the artistic ploughshare that digs the furrow, and the conceptual sword that defends it.

In some respects, this is where *Arte Povera* originated.[8] To a certain extent, the new Italian art was the result of a resurrected process of unifying the different traditions. During the 1960s, there had been a decisive shift from Argan's humanistic anthropology to a social ideology. Celant added experimental activism, a good portfolio of international contacts

---

6 G.C. Argan, *Lucio Fontana* (1960), in *Salvezza e caduta nell'arte moderna*, Il Saggiatore, Milan 1964, pp. 295–297.

7 E. Crispolti, *Ipotesi attuali*, "Il Verri" V, no. 3, 1961, pp. 63–97.

8 Here I am quoting a remark made in *L'arte contemporanea. Il secondo Novecento*, Einaudi, Turin 2013, p. 76.

and a more explicit ideological-militant key. This led to the first unified moment in post-World War II Italian art – and one of the few, by far. In those years, a Mediterranean and 'classical' tradition of Roman art, modernised by Burri, kept alive by the myths of Cy Twombly and continued in the work of Kounellis and Pascali, was merging with the much more analytical and "technological" approach taken in Turin and Milan by Pistoletto, Zorio, Paolini and Fabro. And Mario Merz confirmed how the experience of Informal Painting, by overriding the utopia of the technological avant-garde, could provide a lesson on a new, unprejudiced relationship with matter. Behind many of these things, Fontana's role can be felt.

At one point, Giani, a shrewd observer, very aptly explained it in these terms:[9] 'In his art, Fontana doesn't know what to do with reality.' He was right, in the end. But what did he mean, in that magnificent Italy of 1963, by 'reality'?

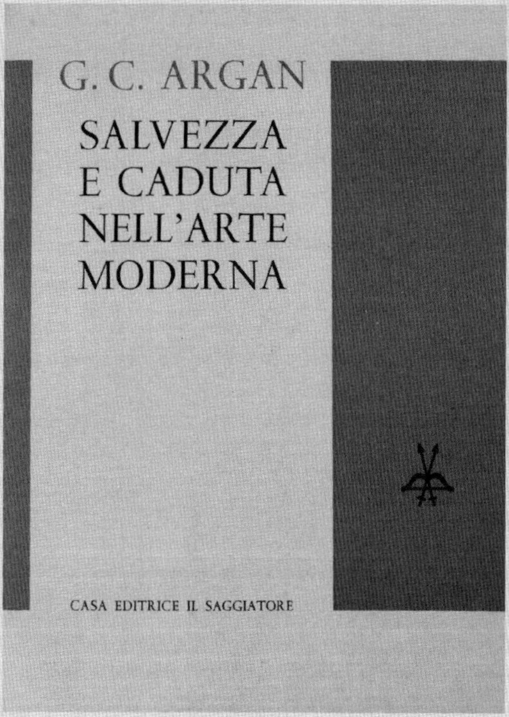

Giulio Carlo Argan, *Salvezza e Caduta nell'Arte Moderna*, Il Saggiatore, Milan 1964

Fontana was giving his answer, and his answer was chipping away at established stances and entrenched patterns. We should then take a step back and return to Argan's *Pittura italiana e cultura europea* (1946). For him, art at that time was not representation but fact; not invention, which always falls into naturalism, but commitment to a way of doing, which was necessarily realistic. Modern painting existed in the morality of concrete facts; it did not represent them, but brought them to completion. Argan clarified things a few years later: "The supporters of representative art care less about reality and more about nature, as a traditional conception or representation of reality."[10]

This observation, anything but trivial for an Italy that was somewhat self-denigrating in those years, could be juxtaposed with that passage lifted from Venturi's *Per la libertà della fantasia creatrice*[11]: "Between the presentation of a form and the representation of an object they [contemporary artists] preferred presentation. Between the existence of an image and the action of the subject of that image, they preferred existence." Sartrean echoes, certainly, but even more irredeemably like Croce.

Venturi and Argan were observing the crisis of art as being representation. But Venturi overturned Argan's assumption, which saw art as the

9 G. Giani, *L'arte di Fontana non sa che farsene della realtà*, "L'Avanti!", 27 June 1963, p. 6.

10 G. C. Argan, *Ancora sull'arte astratta*, 1951, in *Studi e note*, Bocca Editori, Roma 1955, p. 115.

11 L. Venturi, *Per la libertà della fantasia creatrice* (1952), then in *Saggi di critica*, Bocca, Roma 1956, p. 45.

presentation of an object, not a form, and as such situated in history and action. For Venturi, it was the form that imposed itself, the form which existed as such, confirming not the awareness of a historical coming into being, but actually “the rights to imagination, the courage to follow the freedom of the imagination to the end.”

The opposition between Marxism and formalism here was very clear. And on the other hand, Argan’s *Studi e note*, 1955, and Venturi’s *Saggi di critica*, 1956, were respectively the first and second volumes of Bocca’s series “Nuova biblioteca di Cultura”. Of course, culture counted, publishing counted, criticism counted. But Fontana’s work, conceptual and chthonic at the same time, skewed those pages, forcing everyone to go back to the drawing board.

Milan and Venice: Giacometti 1948-1962

Serenella Todesco

Alberto Giacometti was born in Stampa, Switzerland, not far from the Italian border. In fact, though he moved from the Val Bregalia to Paris, he never forsook the Italian language, his mother tongue. Despite his close ties to Milan, he didn't achieve renown in Italy until the Venice Biennale of 1948. The event that brought him to the attention of the Italian public was the presentation of Peggy Guggenheim's important American collection, which had arrived in the Venetian lagoon from the United States that very year and was being hosted in the Greek pavilion. Three of Giacometti's works were on display: *Femme égorgée* (1932, cast in 1940), the plaster cast of *Femme qui marche* (1936), and *Projet pour une place* (1931–32).[1] Albeit limited to his surrealist sculptures, this was the first real opportunity for the Italian public to encounter Giacometti's work. As remarked by Guggenheim herself, the sculptor was all but unknown in Italy, "Before 1948, only Picasso and Klee were known in Italy, apart from the Italian Futurists."[2] At this significant and important Biennale, the Italian public also discovered the ground-breaking works of Lucio Fontana, little known till that moment, who was exhibiting a *Scultura Spaziale* from 1947 in the central pavilion to present his most recent artistic and spatial research.[3]

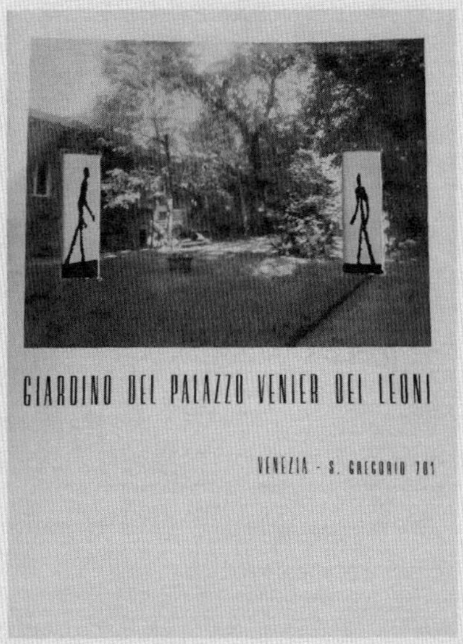

Catalogue of the exhibition of contemporary sculpture in the Garden of Palazzo Venier dei Leoni, 1949, cover. Exhibition of contemporary sculpture, exhibition catalog edited by P. Guggenheim, preface edited by G. Marchiori (Venice, Garden of Palazzo Venier dei Leoni, September 1949), Ferrari, Venice 1949

The works by Giacometti from Guggenheim's collection were shown once again during the *Mostra di scultura contemporanea*, held in Ca' Venier dei Leoni in 1949 and introduced by Giuseppe Marchiori.[4] In the meantime, the collection had grown to include *Piazza* (1948), which was highly representative of Giacometti's new style. In this work we find a number of slender human figures arranged on a broad slab representing an ideal urban square. In the modelling of the bodies, we can already glimpse the manipulation and erosion of matter typical of his later experiments. In this manner the Italian public was able to become acquainted with Giacometti's little known artistic research, though in the mid '30s he had already embarked on a radical change of style that led him away from surrealism towards a more intense and painful figuration.

Nevertheless, in the early '50s neither the Italian art scene nor its critics seemed to be interested in Giacometti or his most recent works. The

1 *XXIV Biennale di Venezia*, exhibition catalogue (Venice, Giardini di Castello, 1 May – 30 September 1948), Edizioni Serenissima, Venezia 1948, pp. 336–350.

2 P. Guggenheim, *Out of this century. Confessions of an art addict*, Andre Deutsch, London, 1979, p. 336.

3 Lucio Fontana exhibited the following works in room XLI of the central pavilion: *Rooster* (1947), *Spatial Sculpture* (1947), *Christ* (1948), *Masque* (1948), and *Masque* (1948).

4 *Mostra di scultura contemporanea*, exhibition catalogue, edited by P. Guggenheim, preface by G. Marchiori (Venice, Gardens of Palazzo Venier dei Leoni, September 1949), Ferrari, Venezia 1949.

exceptions were few but significant; among these, his inclusion in the organising committee of the *Mostra di scultura astratta*, later renamed *Scultori d'oggi*, created by Lionello Venturi for the XXV Biennale in 1950.[5] On this occasion, Giacometti was also invited to exhibit a limited number of works, but because of a disagreement he decided to pull out at the last minute.[6] The organisation of the exhibition was particularly complicated and the end result a partial failure. Another ambitious project for the 1950 Biennale, which however was never brought to fruition was that of an exhibition of the ceramic production of contemporary sculptors and painters with the purpose of prompting the appreciation of the so-called minor arts, among which figured two creations by Lucio Fontana which were nevertheless exhibited in the central pavilion.[7]

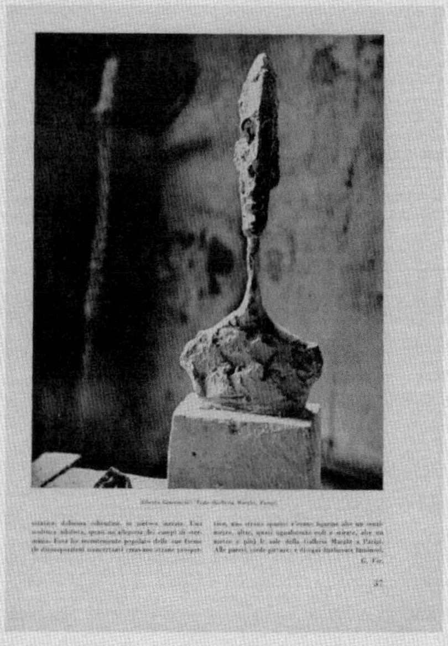

Alberto Giacometti, *Testa*, Saint-Paul-de-Vence, Fondation Maeght, in G. Veronesi, *Paris: Fifty Italian painters today*, "Emporium", CXIV, 679, July 1951, pp. 33-37: p. 37

In the fall of the same year, 1950, Giacometti was invited to show his work at the *Mostra internazionale del disegno moderno* held at Palazzo della Ragione in Bergamo, though even more decisive was his participation in the second edition of the exhibition *Pittori d'oggi. Francia-Italia*.[8] These were in fact the years in which relations between France and Italy were becoming stronger, with increasingly amicable cultural policies. However, his sculptures were greeted with no small amount of amazement and substantial criticism, such as the sarcastic comments of Luciano Pistoi, who in the columns of *L'Unità* described Giacometti's figures as "oversize spaghetti caught in the tines of cyclopean forks."[9] On the other hand, Giuseppe Marchiori expressed a very different opinion, describing Giacometti's work with great interest in *Fiera Letteraria*:

> he is destroying the "corporality" of sculpture, his eye turned towards these slender nuragic figures, so that human beings assume an uncertain dimension and the blank appearance of a caricature viewed from a great distance. Threadlike figurines that we must imagine, as if seen from atop a belltower, in quiet conversation in the square below.[10]

These considerations were most likely inspired by Jean Paul Sartre, who in 1948 devoted a weighty text to the artist by the title *La Recherche de*

---

5 On this same committee there were Giuseppe Marchiori, Giulio Carlo Argan, Alberto Magnelli, and Marino Marini.

6 For this exhibition Giacometti had chosen *Piazza* (1948), which belonged to Peggy Guggenheim's collection, the only cast bronze piece, and three plaster casts: *Composition* (1950), *Head* (1950), and *Figure* (1950).

7 The works by Fontana exhibited in this room were: *Christ* (1950), *Large Plate with Battle* (1950), and *Large Plate with Battle* (1950).

8 L. P. Nicoletti, *Parigi a Torino. Storia delle mostre "Pittori d'Oggi. Francia-Italia,"* PhD thesis, Tutor Prof. Antonello Negri, Università degli Studi di Milano, ay 2011–12.

9 L. Pistoi, "Pittori d'oggi: Francia-Italia," *L'Unità*, 21 September 1952.

10 G. Marchiori, "La Mostra Italia-Francia," *Fiera Letteraria*, 12 October 1952.

l'Absolou (*The Search for the Absolute*), which immediately achieved international renown, influencing, not only in Italy, the critical literature on Giacometti's work for decades to come.[11] In particular, the philosopher explored the nature of the relationship between his sculptures and "the void," especially fascinated by the manner in which the figures asserted their presence in space as solitary beings characterized by a new physicality. Another fundamental feature of the existentialist interpretation was the insistence on the uncertainty that distinguished the work of the sculptor, who – never satisfied – worked untiringly towards an aim that appeared unattainable.

Another exhibition in which the sculptor took part was the *II Rassegna Internazionale di Scultura all'aperto*,[12] held in the park of Villa Mirabello in Varese in 1953 and curated by Lamberto Vitali,[13] whom he soon befriended. On this occasion he showed two sculptures: *Head* (1943) and *Four Figurines on a Base* (1950). Giacometti didn't return to the Venice Biennale until 1956, when he was invited to exhibit a selection of his most recent works, both bronzes and plaster casts, in the French pavilion curated by Raymond Cogniat.[14] Among these was a series of plaster casts destined to become very famous in a very short time, shown here for the first time. Giacometti had worked ceaselessly on these female figures throughout the spring of 1956, as we can read in some of the most evocative passages of Jean Genet's text devoted to the sculptor's atelier.[15] Ever since his first trips to Italy, Giacometti had been captivated by Venice, so much so that after participating in the Biennale he decided to entitle these figures *Femmes de Venise* (*Women of Venice*). This exhibition did much to boost the artist's critical reception in Italy and marked a turning point in his career.

BETWEEN MILAN AND TURIN, FRIENDSHIPS AND EXHIBITIONS

One of the first prominent figures of the Italian art world to dedicate his attention to the works of the Swiss artist was the sculptor Mario Negri, who in 1956 published an essay on Giacometti in the magazine *Domus* just before the inauguration of the Biennale.[16] The two had met in November

---

11 The text was first published in English as an introduction to the exhibition held at the Pierre Matisse Gallery in New York in 1948, and subsequently in French as part of the collection *Situations III* published by Gallimard; *Alberto Giacometti. Exhibition of sculptures, paintings, drawings*, exhibition catalogue, introduction by J. P. Sartre (New York, Pierre Matisse Gallery, 19 January – 14 February 1948), Pierre Matisse Gallery, New York 1948, pp. 2–22.

12 *2a Rassegna Internazionale di scultura all'aperto*, exhibition catalogue, introduction by L. Vitali (Varese, Villa Mirabello, 1953), Manfredi, Varese 1953.

13 Among the personalities on the artistic committee, there were Francesco Arcangeli, Enzo Carli, and Gian Alberto Dell'Acqua.

14 *XXVIII Esposizione Biennale Internazionale d'Arte*, exhibition catalogue (Venice, Giardini di Castello, 16 June – 21 October 1956), Alfieri, Venice 1956, pp. 380–391.

15 J. Genet, *L'atelier d'Alberto Giacometti*, Décines, Barbezat 1958.

16 M. Negri, "Frammenti per Alberto Giacometti," *Domus*, 320, July 1956, pp. 40–48.

1955 when they spent three days together in Stampa. Having seen the sculptor in his homeland far from the Parisian boulevards influenced Negri's approach to the text and led him to give little importance to the more literary aspects of the artist's life which were instead prevalent in the observations of international critics. As Negri himself remarked, "recalling his father, his mother, and his birth town seemed to me a way to become better acquainted with Alberto Giacometti and his development as an artist."[17] In these pages there were a number of original passages, such as an analysis of the role of drawing in the sculptor's creative process. From this moment onwards, the two men established a bond of friendship and reciprocal esteem, as Negri himself tells us in his notes,

> "There was a time when I had the 'Milanese' A[lberto] G[iacometti] all to 'myself,' but then everyone got their hands on him, even though these are the same people who have already forgotten him. I walked down the street with him, here in Milan, in the '50s, and people barely turned their heads to glance at this man who was quite out of the ordinary [...]. For a long time, no one was interested in meeting him, and they barely knew who he was."[18]

Also in 1956, the sculptor Franco Russoli wrote about Giacometti, publishing a review of the room at the Biennale that contained his works in the magazine *Comunità*.[19] He and Giacometti had met a few years earlier in Paris and had soon become friends. This essay contained several allusions to Sartre's writings; here too a central role was given to the analysis of Giacometti's spatial research and a meditation on the subject of distance in his work. The author commented upon "the psychological value of space and distance," adding that, "in this unbelievable emptiness reverberating with sensations, which conditions the images it contains and is in turn conditioned by the presences, forms are freed from every optical and perspective norm."[20] People were beginning to find Giacometti's figures intriguing also because of the reflections they elicited on the tragic existential condition of human beings after the war. Russoli himself remarked that,

> "it seems to us that this was the brilliant and sincere path followed by Giacometti's art, increasingly dedicated to giving reality its true shape, as it is painfully seen and felt by the poet who accepts a human condition of individualistic melancholy."[21]

---

17 Ibid., p. 40.

18 M. Negri, *Note di studio*, edited by S. Esengrini, Pagine d'Arte, Tesserete (Capriasca, Lugano) 2018, pp. 32–33.

19 F. Russoli, "Artisti alla Biennale: Alberto Giacometti," *Comunità*, X, 42, August-September 1956, pp. 74–77.

20 Ibid., p. 74.

21 Ivi, p. 77.

In the second half of the '50s, Giacometti began to visit Milan with increasing frequency and was thus able to become acquainted with Giorgio Soavi, who over the years devoted many pages to the sculptor, as well as Alberto Martini and Lamberto Vitali. It is impossible to say whether during his time in Milan he also met Lucio Fontana, with whom he shared several subjects of inquiry, albeit leading to very different results, among which their meditation on space. Once the Biennale was over, Negri and Giacometti continued their relationship, and in the fall of 1956 the former invited the latter to collaborate in the organisation of *Mostra di scultura all'aperto* (an open-air sculpture show) in Parco Sempione during the XI Triennale di Milano.[22] The exhibition was intended to offer a comprehensive review of international modern and contemporary sculpture, from Rodin and Medardo Rosso to more recent trends. As in Varese, a crucial element was the placement of the works out in the open, a question that was especially dear to Negri. Giacometti's role was to mediate with the Parisians to procure the works for the exhibition. Despite the many difficulties they encountered, the Triennale was inaugurated on 27 July 1957.

In the first half of the '60s, several events devoted to Giacometti took place in Italy, among which his first solo exhibition in the country, organised by Luigi Carluccio in 1961 at the Galleria Galatea in Turin.[23] He exhibited no more than fifteen pieces, but it was still a fairly relevant event as at the time his shows were considered

> "among the most difficult to put together. [...] Giacometti is certainly one of the most important artists of our time. No one can escape the evocative charge of even the smallest of his bronzes: such that could thus far be equalled only by the archaic Etruscan craftsmen."[24]

After the exhibition in Turin, two shows were inaugurated in Milan. In November the Galleria Colonna exhibited a series of "drawings of figurative influence and sincerely human content: not graphic feats, but rather an adherence to the visual fact that is indeed crepuscular and yet intimately dramatic,"[25] as well as "original lithographs and tempera works with a French feel."[26] Soon after, a small exhibition of paintings was held at the Galleria Falanga from December 1961 to January 1962.

---

22 *Undicesima Triennale di Milano*, exhibition catalogue edited by A. Pica, (Milan, Palazzo dell'Arte al Parco, 27 July – 4 November 1957), Crespi, Milan 1957, pp. 265–268.

23 *Alberto Giacometti*, exhibition catalogue edited by L. Carluccio (Turin, Galleria Galatea, 29 September – 25 October 1961), Galleria Galatea, Torino 1961.

24 "Giacometti alla Galatea," *Stampa Sera*, 16 October 1961.

25 "Alberto Giacometti," *Corriere Lombardo*, 21 November 1961.

26 "Alla Galleria Colonna espone Alberto Giacometti," *Gazzetta di Parma*, 17 November 1961.

By this time, Giacometti enjoyed a certain fame in Italy, and in 1962 a retrospective of his works was held at the Venice Biennale. For the occasion, the sculptor cooperated with Secretary General Gian Alberto Dell'Acqua, who had succeeded Pallucchini in 1960. The two established an excellent relationship, and that same year Giacometti presented Dell'Acqua with *Nu debout*, one of the plaster casts exhibited at the Biennale of 1956, today preserved at the Pinacoteca di Brera. The works were selected by Giacometti himself, while the introductory text was written by Palma Bucarelli, who was already working on a great monograph of the artist.[27]

As requested by the sculptor, two large rooms in the central pavilion were devoted to the show, rooms 35 and 36. Giacometti personally curated the set-up, which for him held great importance, as reported by the architect and photographer Bo Boustedt,

> "Giacometti étudiait la disposition des œuvres avec minutie, s'attachant aux moindres détails, et il en résultait une foison de perspectives, un champ infini de prises de vue."[28]

Many recall having seen him during those frenzied Venetian days, and among these Giorgio Soavi:

> "his friends [...] say that Alberto was always somewhere in his rooms, moving sculptures big and small, arranging those wonderful squares crossed by figurines, immersed mostly in his own displeasure."[29]

His frenzy and dissatisfaction were perfectly captured in an eloquent series of photographs by Ugo Mulas. In these rooms, Giacometti played on visual juxtapositions, focusing mainly on the overall impression and the vision conveyed at first glance. The first room was the one that most captivated visitors. Here Giacometti had chosen to display his most recent sculptures, produced between 1958 and 1962, along with a series of drawings hung on the walls. The absolute protagonists were the works arranged in the centre of the space, which entered into a dialogue with one another: *Large Woman I* (*Grande Femme Debout I*, 1960), *Large Standing Woman II* (*Grande Femme Debout II*, 1960), *Large Head* (1960), *Walking Man I* (*L'homme qui*

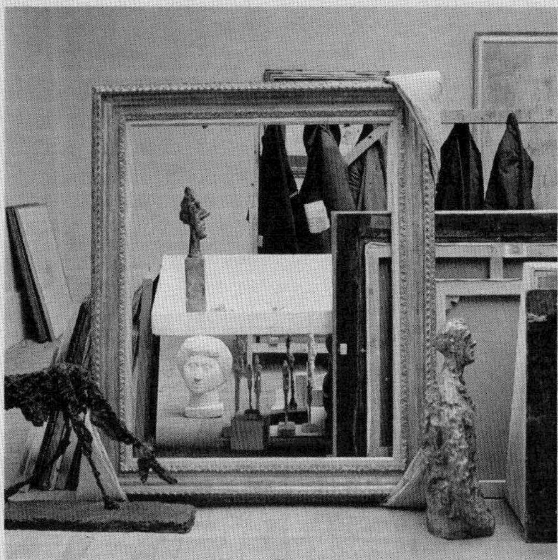

Works by Giacometti discarded during the preparation of the exhibition, photograph by Ugo Mulas, 1962. U. Mulas, *Incontri alla Biennale*, photo reportage by Ugo Mulas, "Pirelli", IV, XV, 4, August 1962, pp. 59-71, p. 63

27 P. Bucarelli, *Alberto Giacometti*, Editalia, Roma 1962.

28 B. Boustedt, "Quand Giacometti plaçait lui-même ses sculptures," *XXème siècle*, XXXI, 33, December 1969, pp. 23–38, p. 25.

29 G. Soavi, *Il mio Giacometti*, Abscondita, Milan 2016, p. 18.

marche I, 1960), and *Walking Man II* (*L'homme qui marche II*, 1960), all belonging to the Galerie Maeght in Paris. Three of these had been imagined as part of an unfinished group of sculptures that was to be exhibited in the Chase Manhattan Plaza area in New York. What stood out most in the room was a powerful sense of verticality, an element that did not fail to impress the public and capture the attention of photographers, "The verticality of Giacometti's figures seems to dilate the space in which they are immersed, punctuating it with a rigorous rhythm."[30] As described in a television commentary devoted to the Biennale,

> "a crowd of solitary beings bestows a new unsettling dimension upon these rooms of the Biennale. They are elongated, gaunt figures that advance towards nothingness, troubled by their own nature, anxious to recognise themselves in a human body."[31]

The second room was instead divided in two by a temporary wall. In the first half Giacometti chose to display a number of his less recent works, a grouping of all the surrealist works he had selected. Here was his famous piece *Invisible Object* (*L'Objet invisible*, 1935), which belonged to the Galerie Maeght, one of his most enigmatic creations that for the sculptor represented a first moment of reflection on the rendition of the whole human figure before a pivotal change in his style. Furthermore, these older works were displayed in such a way as to dialogue with a number of pieces produced between the late '40s and the early '50s, among which *The Chariot* (1950), from the Museum of Modern Art in New York, *Tall Figure* (1949), *The Forest* (1950), and *Three Men Walking* (*Trois hommes qui marchent*, 1949), from the Maeght.

The show was an undeniable success and awoke great interest in Italy. Lengthy articles and essays in magazines and newspapers were devoted to the exhibition, all underlining the importance of the event. The artist's presence at the Biennale was also captured by many photographers who seemed to follow Giacometti in every moment of his time in Venice. Among these, certainly noteworthy were the sequences produced by Ugo Mulas. A number of his shots depicted Giacometti in the first room, the artist captured as he moved among his figures, nearly becoming a sculpture among his sculptures.

Confirming his success in Venice, in 1962 Giacometti was awarded the top prize for sculpture which officially consecrated him as one of the Great Masters of the 20th century. From this moment onward, the sculptor's fame continued to grow, both in Italy and abroad, until his death in 1966. His work undoubtedly left a deep mark in the Italian art scene, a lively and unending stimulus for the next generations.

---

30 U. Mulas, "Incontri alla Biennale, fotoservizio di Ugo Mulas," *Pirelli*, IV, XV, 4 August 1962, pp. 59–71, p. 62.

31 Interview with Alberto Giacometti, audio track, 1962, Paris, Archive of the Fondation Giacometti, folder "Expositions-Biennale Venise", file "Biennale 1962".

The Art of the Void

Marco Senaldi

FONTANA, GIACOMETTI, AND THE (NON)EXISTENCE OF THE MEDIUM

At first glance, it may appear that there is no connection between Lucio Fontana's spatial research and Alberto Giacometti's existentialist approach. Yet, on closer inspection it becomes obvious that the common traits are far more numerous than their differences. If you look carefully, a number of formal correspondences emerges, bringing the two artists closer, such as their habit of installing their figures on metal stems or rods (a common practice for Giacometti, beginning with his *Testa su stelo*, employed by Fontana as well in *Concetto spaziale. Forma*, in 1957), or of leaving their fingerprints in their sculptures, somehow reasserting the pliability of matter. However, the main and unquestionable connection between these two artists is their specific conception of space, of its post-geometrical and topological interpretation, with all that implies.

While in 1946 the signatories of the *Manifiesto Blanco* (*White Manifesto*) had proposed the creation of a 'tetradimensional' form of art, in the ensuing *Primo Manifesto dello Spazialismo* (*First Manifesto of Spatialism*), space was defined as a dynamic force field in which the image became 'aerial, universal, suspended.' And in their *Proposta di un Regolamento* (*Guideline Proposal*) of 2 April 1950, Fontana and his colleagues advanced the idea of 'creating the perception of space with one's own imagination.'

This new conception of space was thus liberated from any previous spatial and geometric categorisation, and ended up resembling the 'flaccid' – that is to say soft, elastic, pliable – space postulated by the inventor of topology, Henri Poincaré.[1]

In the words of Beniamino Ioppolo, an artist and philosopher who was part of this group, "space is for Fontana a new plastic material… space thrown into a ceaseless sequence of events unfolding between a rigid and flustered Euclidean geometry and a geometry governed by the constant movement of forms and colours."[2]

The aim of these wilfully extreme positions was, however, to renew the language of art. In particular, the endorsers of the *Primo Manifesto*

1 H. Poincaré, *La science et l'hypothése*, Flammarion, Paris, 1902, pp. 73–4. According to the French scientist, "space itself" has no dimension, or rather, "*space* has no meaning in itself"; that is to say that it is impossible to ignore the relativity of space, both in a physical and representational sense, and in a more strictly geometrical sense; see P. Simondo, *Il concetto di spazio negli scritti epistemologici di Henri Poincaré*, Università degli Studi di Torino, ay 1961–62, unpublished (by courtesy of Fondazione Simondo, Turin).

2 B. Ioppolo, "L'ambiente spaziale di Lucio Fontana", 1949, in L.M. Barbero, edited by, *Lucio Fontana e gli Spaziali. Fonti e documenti per le Gallerie Cardazzo*, Marsilio, Venezia 2020, p. 45.

proposed to relinquish the old means of expression, such as canvas, bronze, plaster, and modelling clay, in favour of light, vibrations, and air.

Of course, in this case the distance from Giacometti's poetics, forever connected to the coarse material opacity of the medium,[3] could not be greater.[4] And yet, the truth is that for Giacometti matter does not possess a positive, additional essence, but rather he uses it as a negative, by subtraction, as described by his friend Brassaï in recollecting the artist's famous, monastic studio, a clutter of plaster debris scraped from his increasingly evanescent sculptures, which come to form "a hecatomb of condemned, destroyed figures."[5] This subtraction, this 'annihilation,' prevails upon presence and fullness, eventually resembling Fontana's disembodied space: whether it is the intangible object held by the female figure in *Mains tenant le vide. L'Objet invisible* (*Hands Holding the Void. Invisible Object*) from 1934, the atmosphere surrounding his ethereal *Testa su stelo* (1947), or the accessible space separating and yet connecting the *Trois hommes qui marchent* (1948), it is still an empty space, or rather, a space emptied out and reduced to a purely relational concept.

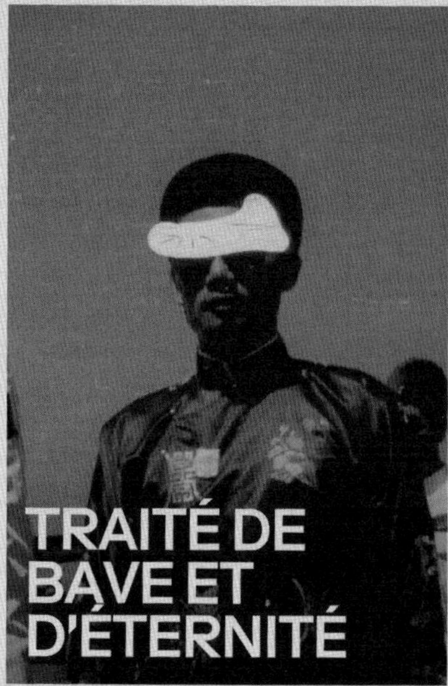

Isidore Isou,
Traité de bave et d'eternité,
1951

Above all, there is one detail that cannot fail to make an impression, recurring, as it does, in a surprisingly similar manner in the visionary poetics of both artists. In fact, though Spatialism is usually associated with the avant-gardist spirit of movements such as Futurism and their penchant for scientific and technological innovation, it also contains a constant reference to the peculiar kind of abstract dimension represented by the medium. The *Manifiesto Blanco* had already addressed the issue of those 'modern artists' who had been incapable of 'conveying movement to bodies' if not 'in a merely illusory fashion using conventional means.' A historical urgency thus led artists to explore 'new technical materials' that would allow them to achieve the aims of this research.

> This circumstance, combined with the development of mechanics, led to the invention of moviemaking, and its success is further proof of the inclination of the spirit towards that which is most dynamic.

Later, the *Manifesto Tecnico dello spazialismo* (*Technical Manifesto of Spatialism*, 1951) affirmed that "the triumph of the film frame is, for

---

3 See J. Genet, "The Studio of Alberto Giacometti", In Fragment of the Artwork, Stanford U.P., 2003

4 *In point of fact, in those years Fontana made broad use of traditional materials such as clay, plaster, and bronze, and continued to do so. We must thus admit that, "unfortunately for critics, and even more regrettably for a hurried and impatient public, Fontana's art does not have a linear development," as observed by Fred Licht in Omaggio a Lucio Fontana*, Guggenheim Foundation, Venice 1989, exhibition catalogue, p. 30.

5 Quoted from A. Del Puppo, *Alberto Giacometti*, Editoriale L'Espresso, Rome 2005, p. 27.

example, definitive proof of the spirit's orientation towards that which is dynamic."[6]

And yet, the art of filmmaking, designated by Futurists as an independent expressive language, albeit limited to the movement of shapes inside a 'frame', was seen by Spatialists as a form of art that could almost be ascribed to the rear-guard. For this reason, they were immediately fascinated by a new medium, directly connected to a novel conception of 'planetary' space: television. In the *Manifesto del Movimento Spaziale* per la Televisione (*Manifesto of the Spatial Movement for Television*, 17 May 1952), television isn't seen so much as a 'video screen', but rather as an electronic image, neither analogical nor photographic, as well as an instrument for transmitting into the 'yet unknown reaches of space.' It is quite significant, in fact, that Fontana and his associates would refer to a form of art 'unimpaired by matter', as in the *Primo Manifesto* they spoke of a matter that was 'pure', dematerialised, and ethereal.

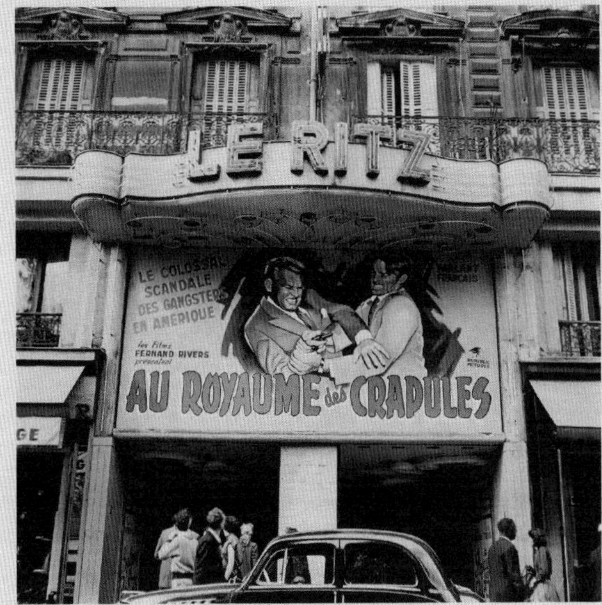

Le Ritz, Paris, 1952

This space is 'communicative', in the sense that it is not a mere *extensio*, indifferent and homogenous, but rather the synthesis of "physical elements: colour, sound, movement, space, integrated in an ideal, as well as material, entity" (*Manifesto Tecnico*). This post-geometrical space is situational and environmental, so much so that as early as 1948, that is to say before the Manifesto per la televisione was written, the artist had imagined a "Spatial Concept transmitted by television into an environment" or, in essence, a work capable of creating an emotional short circuit with the viewer.[7]

Essentially, Fontana interprets television not as a means of expression that produces images within the space of the screen, but rather as a device capable of 'generating spaces in the form of images', or 'environments', in which viewers can abandon the habit of contemplation and be submerged, losing themselves and ceasing to exist.

Now, though the notion may seem extraordinary, we must recall that the shift from Giacometti's early Brancusian and surrealist period to his more mature and universally known – often (unlawfully) defined his 'existentialist' – phase, did not take place thanks to a particular

6 Quotes from E. Crispolti, *Lucio Fontana. Catalogo Generale*, Electa, Milan 1986.

7 See L.M. Barbero, *Lucio Fontana. Catalogo ragionato delle opere su carta*, Skira, Milan 2013, 49 DAS 23.

encounter, a philosophical debate, or an exhibition he had viewed, but – once again – through a medium of communication: the cinema. One evening, presumably in the years immediately after the war (at the same time Fontana was imagining his televised spatial environments), Giacometti had an epiphany as he observed a newsreel in a movie theatre in Montparnasse.

> All of a sudden, I couldn't understand what I was seeing on the screen. Instead of figures moving in a three-dimensional space, all I could make out was black and white spots floating above a flat surface. They had lost all meaning. I looked at the people around me and suddenly, by contrast, I beheld an utterly foreign spectacle. It was amazing. The unknown was the reality surrounding me and no longer that which occurred on the screen! On my way out, on the boulevard, I felt I was faced with something unprecedented, a complete modification of reality.

What we must keep in mind here is that this perceptive shift in space is caused by a reflective backlash originating in the medium. In fact, Giacometti realised that, up till that moment, his vision had been *photographic*, but that

> a photograph or a film cannot be a genuine representation of reality… Everything appeared different to me, entirely new, fascinating, transformed, marvellous. Obviously, I wanted to paint, or sculpt, what I saw, but it was impossible. Yet at least I could try. It was a start.[8]

The effect of Giacometti's epiphany is the opposite of Fontana's jubilation: where the latter intuits that the evanescent, ethereal brightness of television programmes can be the sculptural language of a new art, Giacometti, on the other hand, realises that, if photographic objectivity is 'false', then *truly looking* at material objects – 'a table, a chair, a cup, or a human face' – is a radical experience verging on the impossible.

In this regard, Simone de Beauvoir wrote that "[Giacometti's] attitude was comparable to that of the phenomenologists, since he claimed to sculpture a face *in its context*, as it existed for other people removed from it, and by so doing to avoid the pitfalls both of subjective idealism and pseudo-objectivity."[9] However, this interpreta-

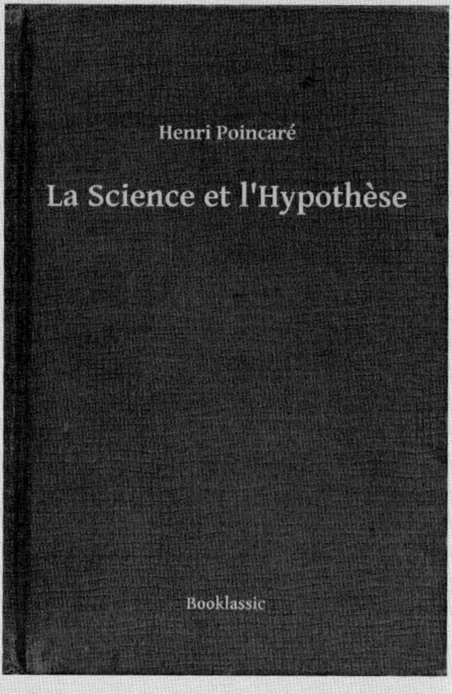

Henri Poincaré,
La science et l'hypothèse,
collection de la Bibliothèque de philosophie scientifique, Bibliothèque nationale de France

8 Cit. in J. Lord, *Giacometti. A Biography*, Farrar Straus Giroux, New York, 1985 (tr. It Giacometti, Allemandi, Torino 1988), cap. 39, pp. 513 ff.

9 S. De Beauvoir, *L'età forte*, Einaudi, Torino 1961, p. 426. *The Prime of Life*, translated by Peter Green, André Deutsch and Weidenfeld and Nicolson.

tion, though quite observant, adheres too closely to a phenomenological-existentialist analysis (originating with Sartre[10]) of Giacometti's art, and though it takes into consideration the optical theme, or the 'distance of the gaze', it still tends to overlook it's origin in the medium. In fact, Giacometti admitted that immediately after perceiving he was seeing the world in a non-photographic way, and having realised the immense difficulty of conveying it, he had been overcome by a piercing sense of discomfort, but also by a totally unprecedented manner of 'seeing space':

I began *seeing heads in the void, in the space that surrounds them.* When I first clearly perceived how a head that I was looking at could be fixed, becoming permanently immobile in time, I shook in terror as I never had before in my life, and cold sweat trickled down my spine. It was no longer a live head, but rather an object that I observed like any other object, or conversely, not like any other object, but like something that was alive and dead at the same time. I screamed in terror, as if I had just stepped across a threshold, as if I were entering a world that I had never before seen.[11]

This world is made accessible by exiting the old world of traditional optical representation, of which photography and cinema were nothing but the most extreme expressions.

It is not at all by chance that Fontana himself, in an interview with Carla Lonzi in the '60s, asked himself, "What is cinema?", and answered without hesitation that "cinema is like producing a 14th century painting today,"[12] clearly distinguishing this type of medium from the 'new eye', the ubiquitous porthole, which was the television screen. However, while Fontana perceives a projective energy in this visual transmission that can potentially be used to 'create forms in space,' 'transmit figures', and 'flood environments with colour',[13] Giacometti captures the devastating and disidentifying element in this duplication of things and people, that is to say the technological witchcraft capable of perpetuating these images in the eternity of the living dead, in a immortality generated by the medium with no escape or redemption.

The terrible stripping to which, from that epiphany onwards, he subjected his figures – his famous 'heads', the female silhouettes, his walking men – stems from the fact that those figures were in fact residues, what was left of the individual after their image, transmitted into space, had been separated from them and had begun, like the portrait of Dorian Gray – to live in their stead. It was not at all by chance that, in 1940, Bioy

---

10 See J-P. Sartre, "La recherche de l'absolu", in *Situations III*, Gallimard, Paris 1966.

11 Lord, op. cit., p. 515 sgg.

12 P. Campiglio (edited by), "Milano, 10 ottobre 1967: Carla Lonzi intervista Lucio Fontana," in Id. (edited by), *Lucio Fontana: sedici sculture*, Silvana Editoriale, Cinisello Balsamo (Milano) 2007, p. 55.

13 Fontana replying to Carla Lonzi, ibid.

Casares had already described this 'disease of the medium' in his novel, *The Invention of Morel*, the story of a machine capable of perfectly reproducing human beings as well as objects (a sort of hyper-television) in three-dimensions, albeit void of soul and basically transformed into eternal zombies.[14] In fact, Casares has the inventor Morel say that, thanks to his machines he has been able to produce not so much a presence (unattainable at that point), but to 'suppress an absence.'[15]

The consequence of this suppression is entirely representative of the schizophrenic condition that still afflicts us to this day: on the one hand, the pure disembodiment of the images in the ether of virtuality and the ubiquitous pervasiveness of the 'televisual' in all its forms, from the video-installation to the metaverse (Fontana); on the other, the bitter, stubborn survival of these residues that are what human beings have become, having lost the uniqueness of 'individuals' and become 'dividual', forever separated from their own image, gaunt and corroded by the acidic torture of this scission, 'afflicted with nonexistence' (Giacometti).

The lesson we may draw from this unexpected dialectic relationship is, as always, that we must interpret a phenomenon in relation with what appears to be farthest from it but, in this odd relational topology that is the contemporary environment of the medium, is at the same time its closest neighbour.

---

14 A. Bioy Casares, A., *La invenciòn de Morel*, Losada, Buenos Aires 1940; Eng. transl., *The Invention of Morel*, New York Review of Books, 2003

15 Ibid., p. 53.

MANIFESTO

DEL MOVIMENTO SPAZIALE PER LA TELEVISIONE

VI

Noi spaziali trasmettiamo, per la prima volta nel mondo, attraverso la televisione, le nostre nuove forme d'arte, basate sui concetti dello spazio, visto sotto un duplice aspetto:

il primo, quello degli spazi, una volta considerati misteriosi ed ormai noti e sondati, e quindi da noi usati come materia plastica;

il secondo, quello degli spazi ancora ignoti nel cosmo, che vogliamo affrontare come dati di intuizione e di mistero, dati tipici dell'arte come divinazione.

La televisione è per noi un mezzo che attendevamo come integrativo dei nostri concetti. Siamo lieti che dall'Italia venga trasmessa questa nostra manifestazione spaziale, destinata a rinnovare i campi dell'arte.

E' vero che l'arte è eterna, ma fu sempre legata alla materia, mentre noi vogliamo che essa ne sia svincolata, e che attraverso lo spazio, possa durare un millenio, anche nella trasmissione di un minuto.

Le nostre espressioni artistiche moltiplicano all'infinito, in infinite dimensioni, le linee d'orizzonte; esse ricercano una estetica per cui il quadro non è più quadro, la scultura non è piú scultura, la pagina scritta esce dalla sua forma tipografica.

Noi spaziali ci sentiamo gli artisti di oggi, poiché le conquiste della tecnica sono ormai a servizio dell'arte che noi professiamo.

Ambrosini, Burri, Crippa, Deluigi, De Toffoli, Dova, Donati, Fontana, Giancarozzi, Guidi, Joppolo, La Regina, Milena Milani, Morucchio, Peverelli, Tancredi, Vianello.

Milano, 17 Maggio 1952

Il "*Movimento Spaziale*" ha sede presso la GALLERIA DEL NAVIGLIO di MILANO, Via Manzoni, 45

Tip. Scarabellin - Milano

VI° manifesto per una trasmissione televisiva di Lucio Fontana. Milano, 1952.

(* L'immancabile refuso tipografico: "millenio" leggi "millennio".

Manifesto del movimento spaziale per la televisione, 17 May 1952

The *Devenir de Fontana*

Towards the Construction of Fontana's Sculptural Language

Cristina Beltrami

Devenir de Fontana is the title of the sumptuous monograph on Lucio Fontana that Michel Tapié published in 1961, tracing the development of the Italo-Argentinian artist's sculptural language.[1] The volume's narration of those first sixty years of relentless experimentation did not advance, or did not solely advance, following the chronological order of Fontana's innovations, proposing instead a synchronic perspective, revealing the simultaneity of his always purely spatial and perceptive exploration.

Indeed, the volume opened with an image of Fontana piercing a canvas in 1949 – a profoundly conceptual act that secured his international fame, almost obscuring more than thirty years of sculpture production – and then went back on the following page to the scratched tablets of the 1930s and a comparison between an abstract drawing from 1934 and the *Silla barocca*, a plaster sculpture from 1946 that Tapié considered representative of one of the furthest extremes of 'Baroque' Fontana.

In his story of how Fontana 'became' Fontana, Tapié deliberately left out his beginnings, when the artist worked as 'a *manufacturer* of granite and marble for architectural construction',[2] which is to say until 'the age of twenty-eight, when he started studying art in Milan at the Brera'.[3]

In fact, Fontana's sculpture career began at a very young age and, inevitably, in the bosom of his family. His father, Luigi Fontana (1865–1946), was a sculptor specialised in decoration and monuments and head of a flourishing business in Argentina. When it was time to start Lucio off on his artistic career, he took him to Italy to ensure his solid academic training. As soon as he finished primary school, Fontana simultaneously attended both the 'Carlo Cattaneo' Technical Institute of Milan and the Brera Academy's Secondary School for the Arts Applied to Industry: two experiences that gave the young man the technical skills, first and foremost drawing, for working in the fields of construction and architecture.

This period of training, which in Tapié's view should be disowned, was in reality the foundation that allowed the artist to progress, experimenting without hesitation, thanks to his total technical mastery of every sculptural means. This was spelled out by Guido Ballo in his introduction to the catalogue for the Milan retrospective in 1972: "We need to say right off that all of this was always supported by the full mastery of his expressive means: his technical confidence gave him a freedom that became conquest, thanks to which his imagination could have free rein."[4]

---

1 M. Tapié. *Devenir de Fontana*, Edizioni d'Arte Fratelli Pozzo, Turin 1961.

2 Ibid., n.p. (introduction).

3 Ibid.

4 G. Ballo, *Lucio Fontana*, exhibition catalogue (Milan, Palazzo Reale, 1972), Arti grafiche Fiorin, Milan 1972, p. 24.

It is also worth considering which Milan Lucio Fontana lived in as a young art student: there was of course the city of the major monument competitions[5] that led to the installation of Ettore Ximenes' equestrian statue of Garibaldi in 1895 and the majestic allegorical group by Giuseppe Grandi in Piazza Cinque Giornate, the city where, in 1906, Ernesto Bazzaro celebrated Felice Cavallotti with a large male nude – *Leonidas* – that was quite similar to academic personifications of river gods. In 1913, another leading figure from the Brera, Enrico Butti, opted for an accurate description of the physiognomy and clothing, although in a 'domestic' pose, for his monument to Giuseppe Verdi.

Instead of the leading figures of celebratory post-Risorgimento art, the mechanisms, advantages and rhetorical limitations of which Fontana was fully aware, the sculptor preferred the 'avant-garde' represented at the time by Futurism and Medardo Rosso. An artist for whom Paris was a second home, Rosso was a recognised beacon of modernity, a 'case', according to Ardengo Soffici, since 1909,[6] who, as Soffici stressed some years later, had freed sculpture from the 'incurable academicism that was the symbol and scourge of every good Italian monument sculptor'.[7] Milan was also the 'rising city' painted by Umberto Boccioni in 1910, a capital teeming with worksites, from the twenty-eight tramways of the Futurist evenings to the Teatro Lirico.

It was with an awareness of the existence of artistic epicentres like Milan and Paris that Fontana returned to Argentina in 1922, where he remained for five years, working in the family business, which was primarily devoted to producing funeral chapels and commemorative decorations, and participating in local exhibitions, in which he was already expressing his originality with innovations that went beyond the monumental canon.

Fontana was building his own, authentic language, one that was inevitably influenced by the big names in European sculpture, known thanks to the increasingly wide circulation of the specialised press and the increasingly internationally oriented Venice Biennale, an event documented also in images and not far from Lombardy, where Fontana had lived for years.

The pose, dreamy expression and puffed-out dress of *La Maternità* from 1926 recalls both Rik Wouters' *Domestic Concerns*,[8] a large plaster

---

5 See *Memorie nel bronzo e nel marmo. Monumenti celebrativi e targhe nelle piazze e nelle vie di Milano*, ed. M. Pietrantoni, F. Motta Editore, Milan 1997.

6 A. Soffici, *Il caso Medardo Rosso: preceduto dall'impressionismo e dalla pittura italiana*, B. Seeber, Florence 1909. Rosso was also, starting in 1910, and therefore during a key period for Fontana's early formation, a constant presence at the most important Italian exhibitions: the *Mostra dell'Impressionismo* in Florence in 1910, the Esposizione Internazionale in Rome in 1911 and the Venice Biennale in 1914.

7 A. Soffici, *Medardo Rosso*, Vallecchi, Firenze 1929, pp. 54–56.

8 *Les soucis domestiques* is a female figure more than two metres high that was sculpted by Rik Wouters in 1913, the plaster cast for which is at the Musées royaux des Beaux-Arts,

sculpture from 1913 displayed at the entrance of the Belgium Pavilion at the 11th Venice Biennale, and the equally monumental *Penelope* (1912) by Antoine Bourdelle, another leading figure of post-Rodin sculpture[9] and who had a solo show in the French Pavilion at Venice that same year.

As regards his two 'fathers' (Belgian and French), Fontana opted for a basic synthesis of forms, as is clear in the detail of the breasts, which already reveals his familiarity with primitive sculpture, reread in part through the lens of the Cubist revolution.

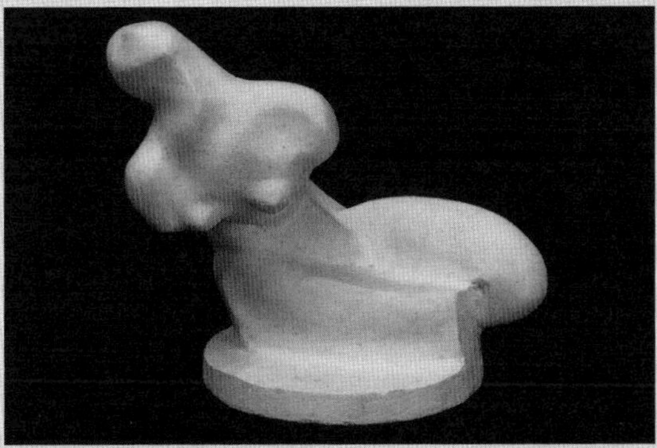

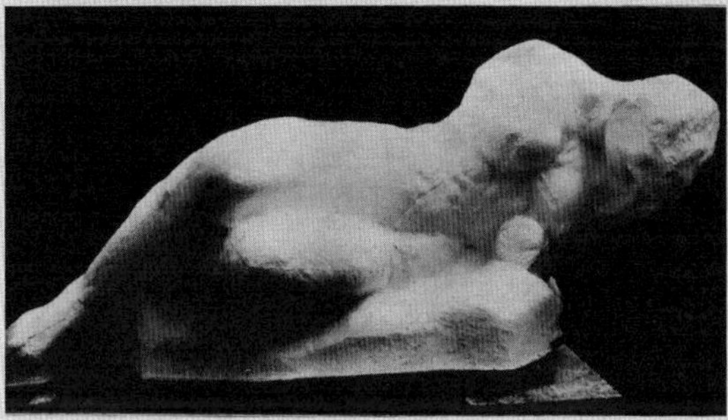

Lucio Fontana,
Nudo, 1926, chalk

Auguste Rodin, *Femme couschée*, Lucca, Fondazione Ragghianti, Fototeca Carlo Ludovico Ragghianti

Also in 1926, Fontana pushed the theme of the nude to disorienting extremes. *Nudo* is a small plaster sculpture that combines the classic pose of the crouching body and its elongation in space, showing Fontana's absorption of both Boccioni's dynamism[10] and the dissolution of contours already implicit in Auguste Rodin's *Femme couschée*, a plaster sculpture known in Italy, at least from 1905 when it was displayed at the Venice Biennale.

When Lucio Fontana returned to Milan in 1927, after an absence of seven years, his plan was to take up his former position in an artistic – and commercial – milieu in which he could continue to mature. A path that also led him to a sculpture class taught by Adolfo Wildt, forty-nine at the time and a recognised master at the Brera Academy[11] who had won the Sculpture Prize at Venice in 1922: an artist fully inserted in the political/cultural climate of the time and a virtuoso with marble[12] who had a free way of working with gold, a material that later became for Fontana a pure spatial tool.[13]

Brussels. At least twelve bronze versions were made, most of which for decorative purposed in public locations. See *Rik Wouters. Exposition rétrospective*, catalogue for the exhibition held at the Musées royaux des Beaux-Arts, Brussels in 2017.

9 See C. Beltrami, *La scultura alla Biennale di Venezia (1895-1914). Una presenza in ombra*, ZeL Edizioni, Treviso 2023 (in press).

10 It was Boccioni who declared, in his *Manifesto of Futurist Sculpture*, published in April 1912, that "Sculpture should give life to objects by rendering their extension into space palpable, systematic and plastic".

11 See P. Mola, 'Wildt a Brera, breve storia di un'utopia', in *Arte Lombarda*, no. 104, 1993, pp. 69–77.

12 A. Wildt, *L'arte del marmo*, 1921, now in A. Wildt, *L'arte del marmo*, ed. E. Pontiggia, Abscondita, Milan 2002, p. 13.

13 On Fontana's use of gold, see *Lucio Fontana. Ceramiche*, ed. L.M. Barbero, Skira, Milan 2022, p. 128, no. 30, which also has an extensive previous bibliography.

The traces of Wildt's influence[14] are palpable in *El Auriga*,[15] a plaster sculpture in which the powerful body of the athlete – not unreminiscent of Bourdelle's *Arciere* – is filled with nervous tension in contrast with the Art Deco stillness of the horse's head. With *El Auriga* Fontana not only took his leave of the Brera but also of figurative sculpture as traditionally understood, starting off his own original sculptural experimentation in the 'Milanese artistic environment' that, to cite Ballo, 'stimulated by the critical intelligence of Edoardo Persico, was in those years renewing itself with other European influences',[16] in particular French.

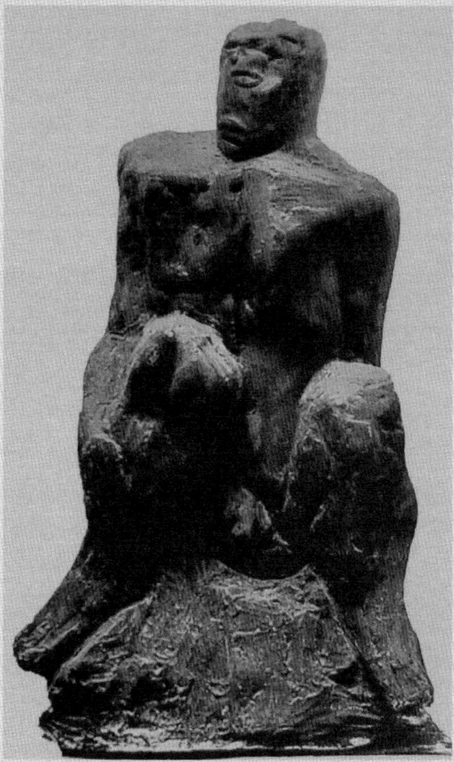

Lucio Fontana, *L'uomo nero*, 1930, painted chalk, lost work

This was the fertile context that gave rise to *L'Uomo Nero*, a sculpture that marked a point of no return for Fontana's sculptural language. His reasoning through deconstructed and geometrical 'blocks' drew him closer to Giacometti's volumetric works from the second half of the 1920s. The works with which the Swiss artist definitively switched to sculpture, *Torso* and *Uomo (composizione cubista)*, sculpted between 1925 and 1927, were clearly influenced by Cubism,[17] in particular Jacques Lipchitz, and are most importantly free from all possible reference to reality. A perhaps even more convincing comparison can be made between the square head of the *Uomo Nero*, understood as a surface upon which the artist traced the features of the face, and Giacometti's 'plaques', flat, four-sided faces, similar to millenary stones with edges eroded by the flow of a river, like *Gazing Head* (1928, Kunsthaus, Zurich), a subject that he presented at Jeanne Boucher's gallery in Paris in 1928 and continued to sculpt for the following two years.

These references are not to be read as the artists chasing after each other formally but rather as a shared feeling about the need to revitalise sculpture, independent of one's own geographic location and personal opportunities.

---

14 Over the years, scholars have often noted Wildt's influence on Fontana's subsequent Spatialist experimentation as well. See E. Pontiggia, *Adolfo Wildt e i suoi allievi. Fontana, Melotti, Broggini e gli altri (exhibition catalogue, Brescia, Palazzo Martinengo, 2000)* and L.M. Barbero, 'L'ensegnement idéal de Wildt: Fausto Melotti et Lucio Fontana', in *Adolfo Wildt. Le dernier symboliste*, exhibition catalogue (Musée d'Orsay – Skira, Paris, 2015), pp. 79–88.

15 *El auriga* (28SC12), keeping its Spanish title, was shipped to Buenos Aires for an exhibition in 1928 and from there all trace of the large plaster sculpture has been lost.

16 Ballo, 1972, op. cit., p. 24.

17 The original study for *Torso*, which was the source for numerous variants, is at the Kunsthaus, Zurich; see object description no. 40 *Torso* and no. 44 *Uomo (composizione cubista)* in *Alberto Giacometti e l'arcaico: a un passo dal tempo*, exhibition catalogue, eds. P. Bellasi and C. Gatti, Man, Nuoro, 2014-2015), Silvana Editoriale, Cinisello Balsamo (Milano) 2014.

In the 1930s, Fontana began to develop a language that 'lives its own life',[18] and so one very difficult to reconcile with what was happening in official Italian sculpture at the time.

Fontana's experimentation was moving towards an increasingly radical abstractionism: his works were certainly not ascribable to the prevailing success of Maraini and the Novecento movement,[19] but were instead, as often stressed in the literature, consonant with the interests of the Galleria del Milione, a place for dialogue with international artists and critics like Carlo Belli who, in 1935 (and with the support of the Ghiringhelli brothers), published *Kn*, a short volume that stressed the value and poetics of abstractionism with maxims like: "Modern art that is not iconoclastic would be nonsense."[20]

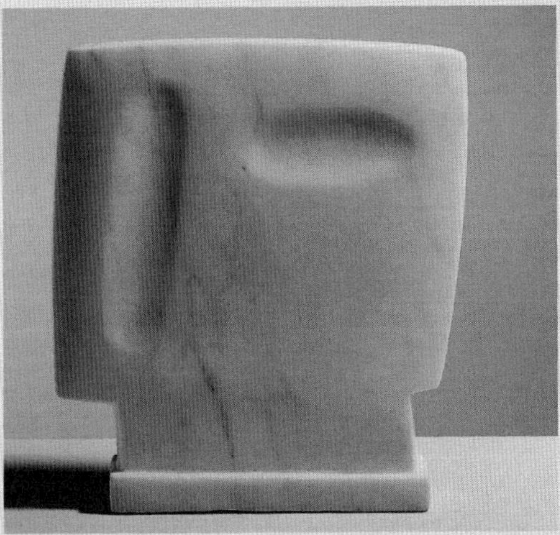

4. Alberto Giacometti, *Tête qui regarde*, 1928, marble, Winterthur, Kunst Museum, Depositum der Alberto Giacometti-Stiftung, 1976

It was at the Galleria del Milione, in January 1935, that Fontana displayed the sculptures he had made the year before, in what was in effect Italy's first abstract sculpture exhibition: works not only free from a tie to the representation of reality but even from the very idea of the existence of a subject. An exhibition that was certainly not easy for most critics to interpret, including Carlo Carrà who, despite having trained his eye on Rosso's dematerialisation, talking about 'mediumistic apparitions' and 'psychic effects',[21] stood in awe of Fontana's radical shift and left judgement up to posterity.[22]

Soon after, but always taking a profoundly anti-natural and most importantly anti-decorative approach, Fontana entered the world of ceramics. In 1936, Fontana created brightly hued still lifes, horses and seabeds in the Albissola kilns with a breaking up of forms that once again, and precociously, led the critics to compare him to Medardo Rosso. Fontana

---

18 E.N. Rogers, "Lucio Fontana alla Galleria del Milione", in *L'Italia Letteraria*, 12 December 1931.

19 The Italy in which Antonio Maraini (1886–1963) – politician, critic and sculptor – played a key role in the country's monumental events as well as the exhibition decisions of the Venice Biennale between 1928 and 1942 (see M. De Sabbata, *Tra diplomazia e arte: le Biennali di Antonio Maraini (1928-1942)*, Forum Editrice, Udine 2006). In 1930, he published *Scultori d'oggi*, which marked out a clear outline of the course of official Italian sculpture, represented to perfection by Napoleone Martinuzzi's *L'Uomo del grano*, displayed at the 1930 Biennale, and the award of the first prize for sculpture at the 1st Rome Quadrennial in 1931 to Arturo Martini, an artist as extraordinary as he was unlike Fontana. fig.10 Martinuzzi

20 C. Belli *Kn*, Il Milione, Milan 1935, p. 47.

21 C. Carrà, typescript preserved in the twentieth-century archive at Mart, Rovereto (Carlo Carrà papers) and now published by B. Avanzi in *Il presente si fa storia. Scritti in onore di Luciano Caramel*, eds. C. De Carli and F. Tedeschi, Milan 2008, p. 58; and in S. Risaliti, 'Medardo Rosso. Vedo cose che il giorno non rivela,' in Solo. Medardo Rosso, exhibition catalogue (Florence, Museo del Novecento), Bandecchi & Vivaldi S.r.l, Pontedera (Pisa) 2020, p. 10.

22 C. Carrà, 'Mostra d'arte', in *L'Ambrosiano*, n. 15, Milan, 17 January 1935: 'But where does one get, I wonder, by dint of purity? Only time will tell'.

certainly shared that artist's 'immediacy and ease',[23] which he couldn't help but feel in his bones, that sensitivity to the relationship between light and space and his view of the sculptural object as pure perception. Years later, Fontana himself, writing the *Manifesto dello Spazialismo*, recognised Rosso as a fundamental force in the development of his work: 'The Spatial movement is in my view the final, logical consequence of fifty years of contemporary art that began with Medardo Rosso's sculptural revolution.'[24]

The vicinity of the two artists becomes even more convincing in ceramics like *Conversazione* from 1936, in which the stripping down of the figures, resolved in the chromatic contrast between black and white, is clearly indebted to Rosso's *Conversazione in Giardino*. As also stressed by Sergio Risaliti in a recent catalogue on the Turin artist, in which he writes: "Fontana found in Rosso an extremely precocious path to anti-naturalism, and so to anti-heroism, and a similar way of handling light. This manipulation of material is what makes both Rosso and Fontana forerunners of Art Informel."[25]

The next year, Fontana finally had the opportunity[26] to go to Paris and, at a time when it still makes sense to talk about centre and periphery, he experienced the city to the full, when it was still the capital of modern art, and was literally dazzled. He had the chance to dive into 'one art exhibition after the other, each more amazing than the last'[27] and, among them, we certainly need to mention the impressive *Sculpteurs du Midì*[28] at the Petit Palais, an event devoted to the great 'Maitres de l'Art indépendant' of the Paris School, bringing together 33 works by Bourdelle, 52 by Despiau and 60 by Maillol, the latter an artist who, still in 1937, Lionello Venturi considered an inescapable model.[29]

---

23 A. Podestà, 'Statue e ceramiche di Lucio Fontana', in *Il Broletto*, April 1938 p. 42.

24 Lucio Fontana quoted in: R. Carrieri, *Pittura, scultura d'avanguardia (1890-1950) in Italia*, Edizioni della Conchiglia - Istituto Editoriale Domus, Milan 1950, p. 288.

25 Risaliti, 2020, op. cit. p. 9.

26 At the 1937 World Exhibition in Paris - an international event that included both Picasso's *Guernica* and Alexander Calder's *Mercury Fountain* - the sculptor showed his work in two pavilions: *Italia* (1937), a still fairly classicising sculpture, for the pavilion designed by Marcello Piacentini, and four sculpture groups in painted plaster - *Vittoria marinara*, *Marinai che salpano*, *La rotta del sole* and *La Dea del Mare* - literally hoisted up on high poles outside the pavilion of the Compagnia Italiana di Navigazione. See M. Villa, 'A Life in Art', in *Lucio Fontana. Sculpture*, exhibition catalogue, ed. L.M. Barbero (New York, Hauser & Wirth Gallery, 3 November 2022 - 4 February 2023), H&W Publishers, Zurich 2022, p. 205.

27 Letter from L. Fontana to T. d'Albissola, in *Lucio Fontana. Lettere 1919-1968*, ed. P. Campiglio, Skira, Milan 1999, pp. 56–57.

28 J. Giro, *Sculpteurs du Midì. Bourdelle, Maillol, Despiau, Dardé, Malacan, Costa, Parayre, Iché*, Libraririe Floury, Paris 1938, p. 47.

29 L. Venturi, 'Arturo Martini', in *L'Arte*, Turin, November, XXXIII; fasc. VI, 1930, p. 561: 'It is difficult to imagine a sculptor today without relating him to Maillol. [...] Maillol is to sculpture today [...] what Cézanne is to painting'.

But most importantly he had the chance to compare himself to artists from his own generation, like Jacques Lipchitz, Juan Miró and Tristan Tzara, as well as the older Ossip Zadkine, already known in Italy through the 1932 Biennale, when he was immediately singled out in an article by Ugo Nebbia.[30]

Tapié instead drew attention to the heated debates over issues of 'space' and 'volume' with the older Brancusi,[31] with whom Fontana certainly disagreed about ways of using gold: "He would say that what I did was not sculpture. I would say, I know, OK; but I'm not looking for volume. In his work, it's the light that breaks on a perfect form and smooths it."[32]

It was during this period in Paris that Fontana also pitted himself against the centuries-old traditions of the Manufacture de Sèvres: he entered those factories "that had served the tables of all the Louis of France[33] like a 'Minotaur on a leash butting the porcelain baskets and bisque allegories with his horns".[34] To paraphrase, Fontana created large-format works – in opposition to the culture of the porcelain knick-knack – and experimented with an even broader palette than the one he had used in Liguria, leading ceramics out of the decorative milieu.

Bolstered by his experience in the French kilns, Fontana returned to Italy and created *Paulette*: a life-size bust in painted ceramic that depicts the sitter while fixing her hair. An extremely bold portrait that, despite the gurgle of material and sharp colour contrast, keeps the features intact and maintains the woman's recognisability, complete with a deeply introspective note. 1938 was a crucial year for Fontana's ceramic production, with two major exhibitions, both at the Galleria del Milione, one in April and the other between December and January of the following year, when it became clear that he had "taken a stick to all the old symbolism of majolica and porcelain, inventing new forms and radiant colours".[35] Works that, to cite Sandro Bini, were like a 'prophecy',[36] able to anticipate the Fontana of the future. In a certain sense, even Giulio Carlo Argan, a critic who often spoke unflatteringly of Fontana, admitted the impressive modernity of *Paulette*, which he attributed to the clear, dramatically contrasting palette of black and white that provided

---

30 U. Nebbia, 'La diciottesima Biennale. Gli italiani', in *Emporium*, vol. LXXV, n. 450, June 1932, p. 386: Nebbia summed up Zadkine's sculpture as the result of the deconstruction of Cubist planes, 'alternated with a crude and refined synthesis game of black derivation [and] overturning the balance of masses and reliefs'.

31 Tapié, 1961, op cit.

32 I. Amaduzzi, *Io sono uno scultore. Lucio Fontana a Milano negli anni Trenta*, Edizioni Angelo Guerrini e Associati, Milan 1999, p. 69.

33 L. Fontana, 'Le mie ceramiche', in *Tempo*, 21 September 1939.

34 Ibid.

35 R. Carrieri, 'Le maioliche geologiche di Lucio Fontana', in *L'illustrazione Italiana*, 8 January 1939, p. 63.

36 S. Bini, 'Lucio Fontana scultore', *il Secolo XIX*, 7 January 1939, p. 3.

'continuity of rhythm... from any point of view'.[37] In the equilibrium between the 'dull black' – that Fontana had also used for *Donna Sdraiata* in 1938, also at the Museo del Novecento, Florence – and the 'glossy shadows of the skin', Argan found the key with which 'Fontana fully freed the artistic image from the empirical condition of space'.[38] Already in 1939, the Roman critic used the term – *space* – that was to become the key to understanding all of Fontana's postwar production.

When he returned to Milan in 1947, after six years in Argentina to compete for the commission for the Flag Monument and above all to avoid the war, the artist found a city ready to rise again, even more dynamic than before and, inevitably, with a new awareness of human events.

Fontana visited his studio, destroyed by the bombs, and it was literally from the rubble that he conceived *Concetto spaziale – L'Uomo Atomico* (*Spatial Concept – Atomic Man*), atomic being an adjective that could never be separated from the ruinous deployment of the nuclear bomb, an event that created a rift in history and society and that the artist translated into an umpteenth sculptural revolution. The *Uomo Atomico* is a human wreck, a figure that reasons though skeletal forms and, in a contemporary photograph also reproduced in *Devenir de Fontana*, looks almost ready to topple over, standing out against a row of gaunt trees.

Although in a certain way formally similar, Fontana's *Uomo Atomico* does not embody the existentialist message that distinguishes the slender figures that Giacometti began to sculpt in 1947, often marching, almost a mirror of the fragile, ephemeral human condition. Giacometti's work found its ideal exegete in Jean-Paul Sartre, the philosopher of existentialism who, in 1948, wrote the introductory text 'The Search for the Absolute' for the Swiss sculptor's first exhibition in the United States, held at the gallery of Pierre Matisse.[39] What might be the biggest point of contact between the two artists is highlighted in Sartre's text: the 'desire to situate oneself at the beginning of the world', which in Fontana takes on the features of a marked sense of 'primitive'.

1948 was also the year of the first post-war Biennale, at which Fontana displayed the extraordinary *Scultura spaziale* – a 'magmatic' work that, as recently observed by Luca Massimo Barbero, 'gave concrete form to the ideal gravitational force of the cosmos over matter',[40] stressing that, at this date, there were few possible comparisons in European sculpture,

---

37 G.C. Argan, 'Su alcuni giovani. Fontana', in *Le Arti*, a.I, file III, February–March 1939, p. 293.

38 Ibid.

39 See S. Bucalo-Mussely, 'Alberto Giacometti et Pierre Matisse. De l''atelier à la galerie', in *Pierre Matisse. Un marchant d'art à New York*, exhibition catalogue, ed. J. Matisse-Monnier (Nice, Musée Matisse, June–September 2021) Paris 2021, pp. 47–53.

40 L.M. Barbero, *Lucio Fontana. Ceramiche. Catalogo ragionato*, Skira, Milan 2022, p. 63.

the most important being Giacometti, as also noted previously by Enrico Crispolti.[41]

Once again, it is the sensibility of Michel Tapié that provides us with a visual illustration of the continuity of Fontana's spatial experimentation, independent of medium, through the juxtaposition, in 1961, of the *Scultura Astratta* from 1947 with a drawing from the following year.

This was the moment when Fontana, with the usual absolute consistency, comes to the exercise of the '*hole*', that extreme gesture of slicing through the canvas (or paper, as it was at first), which had deep roots in his acting on material in the previous years.[42] Fontana's conceptual approach is also the result of his reflection on sculpture in the 1920s and 30s, and as well as in its maturation at the end of the 1940s. The critical juncture during which the same question gripped Giacometti as well, as he observed: "Any sculpture that takes space as a fact is wrong, there is only the illusion of space" (about 1949).[43]

---

41 See E. Crispolti, *Lucio Fontana. Catalogo ragionato di sculture, dipinti, ambientazioni*, Skira, Milano 2006, p. 58: "They are experiments with which Fontana originally presented himself on the horizon of the nascent European Informel sculpture, with very few possibilities for comparison at that time: Theodore Roszak and David Smith in the United States, Étienne-Martin, Germaine Richier, Alberto Giacometti and the few examples of Fautrier's sculpture, in Europe."

42 When asked about his famous 'cuts' in 1966, Fontana himself stressed that everything is rooted in 'tradition': 'The cuts and holes? Ah yes, that's my exploration beyond the usual picture plane, towards a new dimension. Space. An act of defiance … matured in the honest knowledge of tradition, in the academic use of the scalpel, pencil, paintbrush, colour' (L. Fontana, in *La Nazione*, Florence, 24 June 1966).

43 See *Alberto Giacometti. Scritti*, eds. M. Leiris and J. Dupin, Nodi, Sestante, 1995, p. 40.

La recherche de l'absolu

Marco
Fagioli

I.

In what is a key text on modern sculpture, the first *Letter to Pierre Matisse* (1948), Alberto Giacometti rendered in the form of an autobiographical account the essential features of the language of sculpture. It is worth quoting some passages from the letter in full, because its theoretical and cultural implications represent advanced points in the inquiry into the nature of art as language, an inquiry that started with Cézanne and ran through the whole of the twentieth century and even up to the present day, when, for reasons of opportunity and the ideological hegemony of the power elite that manages the art market, such inquiry has been completely suffocated.

In his letter Giacometti nailed down all the points of the matter: the relationship between representation (mimesis) and form, central to Western artistic culture; the relation between totality and detail; the conception of space and that of structure; the transparency of volumes; the relationship between space and movement; the non-tie between isolated object (form) and space; the idea of the circularity of time (the *simultaneity* of Henri Bergson); and, finally, the difficulty of defining the concept of portrait and that of figure, the relation between reality and memory. Paradoxically, all the issues of the conceptual elaboration of art understood as *language* seem to have been channelled into the letter, which is the story of Giacometti's sculpture.

Regarding his first trip to Italy in 1920–21, the sculptor wrote that after visiting Venice, where he spent "les journées a regarder les Tintoret surtout [...] Tintoret fut un peu détrôné, à une grande peine, la jour même où je quittai Venise par les Giotto de Padoue, et celui-ci, à son tour, quelques mois plus tard, par Cimabue à Assisi", he stayed for nine months in Rome, during which he painted figures and landscapes that were "un peu pointillistes (je avais acquis la conviction que le ciel n'est bleu que par conviction mais rouge en réalité)". In Rome Giacometti began to model two busts, "et, pour la première fois, je ne m'en sortais pas, je me perdais tout m'échappait, la tête du modèle devant moi devenait comme un nuage, vague et illimité. Je finis par le détruire à la fin de mon séjour. Je passais une grande partie du temps dans les musées, les églises, les ruines". These signs of a crisis in the relationship between subject and object, which at the same time were the sign of a crisis and an utter abandonment of artistic language as a "representation" of the real, also continued later during his apprenticeship at the school of Émile-Antoine Bourdelle in Paris: "De 1922 à 1925, et plus j'étais à l'Académie de la Grande-Chaumière, chez Bourdelle. Le matin je faisais la sculpture et les mêmes difficultés qu'à Rome recommencèrent".[1] The difficulty Giacometti had in "representing" the subject of a portrait also recurred when he was tackling figures: "Impossible de

---

1 *Alberto Giacometti*, Galerie Beyeler, Basle 1964, introduction by Michel Leiris, including the anastatic reproduction of the typewritten letter to Pierre Matisse, unnumbered page.

saisir l'ensemble d'une figure (nous étions beaucoup trop près du modèle et si on portait d'un détail, d'un talon ou du nez, il n'y avait aucun espoir de jamais arriver à un ensemble".[2]

When Giacometti arrived in Paris in 1922, precursory signs of Surrealism had already been appearing for some time, though the *Manifeste du Surréalisme* did not come out until the autumn of 1924: André Breton, Louis Aragon and Philippe Soupault had begun to publish the magazine *Littérature* in 1919, the last issue of which came out in 1924. But in 1922 Giacometti entered the studio of Antoine Bourdelle at the Académie de la Grande Chaumière. Giacometti was recorded in the list of students as "élève suisse". In 1922 Bourdelle was regarded as the leading French statue sculptor after August Rodin. Being a pupil of Bourdelle rather than of Aristide Maillol meant that Giacometti devoted more attention to Romanesque and Gothic rather than to Classical and Hellenistic sculpture, and a rougher conception of primitivism with a tendency towards rigidity and a quadrifrontal perspective far removed from the chiasmuses and curls, volutes and flourishes of Baroque taste.

Moreover, some of Bourdelle's sculptures, like the very pure portrait *La chilienne*, 1920, sculpted from polychrome plaster, and the bronze *Torse de Pallas*, 1901, whose lean modernity had impressed Henri Matisse, also made an impression on Giacometti and pushed him towards his purer forms.[3] By 1922, Constantin Brancusi had also already produced some of his masterpieces and was on the path to a pure and abstract modernity: the *Portrait de M.me Eugène Meyer*, 1910, the versions of *La muse endormie*, 1910, *La muse*, 1912, the first version of *Mademoiselle Pogany*, 1913, *La princesse X*, 1918, *La maiastra*, 1912 and, in 1924, two key works in the history of modern sculpture, *Le commencement du monde* and *La Léda*, both in marble.

Why Giacometti went to Paris in 1922 rather than to Vienna, where the leading artists Cuno Amiet and Ferdinand Hodler (godfathers respectively to Alberto and his brother Bruno) advised him to go, remains a mystery that has yet to be fully clarified. The decision was taken towards the end of 1921, after his return to Stampa from his third trip to Italy. Bonnefoy has linked his choice of Paris over Vienna with one of the core features of Giacometti's work, the absence of what he calls erotic indulgence towards the depicted subject, which was to be one of the principal denotations in the way women were seen by painters like Gustav Klimt and Egon Schiele, the dominant figures in Viennese culture at the beginning of the century. According to Bonnefoy, Giacometti, whose eyes had doubtless feasted on the figures of the prostitutes in the Parisian brothel, Sphynx, never invested his female figures with dreams of pleasure, but always affirmed in

---

2 Ibid.

3 Ionel Janou-Michel Dufet, Bourdelle, Arted, Paris 1965, nos. 21, 26, 32.

the naked body of the woman the amazement, fear and enigma of being.[4] As evidence for his hypothesis, which postulates that Giacometti moved away from the tradition of eros as imaginative pleasure, an enduring feature of European artistic culture from the Renaissance through to the nineteenth century, Bonnefoy points to some of the sculptor's more specifically surrealist works. These included *Boule suspendue*, 1930–31, and *Femme égorgée*, 1932, which allude to eros as an act of reflection, and, even more so, later works such as *Quatre figures sur socle*, 1950, which Bonnefoy describes unhesitatingly as wrinkled, lacerated, compulsive and far removed from sensual imaginings (ibid., p. 112).

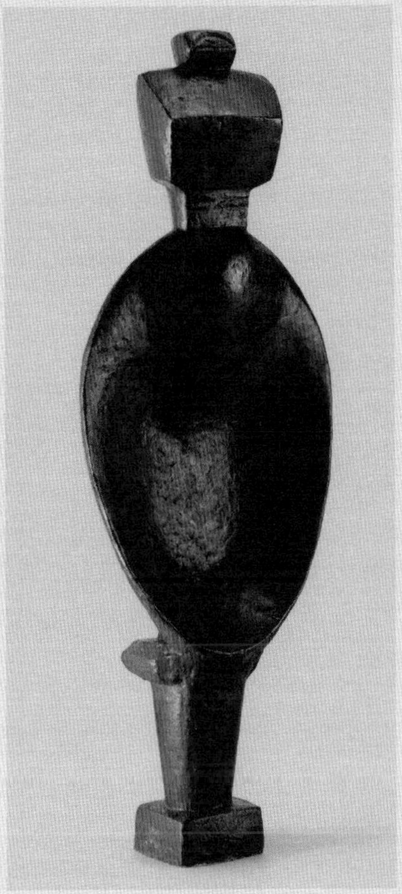

Alberto Giacometti,
Femme cuillère, 1926-1927
bronze, Saint-Paul-de-Vence,
Fondation Maeght

In Paris, then, Giacometti appeared to find the place in which "the woman in the sun, in her beautiful bourgeois attire in the midst of flowers in the garden" would be perceived as more than a sign in a discourse: "Being a presence that is in itself inextinguishable, absolute, the very silence of what is". And yet, though "Giacometti's object is not eroticised [...] despite the violent non-realism of its manifestation in colour or in plaster, it is not anti-sensorial at all. It was born in life, understood through the sound of sensory perception". It thus appears evident that in this process of liberating the figure from the aesthetically graceful, erotic, earthly elements and staged beauty dear to Belle Époque painting, and in the re-evaluation of bodies grasped in their phenomenal and sensorial brutality, Giacometti must necessarily have encountered the painting of Paul Cézanne on the one hand and tribal and primitive art on the other, a path he had to take to construct his forms. It is not, however, this line of Giacometti's inquiry that should be likened to the *antigracefulness* of the Futurists and, albeit in a closer way, the Cubists' recovery of African tribal art.

Giacometti was influenced decisively by Cubist sculpture between 1925 and 1929, as shown not just by his portraits of *Josef Müller*, 1925–26, that of *Padre I*, in bronze, and the granite version of 1927, which are still figured, but also a long series of abstract compositions, such as *Le couple*, 1926, *Personnages*, 1926–27, *Composition cubiste (Homme)*, 1926–27, *Composition (Homme et femme)*, 1927, *Femme*, 1928, and *Tête qui regarde*, 1927–29, gradually associated with Fernand Léger's costumes for *La création du monde*, 1923, a ballet composed by Darius Milhaud and featuring the sculptures of Arp. Giacometti moved in two directions, on the one hand tapping into the fascination of African tribal culture, expressed most evidently in works like *Femme-cuillère*, 1926, and on the other into the three-millennia long history of ancient Mediterranean and European plastic art, ranging from Cycladic figures to Etruscan canopies and Gallic-Roman coins, as attested by sculptures which achieved a synthesis unthinkable for others but

4 Yves Bonnefoy, *Alberto Giacometti. Biografia di un'opera*, Leonardo Editore, Milan 1991, pp. 111–13.

not for the brilliance of Giacometti: *L'objet invisible* (*Mains tenant le vide*), 1934, *Femme qui marche*, 1932–34.

It was in these short but intense years between 1930 and 1934, culminating in the disturbing, magical bronze monolith of *Le cube*, 1933–34, about which, in 2008, George Didi-Huberman wrote one of the most original critical studies about the sculptor, that Giacometti had an almost shaman-like grip on the future destiny of the whole of twentieth-century European plastic art – neo-plastic abstraction with *Le vide-poche*, 1930, a manual millet mill; *Objet désagréable à jeter*, 1931, *La vie continue*, 1932 and *Caresse* (*Malgré les mains*), 1932, which are Megalithic *menhir* and *dolmen*; and *Fleur en danger*, 1933, *Femme couchée qui rêve*, 1929 and *Homme* (*Apollon*), 1929, which anticipate by years certain later solutions by sculptors such as Fausto Melotti and David Smith. In those few years Giacometti was the first, I believe, to invent that element of spatial language, the polyform cube or cuboid, that is *la cage*. This cage made its first appearance in *Boule suspendue*, 1930, exhibited at the Pierre gallery in spring of the same year, attracting the admiration of Breton, Dalí and the other Surrealists. From that moment on the *cage* became not just one of the constituent spatial elements of the new sculpture, but also an extraordinary metaphor of an existentially circumscribed and narrow human space, a metaphysical delimitation of existence, expressed in literary language by writers ranging from Franz Kafka to Samuel Beckett, and recurring, in more recent times, in the linear topography delineated on the floor of the set of Lars von Trier's *Dogville*. Those handful of years between 1929 and 1934, during which Giacometti embraced Surrealism with the original fullness of the total artificer – and the earlier bond with Max Ernst and his work would be decisive in this – also saw him moving closer to Georges Bataille and the magazine *Documents*, rightly emphasised by Bonnefoy.

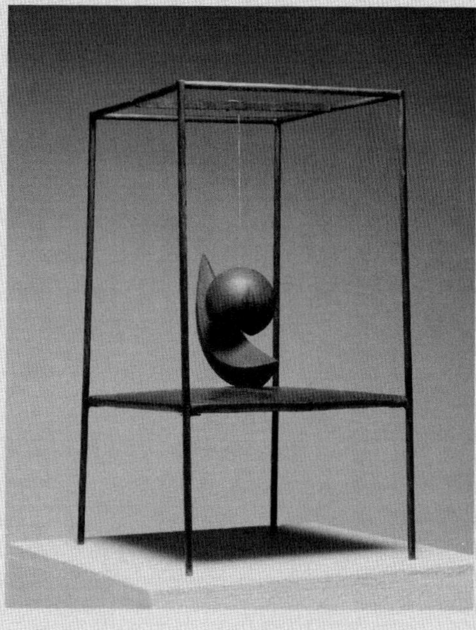

Alberto Giacometti, *Boule suspendue*, 1930-1931, wood, iron, rope. Paris, Centre Georges Pompidou

The first issue of *Documents*, published in April 1929 with the programmatic and thematic sub-heading "Doctrines-Archéologie-Arts-Ethnographie", contained numerous articles about non-European cultures and ethnography: Contenau wrote about the statuary of the Sumerians and Paul Pelliot about the relationship between Chinese and "Siberian" bronzes. Carl Einstein, already the author of an important book on Negro art, wrote about some paintings by Picasso, Michel Leiris about two "figures microcosmiques", Georges Limbour about Paul Klee, Georges Henry Rivière about the Musée d'ethnographie du Trocadero, Jean Babelon about the Evangelaire de Saint-Lupicin and Abdré Schnaffner about Igor Stravinsky. In the fifteen issues that came out between 1929 and 1930, *Documents* was the magazine in which Bataille coherently developed his line of thought until he clashed and split with Breton and the Surrealists after they attacked him violently in the *Second manifeste du Surrealisme* in 1930.

In 1929 and 1930, a series of events and exhibitions took place in Paris that would play a key role in the debate surrounding ethnocentrism and the discovery of non-European cultures. In 1928 Paul Rivet had mounted an exhibition on *Les arts anciens de l'Amérique* at the Musée des Arts Décoratifs. In 1930 the old ethnographical museum of the Trocadero, which would then become the Musée de l'Homme, was reorganised; previously, the *Exposition de l'art indigène des colonies d'Afrique et Océanie* had been held at the Musée des Arts Décoratifs from November 1923 to January 1924. Lastly, in 1931, at the end of a decade of discoveries, there had been the major *Exposition coloniale*, and those same years saw the publication of some of the books that proved decisive for the renewal of ethnography and the birth of modern anthropology. In 1929 the writer, ethnographer and militant surrealist Michel Leiris met Marcel Griaule, one of the founders of the new anthropology and the organiser of the Dakar-Djibouti mission in 1931–33, in which Leiris would take part, publishing several texts about the collected materials in the journal *Minotaure*. Earlier, from 1903, Marcel Mauss, the master of the modern École sociologique française, had published a series of works on *Représentations collectives* with Émile Durkheim, 1903, the *Mentalité archaïque et catégories de pensée*, 1921, and the key work entitled *L'origine des pouvoirs magiques dans les sociétés australiennes*, 1904, which would make a crucial impression on the thought of younger anthropologists all the way through to Claude Lévi-Strauss. In 1908 Mauss had published an important review of the monumental work of Wilhelm Max Wundt, *Völkerpsychologie*, 1904, in which he discussed the German scholar's conception of art and myth.[5]

Giacometti arrived in Paris when this lively renewal in the fields of ethnography and anthropology was in full swing, and he proved to be very much in tune with the new thinking. In historic and political terms these orientations, which all started with a pressing critique of Lucien Lévy-Bruhl's view that the "mentality" of the "primitives" was "prelogical", contained a decisive rejection of ethnocentrism and the affirming of the equal value of every culture, concepts that would then form the foundations of cultural anthropology. Mauss himself had taken issue with Lévy-Bruhl's ideas when reviewing the latter's *Le mentalité primitive* in 1923. In the pages of Mauss' review of Wundt's *Völkerpsychologie* are some ideas that proved crucial for understanding surrealist sculpture, reflected more generally in the works of Giacometti, Arp and Max Ernst between 1920 and 1935. The attitude of ethnographic research towards non-European and so-called primitive cultures had changed after 1920 compared to that which had distinguished the first *passionate amateurs* active at the beginning of the century, including travellers and collectors, artists and gallerists, in the years of the African link between the Fauves and the Cubists. The attitude

5 Minotaure 2, *Mission Dakar-Djibouti*, Albert Skira, Paris 1931–33; Geneviève Calame-Griaule and Jean Guiart, *Dakar-Djibouti. Minotaure and Marcel Griaule*, Musée d'Art Moderne de la Ville de Paris, Paris 1988, pp. 89–93; Marcel Mauss, *Oeuvres*, vol. 2, *Representations collectives et diversité des civilitations*, introduction by Victor Karady, Les éditions de Minuit, Paris 1974, pp. 13–89. 121–68, 319–69.

towards the tribal artefacts of Africa and Oceania of Paul Guillaume, Maurice Vlaminck, André Derain and, though to a lesser degree, of Henri Matisse and Pablo Picasso, André Salmon and Carl Einstein – with the latter two writers already on the way to an anthropologically correct understanding – was not the one assumed two decades later by Michel Leiris, André Breton, Georges Bataille, Henri Michaux and Roger Callois. The writings of Mauss provided theoretical support for a more functional use of primitive art, and his descriptions seemed to suit this function. By offering an introduction to the use of the distinction between the almost linguistic terms *signes* and *symbole*, Mauss enabled the forms of non-European arts to be interpreted as languages with a code of their own, and not simply as expressions of a "prelogical" or even crude thought, as had been the case in traditional ethnography.[6]

For the large-scale exhibition on *Primitivism* at the Museum of Modern Art in New York in 1984, Rosalind Krauss conducted a detailed analysis of the relationship between Giacometti and the sculptural models of the Wobé and Dan tribes from the Ivory Coast (Liberia), with spoon examples very close to works by the sculptor, such as *Donna*, 1926–27, in plaster, later destroyed, and of *Malanggan Figures* from New Ireland, exceptional examples of Melanesian polychrome sculptures, formerly belonging to Max Ernst and undoubtedly analogous to *La cage*, 1931, in terms of spatial structure.

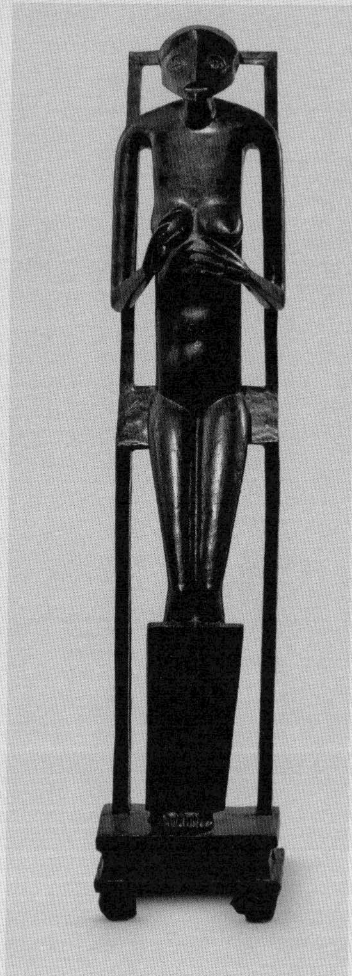

Alberto Giacometti, *Objet invisible (Mains tenant le vide)*, 1934-1935 bronze, Saint-Paul-de-Vence, Fondation Maeght

But apart from the direct and documented derivations, as in the case of the *Sculture tribali* drawing of 1929, the formal analogies principally attest that Giacometti, by rejecting the formal code of Western art founded on *mimesis*, went back to a "zero degree" of sculpture and raised the question of establishing a new code. The surprising resemblance between the bronze *Uomo*, 1929, with the structure of the body configured as a grille of parallel axes, and the Mbole and Zulu *Figures* from Zaire and South Africa respectively, seems to be not so much a direct derivation as a parallel form of the same code. The canonical sculpture of this connection between Giacometti and tribal art is, however, *L'objet invisible* (*Mains tenent le vide*), 1934, which Breton published in *L'amour fou* in 1937, photographed by Dora Maar. It is with regard to this sculpture, which Krauss relates variously to figures associated with the Solomon Islands and the Kopar culture, Sepik region, that we can attempt a new synopsis. Indeed, *L'objet invisible* seems to be the brother of an exemplary piece of Italian archaic sculpture, the larger-than-life size *Guerriero* found in the Etruscan necropolis of Capestrano (L'Aquila) and dating to the sixth century B.C. The rigid, quadrifrontal position is the same, and the posture of the arms, hieratically gathered on the chest, is very similar.[7]

---

6 Bernard Pottier (ed.), *Le langage. Les dictionnaires du savoir moderne*, Centre d'étude et promotion de la lecture, Paris 1973, pp. 485, 514–15; James Clifford, *"On Ethnographic Surrealism"*, in *Comparative Studies in Society and History* 23, 1981, pp. 539–64.

7 Rosalind Krauss, *"Giacometti"*, in William Rubin (ed.), *Primitivismo nell'arte*

Giacometti made a first trip to Italy in May 1920. Accompanying his father, who was Switzerland's commissioner at the Biennale, he visited Padua to see the works of Giotto. A second trip followed in November of the same year, during which he stopped off in Florence and visited the Archaeology Museum, where he was very much taken by the Egyptian art on display. Later, after a stop at Assisi to see Cimabue, he arrived in Rome, where he was fascinated not just by the ancient art and Byzantine mosaics, but also by the Baroque. Whether or not Giacometti saw, while visiting the Archaeology Museum in Florence, perhaps still organised according to topographic regions, examples of Etruscan sculpture and possibly also the many bronze statuettes from votive deposits, has not yet been documented with certainty. It does however seem probable that he walked through those rooms when visiting the museum, if they were open for public viewing at the time. Giacometti's interest in Etruscan sculpture does however appear to be perfectly coherent with his linguistic choices: the rejection of the academic tradition together with classicist aesthetics, and an attention towards pre-classic forms of sculpture from the Cyclades, African sculpture, Egyptian and Etruscan art, all expressions of cultures that in their own way were autonomous and "pure". They were testimony to primitive and original societies, in contrast with the forms of cultures re-elaborated according to subsequently transmitted codes.

Two exceptional exegetes of Giacometti's sculpture, Yves Bonnefoy and Georges Didi-Huberman, have interpreted his work in great depth, establishing the philosophical and literary connections of the age. Didi-Huberman took the artist's enigmatic bronze *Le cube* (1934), the genesis of which is rooted in the absolute form of the cranium and in the polyhedron of Dürer's *Melancolia*, and wove a web of cultural and psychological influences so dense as to make the work a total symbol of modern art. Yet as Giacometti himself said to E. Scheidegger (quoted in Didi-Huberman):

> "I can only speak *indirectly* about my sculptures, in the hope of being able to at least partly explain what motivated them. [...] When the work is constructed, I tend to find in the object images, impressions, and events, transformed and displaced, which have struck me deeply (often unbeknown[st] to me), as well as forms that seem very familiar but which I am often unable to identify, which makes them more and more disturbing."[8]

This is, without question, one of the central features of Giacometti's sculpture, namely, the awareness that the root of a work does not lie in the project, in the operating reason, but in the darkest part of one's nature. In a work written in 1998, Bonnefoy also took the theme of the head, *Tête qui regarde*, 1928, *Tête sur tige*, 1947, *Le nez*, 1947, as the distinguishing

---

del XX secolo. Affinità tra il tribale e il moderno, Mondadori, Milan 1985, pp. 508–22.

8 Georges Didi-Huberman, *Il cubo e il volto. A proposito di una scultura di Alberto Giacometti*, Electa, Milan 2008, p. 152.

element of his output and also found in it one of the paths for arriving at the profound significance of his art:

> "Unlike the art of Picasso, for example, which in a purportedly playful world gives free rein to what is ultimately formal invention, Giacometti's art attends to the essential. It has nothing and being in its spirit; it understands that one can dream of escaping nothingness, it grasps the idea of salvation, though it lacks the means to believe in it."[9]

II.

Among the various portraits of Alberto Giacometti by writers and critics, Jean Genet's stands out for its desolate power. Genet first visited Giacometti's studio at rue Maindron 46 in 1954, and was perhaps introduced to him by Jean-Paul Sartre. Edmund White observes that Giacometti had read the *Fragments*, published in August 1954, with care: "Equally important, he admired Genet's bald head. Giacometti considered hair to be a lie, obscuring the reality of cranial structure, and had tried unsuccessfully to convince his wife to shave her head. When Giacometti saw Genet's tough-guy features, intense eyes, turned-up nose and magnificent dome, which he observed from a distance in a café, he decided that he wanted Genet to pose for him." In exemplary fashion, Genet singled out some of the basic characteristics of Giacometti's work. White rightly points out that his text about the sculptor came after his discovery of Rembrandt, described in *Ce qui est resté d'un Rembrandt déchiré en petits carrés bien réguliers, et foutu aux chiottes*; in 1952 and 1953, he travelled to London and Amsterdam to study the Dutch painter: "According to Genet's singular view, Rembrandt strips his subjects of every merely anecdotal detail"; and he regarded Rembrandt as "the painter who shows the essential heaviness and carnality of human beings who smell, who shit and whose bodies are warm".[10]

According to Genet, the art of Giacometti, like all great art, is not destined for future generations, and offers itself instead "à l'innombrable peuple des morts. Qui l'agréent. Ou la refusent". Partly in the form of a recorded or fabricated dialogue with the sculptor, Genet's essay cuts like a knife into Giacometti's sculpture. In the writer's eyes, Giacometti was like one of his own sculptures:

> "Il sourit. Et toute la peau plissée de son visage se met a rire. D'une drôle de façon. Les yeux rient, bien sûre, mais le front aussi

9 Yves Bonnefoy, *Alberto Giacometti* (1998), edited by Stefano Esengrini, Abscondita, Milan 2004, p. 21.

10 Edmund White, *Jean Genet*, Chatto & Windus, London 1993, pp. 464–66; Jean Genet, *Œuvres complètes*, vol. 5, *Le funambule, Le secret de Rembrandt, L'atelier d'Alberto Giacometti, Les nègres, Les paravents, L'enfant criminel*, Gallimard, Parigi 1979, pp. 42–48.

(toute sa personne a la couleur grise de son atelier). Par sympathie peut-être il a pris la couleur de la poussière. Ses dents rient – écartées et grises aussi – le vent passe à travers."[11]

Giacometti's sculpture is thus a sculpture that evokes death and dust and "au peuple des morts, l'œuvre de Giacometti communique la connaissance de la solitude de chaque être et de chaque chose, et que cette solitude est notre gloire la plus sûre".[12]

Genet's interpretation of Giacometti clearly runs parallel to some of Jean-Paul Sartre's existential themes and aesthetic thought. In the third issue of *Les temps modernes* (December 1945), Sartre had published a draft of Genet's *Pompes funèbres*, and then, in issue ten of the same journal, published in July 1946, some extracts from *Journal du voleur*. In the eighth issue (May 1946), Sartre also published his *Fragments d'un portrait de Baudelaire*, the basis for the 1947 essay that earned him the enmity of philological critics. Sartre had "discovered" Genet in April 1944, having heard about him from Jean Cocteau when *Notre-Dame-des-fleures* came out: "Ces pages nous découvraient à neuf les pouvoirs des mots. Cocteau avait vu juste: un grand écrivain venait d'apparaître".[13]

Giacometti's art, like that of Alexander Calder, Alfred Wols, André Masson, Robert Lapoujade, Paul Rebeyrolle and David Hare, who were all close to the existential movement, could no longer be defined within the aesthetics of Surrealism, and even if existentialism did not have a full-blown aesthetic, as by its very nature it was opposed to any form of regulation, Sartre provided the theoretical justification for the work of these artists. Commencing with *L'imagination*, 1936, Sartre drew inspiration from the phenomenology of Edmund Husserl and criticised the metaphysical tradition of the *image* whereby "l'image mentale existe comme objet". Instead, he affirmed: "Il n'y a pas, il ne saurait y avoir d'images *dans* la conscience. Mais l'image est *un certain type de conscience*. L'image est un acte et non une chose. L'image est conscience *de* quelques chose." In 1940 he published *L'imaginaire, psychologie phénoménologique de l'imagination*, in which he set out the cardinal principles of his conception:

> Il entre dans la nature même de la conscience d'être intentionnelle et une conscience qui cesserait d'être de quelque chose, cesserait par la même d'exister [...]. Poser une image, c'est constituer un objet en marge de la totalité du réel, c'est donc tenir le réel à distance s'en affranchir, en un mot le nier. [...] Pour qu'une conscience puisse imaginer, il faut qu'elle échappe au monde par sa nature même, il faut qu'elle puisse tirer d'elle-même une position de recul par rapport au monde, en un mot, il faut qu'elle soit libre.

---

11 Genet, *Œuvres complètes*, p. 45.

12 Ibid., p. 48.

13 In *Sartre*, edited by Mauricette Berne, Gallimard, Paris 2005, p. 99.

Right from the introduction of *L'imaginaire*, Sartre proposed to establish a new conception of the intentional structure of the image: "Cet ouvrage a pour but de décrire la grande fonction 'irréalisante' de la conscience ou 'imagination' et son corrélatif noématique l'imaginaire". The notion of *beauty* also ended up, in Sartre's thought, having a fusion dependent on the *Imaginary*:

> "De ces quelques remarques on peut déjà conclure que le réel n'est jamais beau. La beauté est une valeur qui ne saurait jamais s'appliquer qu'à l'imaginaire et qui comporte la néantisation du monde dans sa structure essentielle. C'est pourquoi il est stupide de confondre la morale et l'esthétique."[14]

Here we are at the heart of Giacometti's vision, and Genet's writing is a faithful transcription of it. In the (*Première*) *Lettre à Pierre Matisse* Giacometti recounted the primary scene, later returned to by David Sylvester in his introduction to the catalogue of the exhibition at the Tate Gallery in 1965, about when, as a young man, he drew a still life featuring a pear on a table:

> "Une fois, à l'âge de 18 ou 19 ans, j'ai dessiné dans l'atelier de mon père quelques poires posées sur la table à la distance normale pour une nature morte. N'empêche qu'elles devenaient de plus en plus petites. Je recommençai tout, et elle s'atteignaient toujours le même petitesse. Mon père dit avec mauvaise humeur "à présent, fais-les donc une bonne fois comme elles sont, telles que tu le vois". Et, sur ma feuille, il les dessina grandeur nature. J'essayai de les faire à mon tour ainsi, mais je dus les effacer – je fis tant et si bien usage de la gomme qu'une demi-heure plus tard, au millimètre près, mes poires avaient exactement des dimensions des premières".

This passage about pears becoming small due to an optical distancing seems to foreshadow the idea of isolation in space discussed by Genet. And, according to Jean Soldini, it points to two characteristics of Giacometti's early work, "the weakening of the subject" and "impotence before the visible", which would appear to show an almost constitutional disposition on the part of the artist towards certain spatial procedures even before the decisive phases of the story of his expressive language: the influence of Cézanne, the Surrealist experience, the discovery of the purity of the so-called primitive and ethnographic arts.[15] As Genet gradually completed his transcription of Giacometti's art, there appeared, as

---

14 Michel Sicard (ed.), *Sartre et les arts*, in *Obliques* 24-24, special issue, 1979, pp. 15-20, 94-102, 214-20; Jean-Paul Sartre, *L'imaginaire* (1940), Gallimard, Paris 2005, pp. 13, 371.

15 Genet, *Œuvres complètes*, p. 48; David Sylvester, "The Residue of a Vision", in *Alberto Giacometti. Sculpture Paintings Drawings 1913-1965*, Lund, Humphries and Co., London 1965; Jean Soldini, *Il colossale, la madre, il "sacro": l'opera di Alberto Giacometti*, Lubrina, Bergamo 1991.

if evoked by the writing, the constituent elements: earth, the dust that Annette could not remove, and in the painting: "Posée au milieu des vielles bouteilles d'essence, sa palette, des derniers jours: une flaque de boue des différents gris". At this point the two visionaries come together and Genet's calques his writing on the sculptures of his friend: "Ses statues semblent appartenir à un âge défunt, avoir été découvertes après que le temps et la nuit – qui les travaillèrent avec intelligence – les ont corrodées pour leur donner cet air, à la fois doux et dur d'éternité qui passe". Genet's description of Giacometti's female figures seems to combine the existentialist idea of the human body with that of primitive deities, gilded bronzes, associated with the idea of guardians of the dead, and thus retrieves, without saying it, the sacred function. It should however be said that, despite the visually powerful way in which Genet's writing describes Giacometti's sculpture, Sartre's text in *Derrière le miroir* for the exhibition at the Galerie Maeght in Paris in 1954 is an essential and decisive piece for the history of critical writings about the artist, and appeared three years before Genet's 1957 essay, "The Atelier of Alberto Giacometti". Sartre's essay is a kind of "written word" correlating to the form of Giacometti's works.[16]

When writing about Giacometti, Sartre, like Genet, is clearly unable to detach himself visually from the sculpture but produces an imaginary representation: in this Giacometti-Sartre-Genet triangle, it is as if the top vertex is occupied by the sculptor, from which two lines descend to the writings in the angles of the base. In his previous essay, "La recherche de l'absolu", which appeared in *Les temps modernes* (vol. III, no. 28) in January 1948, Sartre had traced these suggestive lines of an interpretation of Giacometti's art that would then dominate in the years to come. He linked Giacometti to a primordial, pre-cultural condition, evoking the antediluvian countenance of his friend, who laughed at culture and did not believe in progress. A man whose preferred contemporaries were the man of Altamura and Eyzies, who believed in the extreme youthfulness of nature in which neither beauty nor ugliness exists. Together with these themes of existential anthropology, Sartre combined a reflection on space, the horror of the infinite and the excess nestling within it, the confusion between real distance and imaginary distance, the indivisibility of stone. Sartre also acknowledged Giacometti's great break with classicism precisely in the conception of the relationship between statue and space: a space no longer measurable and divided, but imaginary, and for this reason *absolute*. Finally, his depiction of characters from a distance, as they are seen, rendering *distance* an absolute condition.

One biographical element of the sculptor's life that has been emphasised by critics, alongside the influence of his painter father Giovanni, who kept a watchful eye over his son until 1915 in an environment involving close

---

16 Genet, *Œuvres complètes*, p. 55; Jean-Paul Sartre, "Les peintures de Giacometti", in *Alberto Giacometti. Sculptures, Peintures Dessins*, Musée d'art moderne de la ville de Paris, Paris 1991, p. 424.

contact with artists such as Ferdinand Hodler and Cuno Hamiet, is the artist's relationship with his mother. The profound relationship with the maternal figure led some critics to produce a series of psychoanalytic conjectures and ethno-psychological interpretations regarding the mother, the prostitute and the idea of the sacred. This line of inquiry, though arduous and despite the necessary reservations that pertain when applying it to art-historical analysis, has yielded an original contribution to the interpretation of Giacometti's work. It was Giacometti's own writings and testimony that guided critics in this direction: one key text in this regard is undoubtedly "Hier, sables mouvants", which appeared in the fifth issue of *Le Surréalisme au service de la révolution* in 1933. This has been analysed in detail by Jean Soldini in relation to a key sculpture from the Surrealist period, *Pointe à l'œil*, 1932. Soldini returns to and discusses a hypothesis advanced by Jean Clair in relation to something Giacometti said in an interview in 1961. On that occasion the sculptor declared that the first drawing he could remember showed Snow White in a coffin with seven dwarves.[17] In the (autobiographical) account, Giacometti recalled the world of his childhood, in which some objects were invested with powerful desire: "Étant enfant (entre 4 et 7 ans), je ne voyais du monde extérieur quel es objets qui pouvaient être utiles à mon plaisir. C'étaient avant tout des pierres et des arbres, et rarement plis d'un objet à la fois". He associated this memory with the discovery of a monolith – "Découverte énorme, tout de suite je considérai cette pierre comme une amie, un être animé des meilleurs intentions à notre égard" – near his native village, which his father used to take him to see. At the foot of the great stone was a double cavern that the boy used to enter with his friends. While Clair associated this monolith and cavern with a drawing from 1928–31, depicting a phallus and vagina (Basel, Kunstmuseum Kupferstich-Kabinett), Soldini draws on a theme from Mircea Eliade regarding the "notion symbolique de centre sacré".[18]

III.

The third writer who, together with Genet and Sartre, forged an organic relationship with Giacometti's artistic vision was the writer and anthropologist Michel Leiris. He was linked to the Surrealist movement, before then joining the splinter group at odds with Breton and Aragon that formed around Georges Bataille and the magazine *Documents*. As Catherine Grenier wrote, Giacometti gravitated towards Surrealism during a complex phase in the story of the movement, when "purges" were underway at the height of the dispute between Breton and Bataille. In 1929, in the final issue of the magazine *La revolution surréaliste*, in which the *Second manifeste du surréalisme* was published, Breton took aim at Bataille, ironically

---

17 Soldini, *Il colossale*, pp. 51–63; Jean Clair, "Le pointe à l'œil", in *Cahiers du Musée National d'Art Moderne* 97, Paris 1983.

18 Alberto Giacometti, "Hier, sables mouvants", in *Le Surréalisme au service de la révolution* 5, 1933, p. 44 ; Clair, "Le pointe", p. 97; Soldini, *Il colossale*, pp. 61–62; Mircea Eliade, *Le sacre et le profane*, Gallimard, Paris 1965, p. 21.

describing his perspective as "basmaterialisme". A month later Bataille hit back, publishing a pamphlet entitled *Un cadavre*, in which he compared Breton to a "lion châtré" and the movement to a religion of which Breton was the self-appointed prophet. In a similar way to Salvador Dalí (whose "paranoia-critique" did however prompt objections from other Surrealists), Giacometti sought reconciliation between the two groups. The sculptor was attracted both by "l'exploration ludique et onirique" of Breton and by the "dimension transgressive" of Bataille. When the two groups became radicalised, one with Breton in favour of "la révolution communiste" and the other with Bataille for "la révolution surréaliste intégrale", Giacometti maintained an independent stance, though he was close to Aragon, Éluard and Crevel in their efforts to mediate. Among the observations made by Grenier is an interesting comparison between Giacometti and Picasso: Alberto partage avec Picasso le fantasme d'un corps féminin manipulable, objectivation d'un désir conjugué de posséder et de détruire[19].

The friendship between Leiris and Bataille began in September 1924, several months before the former joined the Surrealist movement, and lasted until the latter's death in 1962. Leiris began to write about Giacometti in September 1929, with an article in *Documents*,[19] and carried on until his death in 1990:

> J'aime le sculpture de Giacometti parce que tout ce qu'il fait est comme la pétrification d'une de ces crises, l'intensité d'une aventure rapidement surprise et aussitôt figée [...] comme dans le vrai fétiches qu'on peut idolâtre (le vrais fétiches, c'est-a-dire ceux qui nous rassemblent et sont le forme objectivée de notre désir) prodigieusement vivant.[20]

That Bataille's ideas dialogued with Giacometti's sculpture, in particular the theme of the relationship between writing and death, which also aroused great interest from Michel Foucault and Jacques Derrida, has been recognised by the majority of critics.

From the *Histoire de l'oeil*, 1928, through to his final work, *Les larmes d'Eros*, in 1961, Bataille focussed on the relationship between eroticism and death: "[...] and nothing can stop the movement that drags human beings towards an ever more cynical awareness of the erotic bond linking them to death, to corpses and to the horrible pains of the body". And again: "I believe that eroticism is confirmation of life even within death. Sexuality entails death".[21] Even Giacometti's almost obsessive theme of the relationship with the figure of the prostitute, dear to Bataille and

---

19 *Documents* 1, pp. 209–14.

20 Michel Leiris, *Journal 1922–1989* (1992), Gallimard, Paris 2020, p. 99.

21 George Bataille, *La dépense. Contro Breton*, dossier, *Il valore d'uso di D.A.F. de Sade (Lettera aperta ai miei attuali compagni)*, in Id., *Critica dell'occhio*, edited by Sergio Finzi, Guaraldi editore, Rimini 1972, p. 133; Id., "Emile Bronte", in *La letteratura e il male* [1957], SE, Milan 2006, p. 16.

Walter Benjamin, according to which prostitutes "explored the secrets of the free market; goods would no longer have superiority over them" and "The woman in Baudelaire: the most precious treasure [...] life that means death. This quality pertains in the most inalienable way to the prostitute", is in line with Bataille's flat definition of eroticism as "the affirmation of life even within death". In Bataille the motif of the prostitute takes on deliberately and ideologically manifest tones: "I feel no shame about living like a surreptitious adolescent, like an old man. Having ended up, drunk and flushed, in a room of naked women [...] I undressed many women in the brothel. I drank, I was drunk and I was happy only on the condition of being undefendable. One is only free at the brothel".[22]

This introduction to motifs from Bataille in the work of Giacometti does not even seem to contradict Jean Clair's more Lacanian interpretation of his sculpture in *Le nez de Giacometti*, 1992. The common and fixed *circularity* regarding the motifs of death and eros that are found in Bataille and Giacometti also prompts consideration of the motives of the *statue* and of the *portrait* as part of a shared derivation from Baudelaire. According to Bataille, Baudelaire "aspired to the immutability of stone, the onanism of funerary poetry", and, drawing on Sartre's interpretation of the poet, "he chose to consider his life from the point of view of death, as if a premature end had already petrified him".[23] In *La mort de T.*, however, Giacometti seems to shrink from the sensation of ecstasy in the face of death that was a favourite locus for Bataille: "Mais depuis le rêve, depuis la maladie qui me ramène à ce déjeuner, la mort de T. redevient pour moi actuelle [...] En marchant, je revis T. les jours avant sa mort, dans la chambre contiguë à la mienne. [...] Je le revis, au fond de son lit, immobile, la peau, jaune ivoire, ramassé sur lui-même et déjà étrangement loin, et je le revis peu après, à trois heures du matin, mort, les membres d'une maigreur squelettique, projetés, écartés, abandonnés loin du corps, un énorme ventre boursouflé, la tête jetée en arrière, la bouche ouverte. Jamais aucun cadavre ne m'avait semblé si nul, débris misérable à jeter comme le cadavre d'un chat dans une ornière. Immobile debout devant le lit, je regardais cette tête devenue objet, petite boîte, mesurable, insignifiante."

Giacometti's more attentive critics have all noted the centrality of the theme of death in his work, and this represents the fulcrum of the evocation of the *La morte de T.*, which focuses on the dream of the spider, and the memory and news of the closure of the Sphinx brothel. The narrative of the dream ends when he throws the remains of the second, yellow spider into a hole and wakes up.

In the dream-story narrated by Giacometti in "Le rêve, le Sphinx et la mort de T.", a text that is powerfully archetypal and epiphanic at the same time, referring to an episode that occurred at Madonna di Campiglio in

---

22 Michel Surya, *Georges Bataille. La mort à l'oeuvre*, Gallimard, Paris 1992, p. 109.

23 Bataille, *La letteratura e il male*, p. 44.

September 1921 on his way back from his second trip to Rome, but written about in 1946, the sculptor describes his visit to the Sphinx. This was a "salon where, from the day it opened", he had spent "many hours and many evenings, and which for me was the most extraordinary place in the world".[24] The name of the establishment, Sphinx, is all too evocative of one of the subjects dearest to nineteenth-century European painting and therefore way beyond the "copies from the past" of Egyptian statues that recur so often in his drawings.

The theme of Oedipus and the Sphinx was a recurring motif in the culture of Symbolism at the end of the nineteenth century, after the precedent of Jean-Louis-Dominique Ingres' painting, *Oedipus and the Sphinx*, 1808, in which Oedipus is depicted standing side on, one leg resting on a rock, as he deciphers the enigmas posed by the Sphinx. At his feet are the remains of the skeleton of a previous ill-fated competitor. Shown at the Salon of 1827, it was not well received and was later deposited at the Louvre, where Giacometti is certain to have seen it. The work presents the meeting without the typical drama of the event.

That Giacometti's sculpture represents the point of arrival of a dense network of different strands of sculptural expression in the first half of the twentieth century is a principle that critics have now accepted. Giacometti seems to engage in an intense and ongoing dialogue with Rodin, Bourdelle, Despiau and Maillol, and the privileged genre of this conversation is the portrait.

In the first portraits of 1914–20 – Tête d'élève de Schiers, *Tête de Diego, enfant*, *Tête de Bruno enfant*, *Tête d'enfant* (*Simon Bérard*), and through to the *Tête* (*Grand tête de la mère*), 1918–25 – one can note a change with respect to the Secessionist influence present in the portraits of his father Giovanni and his friend Cuno Amiet. Compared to the portraits of his father, Giacometti appears to be more "constructivist", with tesserae-like brushstrokes, as in his *Autoportrait*, 1917, and in the front-on portrait view of his sister *Ottilia*, c.1920. The half-bust figure is wearing an ample blue dress highly reminiscent of certain portraits by Cézanne. Cézanne is an underlying presence in all of Giacometti's painted portraits, from those executed in the 1920s through to the final ones of Caroline in 1965, produced shortly before his death. His dialogue with Cézanne became almost obsessive, as demonstrated by the many drawings from paintings by the French master, those "copies from the past" as Luigi Carluccio called them. Giacometti analysed and deciphered the style of his masters through drawing, which was his true écriture – to a greater extent than any other twentieth-century artist – and he *visited* all of his figural world: from the *Venus of Laussel* to the "idols" of the Cyclades in the Musée de

---

24 Alberto Giacometti, "Le rêve, le Sphinx et la mort de T.", Fondation Giacometti (Hermann), Paris 2016, p. 8; Id., "Le rêve, le Sphinx et la mort de T."-(*Der Traum, die Sphinx und der Tod von T.*, facsimile of the manuscript, edited by Donat Rütimann, Scheidegger and Spiess, Zurich 2005, pp. 38-85).

l'Homme, from the art of Oceania to the Laocoön Group, from Roman busts to the Byzantine *Christ Pantocrator* and the *Souls of Purgatory* of the *Last Judgement* in Torcello Cathedral, from Cimabue's *Saint Francis* in Assisi to Dürer's *Portrait of Willibald Pirckheimer*, Mantegna's *The Parnassus: Mars and Venus*, Masolino's *Original Sin* and Masaccio's *Expulsion from the Garden of Eden* in the Brancacci Chapel, Michelangelo's *Dawn* and Donatello's *Judith and Holofernes*, through to the *Rape of the Daughters of Leucippus* by Rubens, under which Giacometti wrote: "J'ai sommeil, je ferme les yeux, je ne sais plus, où je suis et déjà je rêve, les yeux fermés", and *The Card Players* by Cézanne.

It is striking that Giacometti never included a portrait of Rodin in this interior monologue on the "fathers" of his art. Yet his portraiture would be hard to explain without the portrait head of Baudelaire that Rodin modelled towards 1892 – an apparently atypical work in Rodin's sculptural oeuvre but decisive for a lot of subsequent portraiture. In actual fact, none of the modern masters appear in the volume on the copies from the past edited by Carluccio, neither Rodin nor Bourdelle or Brancusi. But unlike Bourdelle, in whose school at the Académie de la Grande-Chaumière in Montparnasse Giacometti studied from 1922 to 1926, and Brancusi, in whose work Giacometti took an interest from the middle of the 20s, perhaps at the suggestion of Bourdelle who admired him greatly, Rodin never seems to be mentioned in the sculptor's Écrits. We are therefore moving in the realm of pure conjecture, but Giacometti would undoubtedly have carefully observed Rodin's sculptures. In the case of the portrait of Baudelaire, recast by Rodin in Paris on several occasions (1925, 1950, 1953) though it was only shown once in 1900 in the major exhibition devoted to his work at the Pavillon de l'Alma (no. 133), it is possible to demonstrate the influence it had on other modern sculptors, for instance in the plaster *Head of Baudelaire* by Raymond Duchamp-Villon (Rouen, Musée des Beaux Arts).[25]

When viewed superficially, Giacometti's relationship with the sculpture of Rodin might appear inexistent or not as evident as that of Rodin with Matisse, whose sculpture *Le serf* (*The Serf*), 1900–03, is closely related to *L'homme qui marche* (*The Walking Man*), 1899–1907, and with the figure of Jean d'Aire in the *Monument au bourgeois de Calais* (*Monument to the Burghers of Calais*). But more attentive consideration reveals that the principles of Rodin's sculpture formed an underlying element of Giacometti's reflection on and exploration of the figure. The relationship between Giacometti's *L'homme qui marche*, 1960, and that of Rodin is not just thematic, namely, the same subject. Nor is it a formal "external" relationship, and far less a *stylistic* one. Instead, it is "internal", lying in the very idea of the statue's *structure*.

---

25 Luigi Carluccio, *Alberto Giacometti. Le copie del passato*, Botero, Turin 1967, pp. vii–xi.

The presence of Rodin's *Balzac* must also be the phantom concealed behind the extremely avant-garde *Figure en pierre*, 1932, which was in the garden of the Noailles villa in Hyères, executed in the thick of the Surrealist phase and with leanings towards total abstraction. Critics have stuck to a neo-Cubist interpretation of this sculpture, a kind of monolithic totem, for which there is a photo showing the sculptor standing alongside it after making a correction. It is considered to follow on from the Surrealist works of 1925–30, such as *Femme cuillère*, 1927, *Homme et femme*, *Apollon*, and *Femme Couchée qui rêve*, 1929. Apparently, the *Figure en pierre* also references the contemporary sculptures of Zadkine, Lipchitz, Laurens and Csaky, but concealed behind these influences are other suggestions. Giacometti developed this motif in other stele-figures, as is documented by some photos taken in Maloja in 1931, and which were therefore contemporary to the *Figure en pierre*. Their arrangement might also call to mind the *Projet pour en place*, c.1934, the first drawings of which date to 1930, composed of different elements arranged as a menhir, such as the *Cône*, the cube and semi-sphere, and finally the kind of monolith-totem which in one of the drawings of 5 August 1933 appears in the variant of a totem with a skull head. The elaborate conception of the monument-statue to the great writer, to the "Dante" of modern times, documents a kind of torment in Rodin about the idea of space. The slant of the statue with respect to its physical axis in Rodin's definitive *Balzac* (already foreshadowed in the variant of *Balzac nu*, with folded arms and *en march*) anticipates Giacometti's *Figure en pierre* in the statue's yearning to leave the physical space. The concordance is not, it must be emphasised, *stylistic* but *structural*, in the very idea of the relation between statue and physical space. Just as *Balzac* is a statue that tends to leave the physical space that contains it – and this conception appears to be present in most of Rodin's studies relating to the statue, such as *Balzac. Étude drapée avec un capuchon et un jabot de dentelle* – so too does Giacometti's *Figure en pierre* tends to flee, to force the emptiness surrounding it. The profound albeit hidden analogy between these two ideas of space is borne out by the many photos of the two sculptures; by reducing the room and statue to a merely two-dimensional image, the silhouette denotes the virtual impossibility of living in a circumscribed three-dimensional space.

In both works there is, then, a similar structural necessity to get away from classical statuary: *Balzac* by shrinking in the clothes and getting out through the flection of the axis of the body, the *Figure en pierre* by way of the break in the middle of the figure given to the inclination of the cubic "head". The fact that *Balzac* references certain great Baroque works while *Figure en pierre* alludes to the megalithic standing stones of the Bronze Age, like the three comprising *Projet pour une place*, does not make much difference, because the mental process remains similar. What's more, Giacometti's work in progress was marked by an imperious return to statuary in the same year as *Figure en pierre*, 1932, as in *Femme qui marche I*, and then in the subsequent variant of 1936, and lastly in the mysterious female figure of the *Objet invisible* (*Mains tenant le vide*), 1934–35, the year he was expelled from the Surrealist group, offering confirmation of the *circularity* of his sculpture.

The presence of Egyptian statuary was a constant in all of Giacometti's work through to the large thread-like female nudes – the *Femme debout*, 1957, the groups of *La Clairière*, 1950, and *Quatre femmes sur socle*, 1950, often likened by critics to Etruscan votive bronzes, including the famous *Ombra della sera*. Also present in Giacometti's *Homme qui marche*, however, is an idea of a quadrifrontal figure, that is, seen from four points of view, not enveloping and chiasmatic as in Baroque sculpture, but axonometric and basic as in Egyptian statuary. Such an idea had already basically been manifested in the *Femme qui marche*, 1936, in plaster, photographed in the sculptor's studio by Pierre Matisse in August 1936 and by Brassai in October of the same year.[26]

This conception remained central until the groups of *Femme de Venise*, 1956 and *La forét*, 1950, which present once again the relationship between Giacometti and Rodin's *Les bourgeois de Calais*. A photograph taken by Patricia Matisse in 1950 in the grounds of the villa of Eugène Rudier at Vésinet shows Giacometti posing with *Les bourgeois*. He has climbed onto the plinth and is leaning forward, entering and becoming part of the group, resting his hands on those of Jean D'Aire on the right and Pierre de Wissant on the left. Symbolically, it seems to be a programme. Giacometti enjoyed ironically assuming the postures of his sculptures, as shown in some photos by Cartier-Bresson. There is one of him copying the position of *Homme qui marche* at the Galerie Maeght in Paris in 1961, and another of him with the *Femmes de Venise*, in the same gallery in 1964. The motif of *Les bourgeois de Calais* also recurs in *Trois hommes qui marchent*, 1948, which develops the idea of the movement of a group of bodies in space, a motif that had been one of the principal themes of Impressionist painting and which had been tackled and translated into sculpture by Medardo Rosso in the three-figure group of *Impression de boulevard. Paris la nuit*, 1896. This was a life-size group in plaster consisting of three figures, an almost running woman and, behind her, a man and a woman clinging to each other. Rosso's intent had been to render the optical impression received by the nocturnal view of the three bodies, a subject *en plein air* taken from "modern streets".[27]

It is also worth considering that Giacometti may have had a photographic knowledge of some of Rosso's portraits, such as the *Ritratto di Yvette Guilbert*, 1894, the *Ritratto di Madame Noblet*, 1897, and, finally, the extraordinary *Madame X*, 1896–1913, the radicality of which – destructive of naturalistic form and highly "anticlassical" – anticipated many of the finest sculptural works of the twentieth century. In *Madame X* Rosso had achieved that "dissolution of form" of the portrait that also seems to have nagged away at Giacometti. It is not a question of Rossi exerting an influence on Giacometti, with specific and recognisable episodes linking

---

26 *L'atelier d'Alberto Giacometti. Collection de la Fondation Alberto et Annette Giacometti*, Fondation Alberto et Annette Giacometti, Centre Pompidou, Paris 2007, pp. 109–11, figs. 240–45.

27 Marco Fagioli, *Medardo Rosso. Catalogo delle sculture*, Opus Libri, Florence 1993, pp. 100–15.

the two. But in a careful reading of the history of the portrait in twentieth-century sculpture, it seems impossible not to see that the issues of the plastic idiom addressed by the two artists run parallel. Even in Rosso's *pre-Impressionist* phase, with portraits like *La ruffiana*, 1883, *Lo scaccino*, 1883, *La portinaia*, 1883, enlivened by hollow touches on the surface layer, and then in the totally *Impressionistic* portraits like the *Ritratto di Henri Rouart*, 1889, the *Bambino al sole* (*Impression d'enfant*), 1892, and *Bambino alle cucine economiche*, 1892, it is impossible not to see a foreshadowing of some of Giacometti's half-bust portraits, like those of Diego and Annette. Despite the profound difference between the two sculptors, one can reasonably discern a common theoretical concern in their work. This appears to relate to one of the reflections on the question of the relationship between perception, memory and image expounded in exemplary fashion by Henri Bergson in 1904.[28]

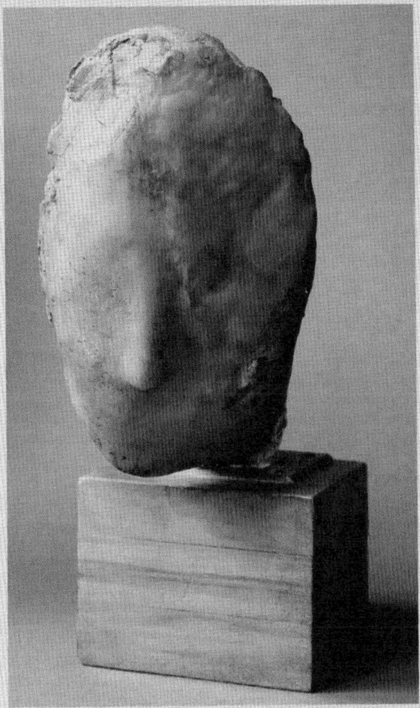

4. Medardo Rosso, *Madame X*, 1896, wax on chalk support. Venezia, Galleria Internazionale d'Arte Moderna di Ca' Pesaro

Two recent exhibitions, *Giacometti entre tradition et avant-garde* at the Musée Maillol and *Giacometti et Rodin* at the Fondazione Gianadda, explored the web of inferences linking Giacometti with other twentieth-century sculptors, from his master Bourdelle to Rodin, and from Maillol to Zadkine, Lipchitz, Csay, Brancusi and Laurens. The result is a very intricate map, much more so than with the sculpture of Matisse and Picasso. Giacometti's conception of plastic-visual form is singular and problematic, but it is apparent in the course of his sculpture: the looking to the past, with the "copies du passé" and at the same time the deep interest in African, Oceanic and primitive sculpture, well documented by his many *d'après*, the *Cahiers d'art*, 1929–37, imploding in the sculptures *Figure* and *Le couple*, 1927, and culminating in *Femme cullière*, 1927, once again presents the relationship of his work with some of the themes of twentieth-century philosophical thought. The idea that there is no beginning or end in art, leading to anxiety about the inability to attain form, and the persistent concern of an incessant inquiry in the portrait that is never completed, seem to be influenced by one of the most controversial and widely discussed themes in Nietzsche's thought. This is the concept of the *eternal return*, possibly indirectly conveyed through the relationship with Georges Bataille and Pierre Klossowski, and which came together in the climate of the magazines *Documents*, in which an article by Michel Leiris about his sculpture had appeared in 1929, and *Acéphale*, 1936. According to the concept of the *eternal return*, there is no *origin* or *end* (last time) in the course of life and history. This notion draws on the principle of "pagan circularity", as opposed to the "linear" path of the Christian vision culminating in redemption. The idea points to "a new conception of time characterised by *immanence* and without even the barest horizon or final destination". Giacometti never mentions the German philosopher in his writings, but his biographers note Nietzsche's

28 Henri Bergson, *Histoire des théories de la mémoire. Cours au College de France 1903–1904*, PUF, Paris 2018, pp. 190–91.

powerful influence on the group of dissident Surrealists gravitating around Bataille, referred to by Giacometti in a television interview with Jean-Marie Drot in 1963: "J'ai connu Masson à une exposition, ce jour même j'ai connu une bonne partie de mes amis qui le sont encore aujourd'hui, c'est-à-dire Masson, Bataille, Leiris, Desnos, Queneau et beaucoup d'autres".[29] In 1929, Masson himself introduced the sculptor to the German writer and expressionist critic Carl Einstein, the author of *Afrikanische Plastik*, a book which would greatly influence the avant-garde movements in their discovery of African sculpture. In 1929 Einstein had founded the magazine *Documents* with Bataille. The latter's interest in Nietzsche was crucial; the philosopher's influence was felt in many works, and he also became a point of reference for the members of the *Collège de sociologie*, founded by Bataille in 1937 together with Leiris and Callois. Yves Bonnefoy also points out the influence of Nietzsche on the thought of Bataille and Leiris, who had written about Giacometti in 1929:

> Mais on a commence, dans ces années 20, de lire Nietzsche, puis Freud; et Mauss, dans son séminaire, a entrepris ses analyses fameuses des usages du corps, cet instrument que le langage n'a ni produit ni jamais totalement contrôlé.
> [Michel Leiris, *Écrits sur l'art*, CNRS Éditions, Parigi 2011, pp. 236 and ff.]

Leiris had abandoned the Surrealist group in 1929, accepting Bataille's offer to become the editorial assistant for *Documents*. In 1931, he had taken part in the Dakar-Djibouti ethnological expedition, writing a diary of the experience, *Afrique fantôme*, 1934, that denounced "la complicité involontaire mais bien réelle de l'enquête des ethnologues et de l'entreprise colonialiste". This represented a fundamental criticism of ethnocentrism, which affirmed the superiority of Western thought over other cultures. Nietzsche's ideas influenced the group of dissident Surrealists associated with *Documents* in 1929, and later in *Acéphale*, 1936, which became a locus for the study of the philosopher's thinking, and reached a peak in 1937 in the notebooks of the *Collège de sociologie*. This group also included the Swiss-born sculptress Isabelle Margaretha Farner, who married the art critic Patrick Waldberg in 1938. She had met Giacometti, who deeply influenced her, and she was a friend of Marcel Duchamp too. In the ambit of the secret society of the *Collège*, she had also translated Nietzsche's *The Will to Power*.[30] Another of Bataille's themes that Giacometti addressed was death: many of the writer's reflections are touched by this theme, which is the central motif of *Le rêve, le Sphinx et la mort de T.* and which became a key element in his sculpture.Death and the preoccupation with the realisation of a form constituting the *absolute* in sculpture are therefore two central themes in Giacometti's work. As had happened in Rome in 1921, when the young sculptor, as he confessed in his letter to Pierre

---

29 Grenier, *Alberto Giacometti*, pp. 72, 314.

30 Georges Bataille, *La congiura sacra (Acéphale). Religion, sociologie, philosophie*, Bollati Boringhieri, Milan 1998, pp. 198, 272.

Matisse, had begun to model two busts and was unable to find his way – "I was lost, everything escaped me, the head of the model before me became like a cloud, vague and undefined. I ended by destroying them" – Giacometti wrestled with these issues all his life.

In *Paris sans fin*, the extraordinary "diary" that was a prelude to the end, which Giacometti planned for Tériade and which comprised one hundred and fifty lithographs and an accompanying text, the sculptor seems to have fixed the key points of his art: "Le silence, je suis seul ici" ("Silence, I am alone here"). This condition of "silence", which in French etymology – "Silence: Fait de ne pas parler: attitude d'une personne qui reste sans parler" – takes on a much more existential and figural value than the English "absence of any noise or sounds", is associated with that "je suis seul ici", and appears to be the essential condition of the "writing, non-writer [sculptor] that Giacometti believes himself to be". But it is the whole page and the sentences following that beginning which capture Giacometti's condition as the end approached: "Le silence, je suis seul ici, dehors la nuit, tout est immobile et le sommeil me reprend. Je ne sais ni qui je suis, ni ce que je fais ni ce que je veux, je ne sais si je suis vieux ou jeune, j'ai peut-être encore quelques centaines de milliers d'années à vivre jusqu'à ma mort, mon passé se perd dans un gouffre gris, j'étais serpent et je me vois crocodile, la gueule ouverte; c'était moi le crocodile rampant la gueule ouverte. Crier et hurler que l'air en tremble et les allumettes de loin en loin là par terre comme des bateaux de guerre sur la mer grise". The first sentence cannot fail to bring to mind a phrase of Charles Baudelaire's, "dans le silence et la solitude de la nuit", indicating the nexus between three essential propositions that link the sculptor and the poet: silence, solitude and the night as constituent images of the language of both.[31] These conditions – silence, solitude and the night – are still the distinctive connotations of his sculpture today.

---

31 Alberto Giacometti, *Paris sans fin*, preface by Mathilde Lacuyer-Maille, Fondation Giacometti, Les cahiers dessinés, Paris 2018, plate 80.

The 'other' Fontana

Maria Grazia Messina

In the overall critical reception of Fontana's work, led early on in Italy by Enrico Crispolti's repeated contributions, there has been a monolithic front of interpretations, though also confirmed by the artist's *Manifesti* and interviews. These place his *Concetti spaziali* [*Spatial Concepts*], holes and cuts in the canvas, in the perspective, an already futurist perspective, of a prophetic dimension in the work of art. This dimension was aerial, immaterial, in tune with scientific discoveries and technological conquests. It ventured into a phenomenalisation of the cosmic void, the void probed by telematic networks or the voyages of the aerospace shuttles that prevailed in the imagery of progress in the late 1950s and early 1960s. The other clear polarity in Fontana's work, the exuberance of the material - from the terracotta works to the congealed oils or polymateric works - was evolving in various ways parallel to the status of matter-energy as established by 20th-century physics as well as by Futurist aesthetics: an activist, transformative nature of matter itself, as Crispolti wrote as early as 1959, drawing a comparison with the existential waste-matter of Dubuffet's[1] informal genre.

Yet another 'alternative' path of interpretation could be attempted, equally motivated because, if properly read, the artist alludes to it in his verbal statements. It is supported above all by the iconographic evidence of his works, mostly destined to be misunderstood in the context of a logocentric culture. In 1972, the insights offered by the Italian translation of French anthropologist Gilbert Durand's notable study, *Les structures anthropologiques de l'imaginaire*, had been taken up solely by Maurizio Calvesi as a strong inspiration for his *Duchamp invisibile* [*Invisible Duchamp*] published not long after, in 1975. I believe that the erudite esoteric-alchemical meaning conferred on Calvesi's insights obscured interest in them, and the incontrovertible fact that Durand's theses should have been tested not on Duchamp, but on Fontana, with the oxymoronic polarities of his imagery. I took on the methodological challenge and attempted it in a university course in the early 1980s. Some of those approaches I now see as functional in an exhibition aimed at intentionally and provocatively comparing Fontana and Giacometti[2].

Durand's study had been published as a qualification thesis for teaching, in 1960, in Grenoble; the definitive edition came out in 1963[3]. Durand had been a student of Gaston Bachelard. His vocation arrived from a crossover of ethno-anthropological interests from both Carl Jung's science of the archetypes in the psyche and Ernst Cassirer's philosophy of symbolic forms. The result was an investigation of the imaginary, mainly focused on the

---

1 See the anthology of writings by Crispolti, 1959-2002, edited by P. Campiglio: E. Crispolti, *Carriera Barocca di Fontana*, Skira, Milan 2004.

2 Again Crispolti in 2002 recalled that the only real aversion explicitly expressed by Fontana concerned Giacometti "giacché sosteneva che fosse falso [since he claimed it was false]", see Crispolti, *Carriera barocca*... cit. p. 313.

3 G. Durand, *Les structures anthropologiques de l'imaginaire. Introduction à l'archétypologie générale*, Grenoble 1960, then Presses Universitaires de France, Paris 1963, Italian translation, Dedalo, Bari 1972.

mythopoetic creations of primitive or archaic cultures, the *mythocritique*. The fact that the book was published only a year after Lucio Fontana's first solo exhibition in Paris at Galerie Stadler, which ran from 17 March to 16 April 1959, is a fortuitous yet meaningful coincidence. It can hardly be assumed that Durand had visited it, even though the Stadler stood out in Paris among avant-garde galleries for being the standard-bearer of the then most fashionable trend, the *informel*. The fact remains that the exhibition sanctioned Fontana's success in France. Until then, he had been unknown; the wide selection of *Concetti spaziali [Spatial Concepts]* exhibited there, especially those from the polymateric phase, lent itself to a correspondence with Durand's theses, especially when one thinks of how it was received by a very surprised public and critics[4]. Unlike the Italian reception, which was sensitive to the artist's spatialist work and futurological projection, both in media innovations and the psychology underpinning them, the French favoured an existentialist, negative and aggressive approach. They threw a spotlight on the sexual metaphors, which contemporary Italian interpretations only alluded to and almost prudishly. Durand's study explained these metaphors thoroughly, finally removing them from the banality of an immediate correspondence with uninhibited erotic impulses or – in Freudian terms – with the sublimation of libido, returning them to the broader dimension of the imaginary already present in the Chthonic myths. This perspective made it possible to probe the deeper meanings of Fontana's gesture, and more completely captures its pervasive inspirational power.

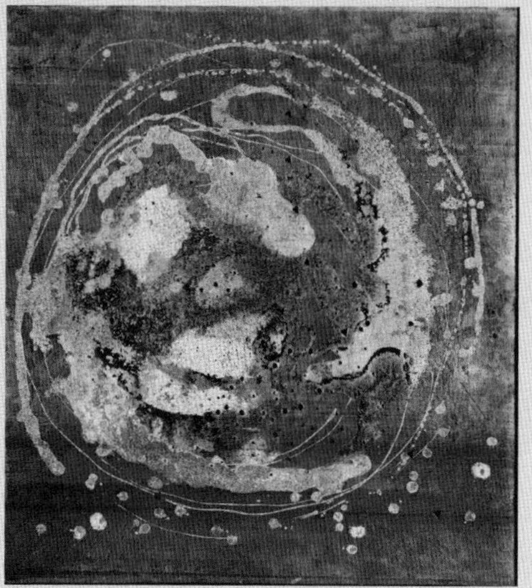

Lucio Fontana, *[Concetto spaziale]*, 1952, mixed media on tin, Milano, Fondazione Lucio Fontana

For Bachelard and Durand, the creative process is a process of imagination. It is reified in the objectual consistency of the work of art. Following the intuition of Jung, who had recognised an energising value in the archetypes it harbours, the imagination is essentially configured as a representation in images of the dynamic path of the gesture, the route by which man relates to the natural and social environment. Upon a deeper analysis of the gesture in light of reflexological studies, Durand points out three primary or dominant reflexes: postural, digestive, and rhythmic-sexual. Many representations or patterns of the imagination correspond to these: the pattern of ascending verticalization and division, visual and manual, corresponds to the first one; the opposite, that of descent, of folding into intimacy, of agglutination, corresponds to the second one; the cyclic one, including both messianic symbols and myths and those centred on the eternal return corresponds to the third one. Durand specifically notes that the symbolising activity of the imagination does not refer as a key to a noun, regardless of whether it is subject or object, but always to the verb, to the gesture that underlies it. This thesis was also

4 See S. Bignami, J. Galimberti, *Lucio Fontana e l'artventure parigina*, Scalpendi editore, Milan, 2014. At the same time, several reproductions of Fontana's *Concetti* were published in the leading specialist periodical, "Aujourd'hui. Art et Architecture", IV, 21, March-April 1959.

upheld by palethnologist André Leroi-Gouran – who also pursued this line of thinking – and in reference to Paleolithic art, he had added the evidence that every gesture implies a material and a technique[5].

Despite Fontana having clearly stated in the 1948 *Spatial* manifesto that "art will remain eternal as a gesture, but will die as matter", he was unaware that he was establishing the contiguity between the intentional and archetypal spheres of his work. Most critics, agreeing to frame Fontana's work in terms of a spatial question, understood this spatiality as the result of a vitalism, circumscribed in the trajectory and calibration of the gesture, but they only investigated the holes and cuts as a sculptural problem, in the results, and a logical-conceptual one, in the motivations, necessarily relegating the gesture to a secondary, operational function. While, on the other hand, the hallmark of Fontana's art is the gesture, and not a graphic one, but one performed with total transport in the material – the films that portray him are enough to convey this –, it is precisely the imaginary, with its essence, that emerges overbearingly. It is the archetypal and symbolic images that recur in it that must be investigated. Taking advantage of Bachelard's intuitions, later systematised by Durand, Fontana's gesture corresponds to the pattern of descent, of penetration, a load-bearing matrix of the so-called "nocturnal regime" of the imaginary, which includes the archetypes of the containing-contained binomial, of the cavity, and the ultimate meaning of womb or uterus, and insularity. A "constellation" of symbolic figures with an isomorphic or convergent meaning – such as the circle, spiral, seed, egg, and embryo – are connected to these archetypes. These figures are arranged in equally distinctive patterns of the same regime: that of "doubling" or "interlocking", which entails the inscription of one within the other; and that of "euphemism" or "inversion", which may imply for the same figure/symbol two opposite directions. This is why the previously mentioned "doubling" entails the ambivalent outcome of concentrated insularity as well as an almost galactic expansion. As a whole, it is an iconographic repertoire that recurs consistently in Fontana, from the spatial environments of the series with the emblematic title *Evoluzione del 1948 [Evolution* of 1948] or *Ambiente spaziale a luce nera di Wood* [*Spatial Environment in Wood's Black Light]* of 1949, to the concentric arrangements in which the holes are preferentially configured in the *Concetti spazial [Spatial Concepts]* of the 1950s, or the turgid and cracked bowls like fruit splitting in its ripening, from the 1960 *Natures*, or the ovular silhouettes of the canvases from the series *La fine di Dio [The End of God]* of 1963. As it manifests itself in these figures, the gesture of descending implies an incoercible aspiration to recovery, to fusion with a primary substance: for the pre-scientific thinking, which Durand covers in his text, the substance has an interior, or rather, an interior whose

5 It is significant that the only critical text that explicitly undertakes an interpretation of Fontana in the light of archaeotypology is that of the French G. Lascault, *Fontana, espace et vide*, "XXéme siècle", XXXII, 35, 1970, pp. 99-105, particularly pp. 103-105, where it refers to the "Expériences élémentaires du trou et de la fente", with a reference to the theses of A. Leroi-Gourhan, *Préhistoire de l'art occidental*, Mazenod, Paris 1965.

intimacy must be penetrated, and every shell, every container is only instrumental in detecting the secret, distinctive substantiality of the contained matter. Fontana himself recalled that, "Not that I pierced it to break the painting: no, I pierced it to find something..."[6]. All the more telling is the fact that, especially from the end of the 1950s, the gesture introduced a second, hidden layer in the thickness of the canvas itself, a veil of loose black gauze, where the mysterious materiality that lies beyond the surface of things, whether cosmic darkness or the indefinable core of matter, becomes tangibly perceptible. An impulse toward the profound that stops and dwells in intimacy appears to emerge from the entire context of Fontana's work; this dimension is also revealed by the title of the paintings with the cuts, *Attese* [*Expectations*], a term that can be understood as contemplative fixation, as well as indefinite expectation, and even cosmic adventure.

Also symptomatic for this interpretation of Fontana are the primary "structures" of the psyche that Durand – in this sense indebted to structuralism – identified as normative protocols governing the three regimes of the imagination. The structures, stable and justified by the isomorphism of archetypes and symbols within the recurring constellations of each regime, reciprocally make themselves guarantors in their margin of objectivity. Responding to the nocturnal regime, Durand singles out four types whose attributes appear to be well reflected in Fontana's oeuvre as a whole. The structure of "doubling" and "perseverance", originating from an obsession with interiority, and expressed in a sort of "viscosity of the theme", like its variation that emphasises the sequential nature of its different versions, is clearly verifiable in the different cycles into which Fontana's work is divided. These cycles are never completed, but practised in synchronic contiguity, albeit with the contingent privilege given to those more directly related to the climate of ongoing artistic research, from Informal art to monochrome research to Pop art. The "viscosity of the representative elements", a sort of linguistic adhesiveness to the theme expressed, is clear in the agglutination on the polymateric paintings, in the cosmic synthesis that emanates from them. The "sensorial nature of the representations", the icastic reification of the images, is characteristic of an artist like Fontana who, beyond verbal assumptions, feels before he thinks; that is, he formulates the images according to the dynamics of the psyche experienced in their primal immediacy, produced and not reproduced. The "miniaturisation", or propensity for detail that becomes a concentration of the whole, is best expressed, rather than by the fact of inscribing the figures one inside the other, by the minimal element of the hole, which gives access to the distilled core of the material.

The comparative study of the archetypes, in light of their structures and constellations, involves a very different connotation for the so-called sexual allusion of Fontana's gesture. Holes and cuts appear to be part of the

---

6 T. Trini, *Colloquio con Lucio Fontana*, "Domus", 466, September 1968. See the unabridged version: https://www.luciofontana.net/testi-lucio-fontana-white

first and vital woman-mother-earth-principle nexus, distinguished, as Durand points out, by an isomorphism between the symbolism of sharp or pointed weapons and ploughing implements, so that the gesture of cutting is mirrored in that of penetrating and fertilising, and the vagina is likened to the furrow, as the access to a generating womb. In Italy, this path was explored at an early stage only by Giulio Carlo Argan, in a text with no great results in 1960, the same year as Durand's study. This at least suggests a horizon of shared interpretations. For the spheres of *Nature*, Argan cites the Chthonian myths, right down to the steatopygian female effigies of Neolithic agricultural cultures, while for the cuts in the *Attese [Expectations]* he writes that 'that cut is a furrow, of the earth and of the woman, the same one that connects the surface, be it earthly or human, with the profound, inscrutable spatiality of the creativity of the cosmos [...] the artist turns back, because now the space that attracts him is no longer the sky but the deep"[7]. These are deeper meanings, which transpire from what Fontana reveals about himself in an interview not long after, in 1962, when, albeit with his usual irreverent jargon-filled style, he responded point blank to the interviewer Jacques Kermoal's game of questions with, "Peinture? Couleur?" "La Terre. Tout Noir", and to the question "La fente?" he reacted with "Vacance avec une belle fille" but also with "La fente c'est une morsure, une déchirure une gestation". In the same dialogue, Fontana bluntly dismisses the hole with its void effect: "c'est un truc philosophique", because "les trous, ça n'existent pas"[8]. In the end, they refer to substance, so that "space has a body", according to Gabriella Drudi's felicitous expression[9].

On the other hand, the polymateric nature of the so-called "baroque" canvases of the mid-1950s – with their backgrounds sprinkled with glassy pebbles, sprays of sequins, lumpy patches of colour – goes well beyond a playful and orgiastic (depending on the case) decorativism, but is filled with the same aspiration to substance as the holes and cuts. The intention is to offer a tangible image of the energetic potential of matter in its making. Fontana's oft-quoted assumption, "I believe in the colour-light of Van Gogh", should therefore be understood as a reference to Van Gogh's pasty, dense, thick, viscous paint, in which light is captured and congealed, changing from an optical to a material phenomenon: it is in this particular sense that light becomes colour in Fontana's works, rather than the diapason of monochromatic backgrounds or the varying incidences of light within the perforations of the canvas. On a symbolic level, the privileged use of certain colours is significant, and the frequency of the gold background, in particular, takes on emblematic value. Leaving aside any in-depth study of alchemy[10], suffice it to say that in the nocturnal regime

---

7 See G.C. Argan, *Fontana*, in U. Apollonio, G.C. Argan, M. Masciotta, *Scultori d'oggi, Moore, Fontana, Mastroianni, Mirko, Viani*, Edizioni Minerva Artistica, Turin 1960, pp. 51-59, here p. 57.

8 J. Kermoal, *Psychoanalyse de Fontana*, "Metro", III, 7, December 1962, pp. 25-27.

9 G. Drudi. *Lucio Fontana*, in *La donazione Lucio Fontana*, exhibition catalogue (Milan, Palazzo Reale, 28 November 1978-31 January 1979) Multhipla edizioni, Milan 1979, pp. 13-19, here p. 14.

10 See G. Dorfles, *Lucio Fontana le ova*, exhibition catalogue, Galleria de L'Ariete, Milan, June

of the imagination, the value of gold is not in its luminous appearance, but its substance, which is symbolic of all inner life. This is indicated by the image of the treasure chest buried at the end of the rainbow that recurs in myths and fairy tales. Since gold is the finest result of the distillation process, it becomes a symbol for everything that is concentrated, a perennial extract, beyond the vicissitudes of the accidental. In this sense, the symbolism of gold is analogous to that of the Mandala, alluding to a centre, to a constitutive nucleus of the material Being, with the result of fulfilment and satisfaction that follows: the canvas *Venezia era tutta d'oro [Venice was all gold]* from the 1961 series on Venice is thoroughly representative of this substantialist intention. Here a whirling spiral, traced on a thick gold background, culminates in a clean cut at the centre, from which the black of a further intimate substance emerges.

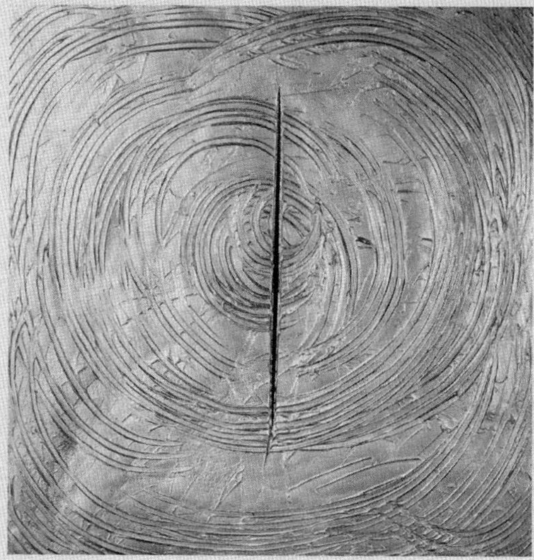

Lucio Fontana, *Concetto spaziale. Venezia era tutta d'oro*, 1961, oil on canvas Madrid, Fundación Colección Thyssen-Bornemisza

Fontana's substantialism appears to contradict the intentions expressed by the series of Manifestos on Spatialism. Yet nature/substance and matter are called into question as far back as the *Manifiesto blanco* of 1946: "We demand an exact understanding of the primary values of existence, which is why we establish the substantial values of nature in art. We present the substance, not the marginality of things [...] We direct ourselves towards matter and its evolution, the generative sources of existence". And again, to emphasise the source of such assertions: "Reason does not create. In the creation of forms, its function is to be subordinate to that of the subconscious". If we apply Jung's assumption of a continuity between imagination and logical-conceptual thinking, whereby the visual archetype is the source of the idea, the hiatus between Fontana's intentions, who defined art as "thought" and continued to name his works *Concetti [Concepts]*[11], and the interpretation of, for example, Argan, who in the quoted text considered his poetics to be exclusively visual, is in fact contradicted. Fontana's work consists of a visualised imaginative process, which is then transposed, with due transitions, adjustments, censures, into the speculative and programmatic plane. Suffice it to recall how, in the 1960s, the artist increasingly placed his work in a minimalist and conceptual sense, precisely because of a harmony – that may or may not have been involuntary - with the avant-garde research of the time[12]. After all, the antinomies inherent to Fontana's work, the polarity between matter

---

1963; G. Celant, *Lucio Fontana, La soglia tra due mondi*, in *Lucio Fontana, Terra e oro*, exhibition catalogue edited by A. Coliva (Rome, Galleria Borghese, 22 May-25 August 2019), Silvana Editoriale, Cinisello Balsamo 2019, pp. 12-25, particularly p. 24.

11 See the introduction to his solo exhibition at the Galleria del Naviglio, Milan 1953: "Non ci può essere una pittura o scultura spaziale, ma solo un concetto spaziale dell'arte [There can be no spatial painting or sculpture, only a spatial concept of art]".

12 See the well-known interview with Lonzi from 1967, unabridged version: *Milano 10 ottobre 1967: Carla Lonzi intervista Lucio Fontana*, in *Lucio Fontana. Sedici Sculture. Sixteen Sculptures. 1937-1967*, exhibition catalogue edited by P. Campiglio (Milan, Amedeo Porro Arte moderna e Contemporanea, 12 December 2007-28 February 2008), Silvana Editoriale, Cinisello Balsamo 2007, pp. 26-65.

and space, between vitalist colourism and achromaticity, between the activistic expansion of the image and the dismaying perception of the void, between the recovery of artisanal craftsmanship and projection into electronic and aerospace futurism, are commonplace. Returning to archetypes, it is precisely that dialectical nature intrinsic to the processes of the imagination that Durand finally intended to systematise, contrasting a diurnal and nocturnal regime of archetypes and symbols that coexist within it, and to which the extremes of Fontana's way of working correspond in precise ways. Above all, the nocturnal regime has a vocation for the coexistence of opposites, for the co-presence of an active and passive meaning of the verb or action on which the symbolising activity is polarised: this is borne out by this regime's load-bearing structures, such as euphemism and the inversion of values. In this sense, the nocturnal regime comes to be configured as a summary of the imagination itself, and, given the power and poignancy exerted by its own archetypes, designates as essentially imaginative the work of those who, like Fontana, gravitate to it.

It is a conclusion that is not called into question by the same yearning for progress that unquestionably marks Fontana's work, inasmuch as it is a striving to go beyond history or a desire to present the future, anticipating it and verifying it with the imagination: the very consistency of his work in synchronic series is an indication of a latent intention to exorcise time through the repetition of temporal instants, in convergence with any messianism, aimed at accelerating history in order to bring it to its fulfilment, and therefore to dominate it. The ultimate reference of Fontana's gesture - beyond matter/space's question - is the temporal condition, transcended in the decanting of matter to the extreme, denied in the withdrawal into a primary and cosmic substantialism, mastered in its otherwise anguished coming into being. It is here, in my opinion, that the comparison with Giacometti is played out. He, on the other hand, is painfully confined in such a temporal condition. While Fontana brings space and matter "closer", involves our gaze in their density, gives us an experience of them in the present, Giacometti, with his figures, makes distance and the corrosive action of time tangible. In Jean Genet's complicit interpretation, his figures are the image that the dead have of themselves, visualising themselves at the moment of their being alive.

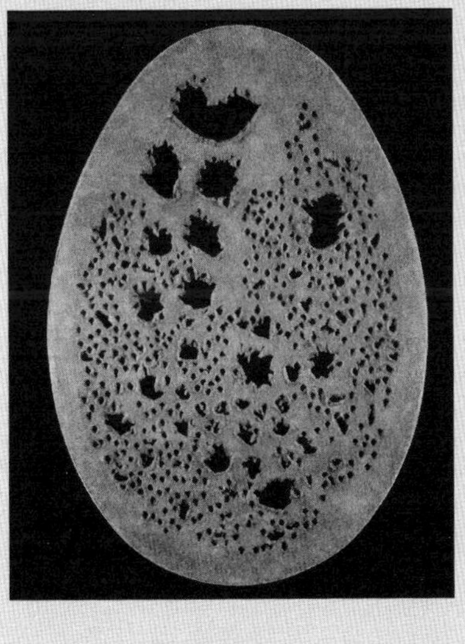

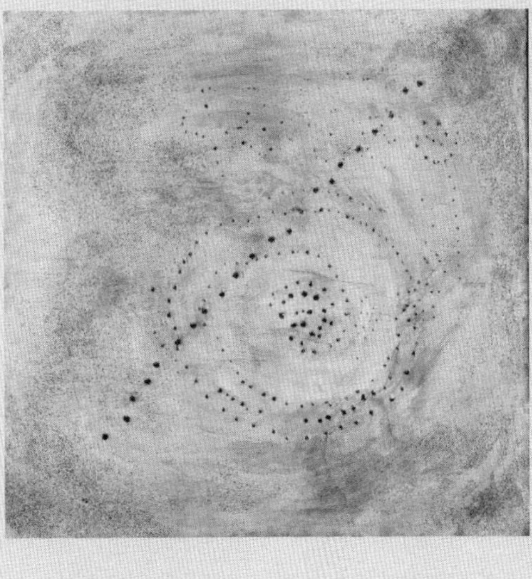

Lucio Fontana, *[Concetto spaziale], La fine di Dio*, 1963, oil, rips, holes, graffiti, and sequins on canvas, Milano, Fondazione Lucio Fontana

Lucio Fontana, *[Concetto spaziale]*, 1951-1952, oil and sequins on canvas, Milano, Fondazione Lucio Fontana

Selected Bibliography

1902
H. Poincaré, *La science et l'hypothése*, Flammarion, Paris 1902

1909
A. Soffici, *Il caso Medardo Rosso: preceduto dall'impressionismo e dalla pittura italiana*, B. Seeber, Firenze 1909

1925
F. Perzyński, *Japanische Masken. Nō und Kyōgen*, Walter de Gruyter & Co., Berlin 1925

1929
A. Soffici, *Medardo Rosso*, Vallecchi, Firenze, 1929
C. Zervos (ed. by), *Fascicule consacré à l'art des Océaniens*, monograph of the magazine "Cahiers d'art. Bulletin mensuel d'actualité artistique" IV, nos. 2-3, Éditions "Cahiers d'Art", Paris, marzo 1929

1930
L. Venturi, *Arturo Martini*, "L'Arte", Torino, November, XXXIII; folder VI, 1930, pp. 556-577

1931
E. N. Rogers, *Lucio Fontana alla Galleria del Milione*, "L'Italia Letteraria", 12 December 1931

1932
U. Nebbia, in *La diciottesima Biennale. Gli italiani*, "Emporium", vol. LXXV, no. 450, June 1932, pp. 339-394

1933
A. Giacometti, *Hier, sables mouvants*, "Le Surréalisme au service de la révolution", 5, 1933, pp. 44-45
"Minotaure", no. 2, *Mission Dakar-Djibouti*, Albert Skira, Paris 1931-1933

1934
A. Breton, *Equation de l'objet trouvé*, in *Intervention surréaliste*, numero monografico della rivista "Documents 34", n.s., no. 1, Paris, June 1934, p. 20

1935
C. Belli *Kn*, Il Milione, Milano 1935
C. Carrà, *Mostra d'arte*, "L'Ambrosiano", no. 15, Milano, 17 January 1935

1938
J. Giro, *Sculpteurs du Midì. Bourdelle, Maillol, Despiau, Dardé, Malacan, Costa, Parayre, Iché*, Libraririe Floury, Paris 1938
A. Podestà, *Statue e ceramiche di Lucio Fontana*, "Il Broletto", April 1938, p. 42

1939
G.C. Argan, *Su alcuni giovani. Fontana*, in "Le Arti", a. I, folder III, February-March 1939, p. 293
S. Bini, *Lucio Fontana scultore*, "il Secolo XIX", 7 January 1939, p. 3
R. Carrieri, *Le maioliche geologiche di Lucio Fontana*, "L'illustrazione Italiana", 8 January 1939, p. 63
L. Fontana, *Le mie ceramiche*, "Tempo", 21 September 1939

1940
A. Bioy Casares, *La invenciòn de Morel*, Losada, Buenos Aires 1940, Eng. transl., *The Invention of Morel*, New York Review of Books, 2003

1945
A. Giacometti, *Un sculpteur vu par un sculpteur. Henri Laurens par Alberto Giacometti*, "Labyrinthe. Journal mensuel des lettres et des arts ", no. 4, Pierre Cailler, Genève, 15 Janaury 1945
A. Giacometti, *À propos de Jacques Callot*, "Labyrinthe. Journal mensuel des lettres et des arts", no. 7, Pierre Cailler, Genève, 15 April 1945, p. 3

1948
XXIV Biennale di Venezia, exhibition catalogue (Venice, Giardini di Castello, 1 May - 30 September 1948), Edizioni Serenissima, Venezia 1948
Alberto Giacometti. Exhibition of sculptures, paintings, drawings, exhibition catalogue, presentation curated by J. P. Sartre (New York, Pierre Matisse Gallery, 19 January - 14 February 1948), Pierre Matisse Gallery, New York 1948

1949
Mostra di scultura contemporanea, exhibition catalogue edited by P. Guggenheim, preface edited by G. Marchiori (Venice, Giardino del Palazzo Venier dei Leoni, September 1949), Ferrari, Venezia 1949

1950
R. Carrieri, *Pittura, scultura d'avanguardia (1890-1950) in Italia*, Edizioni della Conchiglia – Istituto Editoriale Domus, Milano 1950

1952
G. Marchiori, *La Mostra Italia-Francia*, "Fiera Letteraria", 12 October 1952
L. Pistoi, *Pittori d'oggi: Francia-Italia*, "L'Unità", 21 September 1952

1953
2a Rassegna Internazionale di scultura all'aperto, exhibition catalogue, presentation curated by L. Vitali (Varese, Villa Mirabello, 1953), Manfredi, Varese 1953

1955
G. C. Argan, *Studi e note*, Bocca Editori, Roma 1955

1956
M. Negri, *Frammenti per Alberto Giacometti*, "Domus", 320, July 1956, pp. 40-48
F. Russoli, *Artisti alla Biennale: Alberto Giacometti*, "Comunità", X, 42, August-September 1956, pp. 74-77
L. Venturi, *Saggi di critica*, Bocca, Roma 1956
XXVIII Esposizione Biennale Internazionale d'Arte, exhibition catalogue (Venice, Giardini di Castello, 16 June - 21 October 1956), Alfieri, Venezia 1956

1957
Undicesima Triennale di Milano, exhibition catalogue edited by A. Pica, (Milan, Palazzo dell'Arte al Parco, 27 July - 4 November 1957), Crespi, Milano 1957

1958
J. Genet, *L'atelier d'Alberto Giacometti, Les bonnes, L'enfant criminel, Le funambule*, L'Arbalète, Décines (Rhône) 1958

1959
G. Charbonnier, *Le monologue du peintre*, René Julliard Éditeur, Paris 1959

1960
U. Apollonio, G. C. Argan, M. Masciotta, *Scultori d'oggi, Moore, Fontana, Mastroianni, Mirko, Viani*, Edizioni Minerva Artistica, Torino 1960
S. de Beauvoir, *La force de l'âge*, Gallimard, Paris 1960
G. Durand, *Les structures anthropologiques de l'imaginaire. Introduction à l'archétypologie générale*, Grenoble 1960, poi Presses Universitaires de France, Paris 1963, It. translation, Dedalo, Bari 1972
C. Giedion-Welcker, *Contemporary Sculpture, an Evolution in Volume and Space*, New York 1960

1961
S. de Beauvoir, *L'età forte*, Einaudi, Torino 1961
A. Giacometti, *Ma longue marche*, Éditions de "L'Express", Paris, 8 June 1961, pp. 48-50
M. Tapié. *Devenir de Fontana*, Edizioni d'Arte Fratelli Pozzo, Torino, 1961
Alberto Giacometti, exhibition catalogue edited by L. Carluccio (Turin, Galleria Galatea, 29 September - 25 October 1961), Galleria Galatea, Torino 1961E. Crispolti, *Ipotesi attuali*, "Il Verri" V, no. 3, 1961, pp. 63-97
Alberto Giacometti, "Corriere Lombardo", 21 November 1961
Alla Galleria Colonna espone Alberto Giacometti, "Gazzetta di Parma", 17 November 1961
Giacometti alla Galatea, "Stampa Sera", 16 October 1961

1962
P. Bucarelli, *Alberto Giacometti*, Editalia, Roma 1962
J. Dupin, *Alberto Giacometti*, Maeght Éditeur, Paris 1962
J. Kermoal, *Psychoanalyse de Fontana*, "Metro", III, 7, December 1962, pp. 25-27
U. Mulas, *Incontri alla Biennale, fotoservizio di Ugo Mulas*, "Pirelli", IV, XV, 4, August 1962, pp. 59-71
P. Simondo, *Il concetto di spazio negli scritti epistemologici di Henri Poincaré*, Università degli Studi di Torino, a.a. 1961-62, unpublished (courtesy of Fondazione Simondo, Torino)

1963
G. Dorfles, *Lucio Fontana le ova*, exhibition catalogue, Galleria de L'Ariete, Milano June 1963
G. Giani, *L'arte di Fontana non sa che farsene della realtà*, "L'Avanti!", 27 June 1963, p. 6

1964
G. C. Argan, *Salvezza e caduta nell'arte moderna*, Il Saggiatore, Milano 1964
Alberto Giacometti, Galerie Beyeler, Basel 1964

1965
I. J.-M. Dufet, *Bourdelle*, Arted, Paris 1965
M. Eliade, *Le sacre et le profane*, Gallimard, Paris 1965
J.-P. Sartre, *L'essere e il nulla*, Il Saggiatore, Milano 1965
Alberto Giacometti. Sculpture Paintings Drawings 1913-1965, Lund, Humphries and Co., London 1965

1966
J.-P. Sartre, *La recherche de l'absolu*, in *Situations III*, Gallimard, Paris 1966

1967
L. Carluccio, *Alberto Giacometti. Le copie del passato*, Edizioni Botero, Torino 1967

1968
F. Meyer, *Alberto Giacometti. Eine Kunst existentieller Wirklichkeit*, Verlag Huber, Frauenfeld 1968
T. Trini, *Colloquio con Lucio Fontana*, "Domus", 466, September 1968

1969
B. Boustedt, *Quand Giacometti plaçait lui-même ses sculptures*, "XXème siècle", XXXI, 33, December 1969, pp. 23-38
C. Lonzi, *Autoritratto*, De Donato, Bari 1969

1970
C. Huber, *Alberto Giacometti*, Éditions Rencontre, Lausanne 1970
P. Fossati (ed. by), *Lucio Fontana. Concetti spaziali*, Einaudi, Torino 1970
G. Lascault, *Fontana, espace et vide*, "XXéme siècle", XXXII, 35, 1970, pp. 99-105

1971
R. Hohl, *Alberto Giacometti*, Hatje, Stuttgart 1971 (French translation, Éditions Clairefontaine, Lausanne 1971)

1972
G. Bataille, *Critica dell'occhio*, edited by S. Finzi, Guaraldi editore, Rimini 1972
Lucio Fontana, exhibition catalogue edited by Guido Ballo (Milan, Palazzo Reale, 1972), Arti grafiche Fiorin, Milano 1972

1973
B. Pottier (ed. by), *Le langage. Les dictionnaires du savoir moderne*, Centre d'étude et promotion de la lecture, Paris 1973

1974
A. Breton, *L'amour fou*, Einaudi, Torino 1974
M. Mauss, *Oeuvres*, vol. 2, *Représentations collectives et diversité des civilisations*, Les éditions de Minuit, Paris 1974

1977
Fontana/Disegni, exhibition catalogue edited by Paolo Fossati (Milan, Castello Sforzesco, 1977), Electa, Milano 1977

1979
J. Genet, *OEuvres completes*, vol. 5, *Le funambule, Le secret de Rembrandt, L'atelier d'Alberto Giacometti, Les negres, Les paravents, L'enfant criminel*, Gallimard, Paris 1979
P. Guggenheim, *Out of this century. Confessions of an art addict*, Andre Deutsch, London, 1979
M. Sicard (ed. by), *Sartre et les arts*, "Obliques", 24-24, special number, 1979
La donazione Lucio Fontana, exhibition catalogue (Milan, Palazzo Reale, 28 November 1978 - 31 January 1979) Multhipla edizioni, Milano 1979

1981
J. Clifford, *On Etnographic Surrealism*, "Comparative Studies in Society and History", 23, 1981, pp. 539-564

1983
J. Clair, *Le pointe a l'oeil*, "Cahiers du Musée National d'Art Moderne", 97, 1983

1984
W. Rubin (ed. by), *Primitivism in 20th Century Art. Affinity of the Tribal and the Modern*, The Museum of Modern Art, New York 1984

1985
R. E. Krauss, *The originality of the avant-garde and other modernist myths*, Cambridge MA, 1985
J. Lord, *Giacometti. A Biography*, Farrar Straus Giroux, New York 1985 M. Megged, *Dialogo nel vuoto. Beckett e Giacometti*, trad. it., Hestia, Cernusco Lombardone (Como) 1993 (original edition *Dialogue in the Void. Beckett & Giacometti*, Lumen Books, New York 1985)
W. Rubin (ed. by), *Primitivismo nell'arte del XX secolo. Affinità tra il tribale e il moderno*, Mondadori, Milano 1985

1986

E. Crispolti, *Lucio Fontana. Catalogo Generale*, Electa, Milano 1986

1987

P. Beye, D. Honisch, A. Schneider (ed. by), *Alberto Giacometti*, Prestel, München 1987

1988

G. Calame-Griaule, J. Guiart, *Dakar-Djibouti. Minotaure and Marcel Griaule*, Musée d'Art Moderne de la Ville de Paris, Paris 1988

J. Lord, *Giacometti. Una biografia*, Italian translation Umberto Allemandi & C., Torino 1988 (original edition *Giacometti. A Biography*, Farrar, Straus and Giroux, New York 1985)

Omaggio a Lucio Fontana, Fondazione Guggenheim, Venice, 1989, exhibition catalogue, Marsilio, Venezia 1988

1990

G. Celant, *L'infermo dell'arte italiana. Materiali 1946-1964*, Costa&Nolan, Genova 1990

A. Giacometti, *Scritti*, Abscondita, Milano 1990

1991

Y. Bonnefoy, *Alberto Giacometti. Biographie d'une œuvre*, Flammarion, Paris 1991

E. Scheidegger, *Alberto Giacometti. Spuren einer Freundschaft*, Scheidegger und Spiess, Zürich 1991

J. Soldini, *Il colossale, la madre, il "sacro". L'opera di Alberto Giacometti*, Pierluigi Lubrina, Bergamo 1991

Alberto Giacometti, exhibiton catalogue edited by Suzanne Pagé (Musée d'art moderne de la Ville de Paris, 30 November 1991 - 15 March 1992), Musée d'Art Moderne, Paris, 1991

1992

G. Bataille, *La parte maladetta*, Bollati Boringhieri, Torino 1992

Y. Bonnefoy, *Alberto Giacometti. Biografia di un'opera*, Editore, Milano 1991

J. Clair, *Le nez de Giacometti - Faces de carême - Figures de carnaval*, Gallimard, Paris 1992

M. Surya, *Georges Bataille. La mort a l'œuvre*, Gallimard, Paris 1992

1993

G. Didi-Hubermann, *Le Cube et le visage. Autour d'une sculpture d'Alberto Giacometti*, Éditions Macula, Paris 1993

M. Fagioli, *Medardo Rosso. Catalogo delle sculture*, Opus Libri, Firenze 1993

V. Hugotte, *"La présence active du vide" L'Objet invisible de Giacometti*, "Esprit", no. 189, Éditions Esprit, Paris, febbraio 1993, pp. 56-68

M. Megged, *Dialogo nel vuoto, Beckett e Giacometti*, Hestia, Cernusco Lombardo 1993

P. Mola, *Wildt a Brera, breve storia di un'utopia*, "Arte Lombarda", no. 104, 1993, pp. 69-77

E. White, *Jean Genet*, Gallimard, Paris 1993

1995

D. Koepplin, *Warum kopierte Alberto Giacometti ältere Kunst. Zu einigen Zeichnungen hauptsächlich im Kupferstichkabinett Basel*, Wiese Verlag, Basel 1995

M. Leiris, J. Dupin (ed. by), *Alberto Giacometti. Scritti*, Nodi, Sestante, 1995

Alberto Giacometti. Sculture, dipinti, disegni, catalogo della mostra a cura di C. Di Crescenzo (Milan, Palazzo Reale 26 January - 2 April 1995), Artificio, Firenze 1995

1996

J. Bonnemaison, K. Huffman, C. Kaufmann, D. Tryon (ed. by), *Vanuatu. Océanie. Arts des îles de cendre et de corail*, Réunion des musées nationaux, Paris 1996

1997

A. Del Puppo, *Alberto Giacometti*, Editoriale L'Espresso, Roma, 2005, p. 27

J. Genet, *L'atelier di Giacometti*, in *Il funambolo*, Adelphi, Milano 1997

C. Kaufmann, *Vanuatu. Kunst aus der Südsee. Eine Einführung*, Christoph Merian Verlag, Basel 1997

M. Pietrantoni (ed. by), *Memorie nel bronzo e nel marmo. Monumenti celebrativi e targhe nelle piazze e nelle vie di Milano*, F. Motta Editore, Milano 1997

1998

G. Bataille, *La congiura sacra (Acephale). Religion, sociologie, philosophie*, Bollati Boringhieri, Milano 1998

G. Bataille, *L'aldilà del serio e altri saggi*, Guida editori, Napoli 1998

A. Giacometti, *Il mio lungo cammino*, Hestia edizioni, Cernusco Lombardo 1998

R. Hohl, *Giacometti. A Biography in Pictures*, Hatje, Ostfildern 1998

1999

A. Angliviel de la Beaumelle (ed. by), *Alberto Giacometti. La collection du Centre Georges Pompidou, Musée national d'art moderne*, Réunion des musées nationaux, Paris 1999

I. Amaduzzi, *Io sono uno scultore. Lucio Fontana a Milano negli anni Trenta*, Edizioni Angelo Guerrini e Associati, Milano 1999

P. Barone, *Età della polvere. Giacometti, Heidegger, Kant, Hegel, Schopenhauer e lo spazio estetico della caducità*, Saggi Marsilio, Venezia 1999

P. Campiglio (ed. by), *Lucio Fontana. Lettere 1919-1968*, Skira, Milano 1999

R. E. Krauss, *Passaggi, Storia della scultura da Rodin alla Land Art*, Bruno Mondadori, Milano 1998

Y. Le Fur (ed. by), *"La mort n'en saura rien". Reliques d'Europe et d'Océanie*, Réunion des musées nationaux, Paris 1999

D. Radrizzani, *Alberto Giacometti nel paese di Fidia*, "k+a. Kunst + Architektur in der Schweiz", numero monografico intitolato *Griechenland und Moderne*, no. 1, Gesellschaft für Schweizerische Kunstgeschichte, Bern 1999, pp. 57-65

2000

J. Kerchache, V. Bouloré (ed. by), *Sculptures. Afrique. Asie. Océanie. Amériques*, Réunion des musées nationaux, Paris 2000

E. Pontiggia, *Adolfo Wildt e i suoi allievi. Fontana, Melotti, Broggini e gli altri* (exhibition catalogue, Brescia, Palazzo Martinengo, 2000), Skira, Milano 2000

Giacometti. Dialoghi con l'arte, exhibition catalogue edited by Casimiro Di Crescenzo e Simone Soldini (Mendrisio, Museo d'arte, 17 September - 12 November 2000), Museo D'arte, Mendrisio 2000

2001

A. Angliviel de la Beaumelle (ed. by), *Alberto Giacometti. Le dessin à l'œuvre*, Gallimard, Paris 2001

M. Eliade, *Une nouvelle philosophie de la lune*, Essai L'Herme, Paris 2001

A. Giacometti, *Scritti*, presentati da M. Leiris, J. Dupin, Abscondita, Milano 2001

C. Klemm, C. Lachner, T. Bezzola, A. Umland (ed. by), *Alberto Giacometti*, The Museum of Modern Art, New York 2001

C. Klemm, Carolyn Lachner, Tobia Bezzola, Anne Umland (ed. by), *Alberto Giacometti*, The Museum of Modern Art, New York 2001

2002

Y. Bonnefoy, *Remarques sur le regard*, Picasso Giacometti Morandi, Calmann-Lévy, Paris 2002

H. Focillon, *Vita delle forme seguito da Elogio della mano*, Einaudi, Torino, 2002

W. M. Griswold, J. Tonkovich (ed. by), *Pierre Matisse and his Artists*, Pierpont Morgan Library, New York 2002
A. Wildt, *L'arte del marmo*, edited by E. Pontiggia, Abscondita, Milano, 2002

2003
Y.-A. Bois, R. E. Krauss, *L'informe. Istruzioni per l'uso*, Bruno Mondadori, Milano 2003
G. Zanchetti, *"Un futuro c'è stato..." Anacronismo e suggestioni iconografiche in Fontana*, "L'uomo nero", no. 1, 2003, pp. 89-100

2004
Y. Bonnefoy, *Alberto Giacometti* (1998), edited by S. Esengrini, Abscondita, Milano 2004
E. Crispolti, *Carriera Barocca di Fontana*, Skira, Milano 2004

2005
G. Mazza, *La liminalità come dinamica di passaggio. La rivelazione come struttura osmotico performativa dell'interesse trinitario*, Pontificia Università Gregoriana, 2005
J.P. Sartre, *L'imaginaire* (1940), Gallimard, Paris 2005
Alberto Giacometti, exhibition catalogue edited by Claudio Spadoni (Ravenna, Loggetta Lombardesca, 10 October 2004 - 20 February 2005), Ravenna, Mazzotta, 2004
Sartre, direction by M. Berne, Gallimard, Paris 2005

2006
G. Bataille, *La letteratura e il male* (1957), SE, Milano 2006
G. Bataille, *Storia dell'erotismo*, edited by Franco Rella, Fazi editore, Roma 2006
E. Crispolti, *Lucio Fontana. Catalogo ragionato di sculture, dipinti, ambientazioni*, Skira, Milano, 2006
M. De Sabbata, *Tra diplomazia e arte: le Biennali di Antonio Maraini (1928-1942)*, Forum Editrice, Udine 2006
M. Eliade, *Il sacro e il profano*, Universale Bollati Boringhieri, Torino 2006

2007
D. Arasse, *Il dettaglio, la pittura vista da vicino*, Il Saggiatore, Milano 2007
P. Campiglio (ed. by), *Lucio Fontana: sedici sculture*, Silvana Editoriale, Milano 2007
M. Gunn, P. Peltier (ed. by), *Nouvelle-Irlande. Arts du Pacifique Sud*, Five Continents, Milano 2007
L'atelier d'Alberto Giacometti. Collection de la Fondation Alberto et Annette Giacometti, Fondation Alberto et Annette Giacometti, Centre Pompidou, Paris 2007
Lucio Fontana. Sedici Sculture. Sixteen Sculpture. 1937-1967, exhibition catalogue edited by P. Campiglio (Milan, Amedeo Porro Arte moderna e Contemporanea, 12 December 2007 - 28 February 2008), Silvana Editoriale, Cinisello Balsamo 2007

2008
C. De Carli, F. Tedeschi (ed. by), *Il presente si fa storia. Scritti in onore di Luciano Caramel*, Vita e Pensiero, Milano 2008
G. Didi-Huberman, *Il cubo e il volto. A proposito di una scultura di Alberto Giacometti*, Electa, Milano 2008
Carlo Cardazzo. Una nuova visione dell'arte, exhibition catalogue edited by L. M. Barbero (Venice, Peggy Guggenheim Collection, 1 November 2008 - 9 February 2009), Electa, Milano 2008
Lucio Fontana 1946-1960. Il disegno all'origine della nuova dimensione, exhibition catalogue edited by Simone Soldini and Luca Massimo Barbero (Mendrisio, Museo d'arte, 20 September - 14 December 2008), Mendrisio, 2008

2009
C. Wildung, D. Klemm, *Giacometti. Der Ägypter*, Deutscher Kunstverlag, München/Berlin 2009
Giacometti, exhibition catalogue edited by Ulf Kuster (Basel, Fondation Beyeler, 30 May – 11 October 2009), Hatje Cantz Verlag, Berlin 2009

2011
M. Leiris, *Ecrits sur l'art*, CNRS éditions, Paris 2011
A. Wieczorek, W. Rosendahl (ed. by), *Schädelkult. Kopf und Schädel in der Kulturgeschichte des Menschen*, Schnell und Steiner, Regensburg 2011
Giacometti et les Étrusques, exhibition catalogue edited by Claudia Beltramo Ceppi Zevi, Marc Restellini (Pinacothèque de Paris, 15 September 2011 - 8 January 2012), Giunti, Firenze 2011

2012
L. P. Nicoletti, *Parigi a Torino. Storia delle mostre "Pittori d'Oggi. Francia-Italia"*, doctorate thesis, Tutor Prof. Antonello Negri, Università degli Studi di Milano, A.A. 2011-2012
V. Wiesinger (ed. by), *Alberto Giacometti. Les copies du passé*, Éditions Fage, Lyon 2012

2013
L. M. Barbero, *Lucio Fontana. Catalogo ragionato delle opere su carta*, Skira, Milano 2013
A. Del Puppo, *L'arte contemporanea. Il secondo Novecento*, Einaudi, Torino 2013
M. Gounelle, *Météorites. A la recherche de nos origines*, Flammarion, Parigi 2013
C. Paglia, *Seducenti Immagini*, Il Mulino, Bologna 2013

2014
G. Bataille, *Lascaux, La nascita dell'arte*, Ascondita, Milano 2014
S. Bignami, J. Galimberti, *Lucio Fontana e l'artventure parigina*, Scalpendi editore, Milano 2014
Alberto Giacometti e l'arcaico: a un passo dal tempo, exhibition catalogue edited by P. Bellasi and C. Gatti (Man, Nuoro, 2014-2015), Silvana Editoriale, Cinisello Balsamo 2014

2015
L. Fontana, *Manifesti Scritti Interviste*, Abscondita, Milano 2015
Adolfo Wildt. Le dernier symboliste, exhibition catalogue (Musée d'Orsay), Skira, Paris, 2015
Lucio Fontana, exhibition catalogue with texts by E. Crispolti, L. M. Barbero, E. Lucie-Smith (London, Tornabuoni Art, 8 October – 5 December 2015) Forma edizioni, Firenze 2015

2016
A. Giacometti, *Le rêve, le Sphinx et la mort de T.*, Fondation Giacometti (Hermann), Paris 2016
M. Schultz, *Arthur Speyer – drei Generationen Sammler und Händler*, "kunst&kontext", no. 2, Vereinigung der Freunde afrikanischer Kultur, Berlin 2016, pp. 5-7
G. Soavi, *Il mio Giacometti*, Abscondita, Milano, 2016
J. Soldini, *Alberto Giacometti. Lo spazio e la forza*, Mimesis, Milano-Udine 2016

2017
J. M. Fiduccia, *Hollow Man. Alberto Giacometti and the Crisis of the Monument, 1935-45*, doctorate thesis in art history, University of California, Los Angeles (CA) 2017
L. Fontana, *La fine di Dio*, edited by Enrico Crispolti, Forma edizioni, Firenze 2017
C. Grenier, *Alberto Giacometti*, Flammarion, Paris 2017
J. MacLaren Walsh, B. Topping, *The Man Who Invented Aztec Crystal Skulls. The Adventures of Eugène Boban*, Berghahn Books, Oxford 2018
M. Negri, *Note di studio*, edited by S. Esengrini, Pagine d'Arte, Tesserete (Capriasca, Lugano) 2018, pp. 32-33
L. Sacco, *Alberto Giacometti e Maurice Merleau-Ponty, un dialogo sulla percezione. Fenomenologia dell'esperienza artistica*, Gangemi Editore, Roma 2017

2018
A. Giacometti, *Paris sans fin*, prefazione di M. Lacuyer-Maille, Fondation Giacometti, Les cahiers dessinés, Paris 2018

H. Bergson, *Histoire des theories de la memoire. Cours au College de France 1903-1904, PUF, Paris 2018*
Giacometti, exhibition catalogue edited by Megan Fontanella, Karole P.B. Vail (New York, Guggnheim Museum , 8 June - 12 September 2018), Guggenheim Museum Publication, New York 2018

2019
G. Gaggiotti, *La visione verticale*, Morlacchi editore, Perugia 2019
C. Grenier, *Alberto Giacometti, Biografia*, Johan& Levi, Varese 2019
Lucio Fontana, Terra e oro, exhibition catalogue edited by A. Coliva (Rome, Galleria Borghese, 22 May - 25 August 2019), Silvana Editoriale, Cinisello Balsamo 2019

2020
L.M. Barbero (ed. by), *Lucio Fontana e gli Spaziali. Fonti e documenti per le Gallerie Cardazzo*, Marsilio, Venezia 2020
Alberto Giacometti. 1901-1966. Grafica al confine tra arte e pensiero, exhibition catalogue edited by Jean Soldini and Nicoletta Ossanna Cavadini (Chiasso, Centro Culturale m.a.x. museo, 09 June – 21 December 2020), Skira, Milano 2020
Solo. Medardo Rosso, exhibition catalogue (Florence, Museo Novecento), Bandecchi & Vivaldi S.r.l, Pontedera (Pisa), 2020

2021
P. Florenskij, *Le porte regali. Saggio sull'icona*, Adelphi, Milano 2021
A. Leonardi, S. Petrillo (ed. by), *Leoncillo. Natura ed espressione*, Electa, Milano 2021
I. Yanaihara, *I miei giorni con Giacometti*, Giometti&Antonello, Macerata 2021
Pierre Matisse. Un marchant d'art à New York, exhibition catalogue edited by J. Matisse-Monnier (Nizza, Musée Matisse, June-September 2021), Bernard Chauveau Editeur Couleurs Contemporaines, Paris 2021

2022
L. M. Barbero, *Lucio Fontana. Ceramiche. Catalogo ragionato*, Skira, Milano 2022
A. Tura, *Il Novecento di Baudelaire. L'arte evanescente*, Johan & Levi, Varese 2022
Lucio Fontana. Sculpture, exhibition catalogue edited by L.M. Barbero (New York, Hauser & Wirth gallery, 3 November 2022- 4 February 2023), H&W Publishers, Zurich 2022

2023
C. Beltrami, *La scultura alla Biennale di Venezia (1895-1914). Una presenza in ombra*, ZeL Edizioni, Treviso, 2023 (in press)

Contents

GIACOMETTI FONTANA

The Research of the Absolute

**2 MARCH
4 JUNE 2023**

An exhibition promoted by
Comune di Firenze

Conceived by
Sergio Risaliti

Curated by
Chiara Gatti
Sergio Risaliti

Scientific coordination
Eva Francioli, Francesca Neri – MUS.E
Jacopo Manara

Press office and communication
Costanza Savelloni,
Lara Facco P&C
Lara Facco, Claudia Santrolli
Elisa Di Lupo, Comune di Firenze
Sara Camaiora, Comune di Firenze

Social media
Giulia Spissu

Visual identity
Forma Edizioni

Education department
MUS.E

Graphic prints on display
Litografia IP srls

Translations
NTL – Il Nuovo Traduttore Letterario S.c.

Insurance
Aon Spa | Fine Arts, Jewellery & Private Client Solution

Handling and artworks preparation
Apice Firenze S.r.l.

Condition report
Chiara Valcepina

Bases
Galli Mostre

Lighting installation
Vannetti Andrea S.r.l.

Security
REAR Società Cooperativa

Photographs
Serge Domingie

Thanks to
Dario Nardella,
Mayor of Florence
Alessia Bettini,
Vice Mayor and Councillor for culture
Matteo Spanò,
President of MUS.E

The lenders
Ben Brown Fine Arts, London, Hong Kong and Palm Beach
Collezione Piero Gnudi
Fondazione Marguerite et Aimé Maeght
Fondazione Lucio Fontana, Milano
Museo del Novecento, Milano

And all the private lenders who wished to remain anonymous

Also thanks to
Ignazio Amuro, Laura Andreini, Silvia Ardemagni, Claudia Bardelloni, Andrea Batistini, Cristina Beltrami, Andrea Bianchi, Paolo Campione, Mariella Carlotti, Marco Casamonti, Francesca Cattoi, Laura Chimenti, Emanuele Coccia, Silvia Colucci, Cathy Cordova, Rita Corsini, Emanuele Crocetti, Alessandro Del Puppo, Mirco Donati, Silvia Evangelisti, Marco Fagioli, Gabriella Farsi, Francesco Fricelli, Manuela Galliano, Marina Gardini, Piero Gnudi, Gianfranco Maraniello, Ilaria Nerli, Antonella Nicola, Cecilia Pappaianni, Silvia Pareschi, Silvia Penna, Franca e Lorenzo Pinzauti, Barbara Rapaccini, Stefania Rispoli, Stefanie Roggensack, Cristiano Giulio Sangiuliano, Paolo Sani, Andrea Sandri, Marco Senaldi, Serenella Todesco, Chiara Useli, Maria Villa, Marco Voena, Valentina Zucchi

Alle the offices of the city of Florence involved, in particular
The Mayor's Office, the Culture Directorate, the Ceremonial, the Monumental Halls

Supported by
Fondazione Lucio Fontana, Milano
AON Spa | Fine Arts,
Jewellery & Private Client Solution

COMUNE DI FIRENZE   MUSEO NOVECENTO   MUS.E musei // eventi firenze

Silvana Editoriale

Chief Executive
Michele Pizzi

Editorial Director
Sergio Di Stefano

Art Director
Giacomo Merli

Editorial Coordinator
Maria Chiara Tulli

Copy Editing
Lorena Ansani, Micol Fontana

Layout
Mirco Ameglio

Production Coordinator
Antonio Micelli

Editorial Assistant
Giulia Mercanti

Photo Editor
Silvia Sala, Barbara Miccolupi

Press Office
Alessandra Olivari, press@silvanaeditoriale.it

ISBN 9788836655014

Silvana Editoriale S.p.A.
via dei Lavoratori, 78
20092 Cinisello Balsamo, Milano
tel. 02 453 951 01
www.silvanaeditoriale.it

Reproductions, printing and binding
in Italy
Printed by Grafiche Antiga,
Crocetta del Montello (TV)
in March 2024

MIX
Paper | Supporting responsible forestry
FSC® C008309

Photo credits

© Archivio Giancolombo
Courtesy Kröller Müller Museum Otterlo /
Photo Ad Petersen
© Fondazione Lucio Fontana, Milano
by SIAE 2024
© Fondazione Musei Civici di Venezia
© Succession Alberto Giacometti
by SIAE 2024
© Succession Alberto Giacometti (Fondation
Giacometti, Paris et Adagp, Paris)
© The Estate of Alberto Giacometti (ADAGP,
Paris), licensed in the UK by DACS, London
2023 / Bridgeman Images
Bibliothèque de philosophie scientifique,
Bibliothèque nationale de France
Courtesy BCL Biblioteca Campus Leonardo
Philippe Migeat - Centre Pompidou,
MNAM-CCI /Dist. RMN-GP
DACS, London 2023 / Bridgeman Images
Foto Scala,Firenze - su concessione Ministero
della Cultura
Fotografie Ugo Mulas © Eredi Ugo Mulas.
Tutti i diritti riservati
Gabinetto Disegni e Stampe Gallerie degli
Uffizi, Firenze - Ministero della Cultura
Kunsthaus Zürich
Kunstmuseum Basel, Inv. P 49
François Fernandez – Archives François
Fernandez, Archives Fondation Maeght,
Saint-Paul-de-Vence
RMN-Grand Palais /Dist. Foto SCALA, Firenze
Shunk-Kender © J. Paul Getty Trust.
Tutti i diritti riservati
Su concessione di Fondazione Ragghianti,
Lucca, Fototeca, Arte contemporanea, b. 388,
n. 00043376